How it starts
and How it ends.

Human Trafficking, Human Misery

**Recent Title in
Global Crime and Justice**

Outsmarting the Terrorists
Ronald V. Clarke and Graeme R. Newman

HUMAN TRAFFICKING, HUMAN MISERY

The Global Trade in Human Beings

ALEXIS A. ARONOWITZ

Global Crime and Justice

Graeme R. Newman, Series Editor

Westport, Connecticut
London

Library of Congress Cataloging-in-Publication Data

Aronowitz, Alexis A., 1956–
  Human trafficking, human misery : the global trade in human
beings / Alexis A. Aronowitz.
    p. cm. — (Global crime and justice, ISSN 1931-7239)
  Includes bibliographical references and index.
  ISBN 978-0-275-99481-5 (alk. paper)
1. Human trafficking. 2. Human smuggling. 3. Human trafficking—
Prevention. 4. Human smuggling—Prevention. I. Title.
  HQ281.A76   2009
  364.1′37—dc22   2008045310

British Library Cataloguing in Publication Data is available.

Library of Congress Catalog Card Number: 2008045310
ISBN: 978-0-275-99481-5
ISSN: 1931-7239

First published in 2009

Praeger Publishers, 88 Post Road West, Westport, CT 06881
An imprint of Greenwood Publishing Group, Inc.
www.praeger.com

Printed in the United States of America

The paper used in this book complies with the
Permanent Paper Standard issued by the National
Information Standards Organization (Z39.48-1984).

10 9 8 7 6 5 4 3 2 1

*This book is dedicated to the victims of human trafficking and
all those who are working to make a difference in their lives.*

Contents

Series Foreword

HOW FITTING THAT one of the first books in this new Praeger series *Global Crime and Justice* should be on human trafficking, *the* global crime of the twenty-first century. Though how disappointing that human trafficking is not recognized as a crime in every part of the world, and that its global nature defies nations that outlaw it and challenges international governmental and nongovernmental efforts to police it. And how shocking it is that slavery—a global enterprise for centuries—still exists, flying in the face of its heralded abolition in the eighteenth and nineteenth centuries. Human trafficking is a very, very old practice, feeding very, very old vices.

In this thoroughly researched book, Alexis Aronowitz exposes the human misery of trafficking, examining every nook and cranny of its practice. She shows how innocent families and their children, looking for a better life, are tricked and exploited into the nether world of modern slavery—a world in which they live hidden, yet in plain sight of those who benefit from the services they provide—the indentured sex, domestic, farm, garment, and factory workers.

One cannot doubt the authenticity of this book, the best documented exposition on human trafficking available, presented by an author whose years of experience in interviewing stakeholders and victims as she researched human trafficking in many parts of the world shines through. The message is clear enough, repeated on just about every page (and it needs to be): Readers, wake up. Nations and international organizations, do more. Governments and authorities, acknowledge the victim status of trafficked persons, regardless of whether they are legal or illegal immigrants, and even if they are the latter, know that they are victims first, offenders last.

All those who read this book will be forced to ask themselves: how civil are we? If the question elicits an honest answer, it may be painful; but even then, the pain of honesty is better than the consequences of hypocrisy.

Graeme R. Newman
Philadelphia, August 2008

Preface

FOR A PERIOD of over five years, I worked in various capacities for the United Nations Interregional Crime and Justice Research Institute and the United Nations Office on Drugs and Crime as a researcher and consultant on human trafficking projects in the Philippines, the Czech Republic, Benin, Nigeria, and Togo. My work for the United Nations brought me to these countries on numerous occasions. I returned to Nigeria while working as a consultant for Winrock International and visited Albania while carrying out an assessment on trafficking for Management Systems International in that country in 2003.

All of these missions involved meetings with stakeholders in the country—from high-ranking government officials, to police officers and immigration officials, representatives of local nongovernmental organizations (NGOs) and international and intergovernmental organizations, and trafficked victims. We heard moving stories from those who were working with the young victims in an NGO in Benin—of how children had died of starvation and hunger while in transit to Gabon and how children on the boat were told to dispose of the corpses. We spoke to two child victims of trafficking and their parents at an NGO in Togo. The parents, poor and uneducated, explained to us how they only wanted to provide their young sons with an education and thought they were doing the right thing when they gave the children to the care of a man who promised to educate them. In Nigeria I spoke with a nine-year-old child who didn't know which village or country she had come from. At the age of six, her older sister had left her with a family in Nigeria to become a domestic slave. In Albania, while visiting a shelter run by the International Organization for Migration for repatriated trafficked victims, I sat in the living room and spoke to the young women in English, German, Dutch, and Italian. I could speak those languages because I had lived, studied, or worked in those countries. They spoke those languages because they, too, had worked in those countries—as prostitutes. After I left, it suddenly dawned on me that perhaps they thought I, too, had been trafficked and that's why I lived in so many countries to which they had traveled and spoke some of the same languages. How different our lives were.

To look into the eyes of a trafficked victim or survivor and to hear their stories is an unforgettable experience—one that should be passed on so that others can become aware of their plight and the plight of millions of others like them around the world. They are terrible, moving stories, yet many people, perhaps most, have difficulty in accepting the clear fact that "slavery and bondage still exist in the twenty-first century," as U.N. Secretary General Kofi Anan noted in 2006. Ambassador John R. Miller, Ambassador-at-Large on International Slavery in a speech presenting the U.S. State Department's 2006 *Trafficking in Persons Report*, further noted: "Here we are in the twenty-first century and we're talking about slavery. Wouldn't this be a shock to our abolitionist ancestors who thought they finished the job back in the 19th century."[1] The U.S. State Department estimates that up to 800,000 people, primarily women and children, are trafficked across national borders while millions more are victims of trafficking within their own countries each year.[2] This is a crime of violence, and an inconceivable violation of human rights and dignity. We talk of trafficking in terms of the sheer number of persons exploited or the amount of money generated by the trafficking practice. But behind every number and every dollar, pound, euro, ruble, rupee, or yen is a story of human misery.

This book combines scientific, academic, and government reports; studies generated by nongovernmental, international, and intergovernmental organizations; popular literature and media; and the author's experience coordinating research and conducting trafficking assessments in various countries to provide the reader with a deeper understanding of human trafficking. The reader will come to understand why victims are lured into dangerous situations, who is behind the trafficking networks, and why it is so difficult to determine the extent of the crime. Victims and their stories provide an understanding of how and why this crime occurred and the impact it had on their lives. More unusual forms of trafficking—in child soldiers, mail-order brides, and trafficking in human beings for their organs and illegal adoptions—will be exposed. The book examines new markets and opportunities for trafficking as a result of the growth of the Internet, international travel, military operations, sporting events, and natural disasters. The last chapter presents good practices— and the role played by various stakeholders in the prevention, enforcement, and victim assistance projects in an unceasing battle to stem the tide of human trafficking.

Acknowledgments

I WOULD LIKE to thank the United Nations Interregional Crime and Justice Research Institute and the United Nations Office on Drugs and Crime for the opportunity to work on a number of U.N. trafficking projects and for the invitation to attend the UN.GIFT (Global Initiative to Fight Human Trafficking) Vienna Forum to Fight Human Trafficking. Special gratitude goes to all those with whom I spoke during my years of work on trafficking in various countries. Their knowledge, experiences, and opinions have shaped my understanding of human trafficking and have left a deep impression on me—not only for the horror of victims' stories, but also for the dedication and commitment shown by those working to help them. My appreciation goes to University College Utrecht, which gave me research time to work on the book.

I am grateful to Graeme Newman, my mentor, for suggestions on improvements to earlier versions of the manuscript, and to my niece Shavon, for her assistance with the Index.

Most importantly, thanks to Gert-Jan, Marilyn, Julius, Jay and Andrée (and their children, Jenna, Jeboa, Shavon, Tony and Jason)—my sources of love, support and friendship, past, present and future.

Acronyms and Abbreviations

APLE	*Action Pour Les Enfants*
ASEAN	Association of Southeast Asian Nations
BKA	Bundeskriminalamt (German Federal Criminal Police)
BNRM	Bureau National Rapporteur Mensenhandel (Bureau of the Dutch National Rapporteur on Trafficking in Human Beings)
CETS	Child Exploitation Tracking System
CIS	Commonwealth of Independent States
CRC	Child Rights Committee (Pakistan)
CTM	Counter-Trafficking Module [database]
DPKO	Department of Peace Keeping Operations
ECPAT	End Child Prostitution, Child Pornography and the Trafficking of Children
ELN	National Liberation Army (Colombia)
EU	European Union
EUROPOL	European Law Enforcement Organisation
EXIT	End Exploitation and Trafficking
FARC	Revolutionary Armed Forces of Colombia
FBI	Federal Bureau of Investigation
FUC	United Front for Change (Chad)
ICE	Immigration and Customs Enforcement
ICMEC	International Centre for Missing and Exploited Children
ICMPD	International Centre for Migration Policy Development

ICT	information and communication technology
IJM	International Justice Mission
ILO	International Labour Organization
IMBRA	International Marriage Broker Regulation Act
INTERPOL	International Police Organization
IOM	International Organization for Migration
IPTF	International Police Task Force
LAC	Latin America and the Caribbean
LRA	Lord's Resistance Army (Uganda)
LTTE	Liberation Tigers of Tamil Eelam (Sri Lanka)
MOHAN	Multi Organ Harvesting Aid Network Foundation
MP3	Digital Audio Player
MTV	Music Television
NAPTIP	National Agency for the Prohibition of Traffic in Persons and Other Related Matters (Nigeria)
NATO	North Atlantic Treaty Organization
NGO	nongovernmental organization
OAS	Organization of American States
OHCHR	Office of the High Commissioner for Human Rights
OSCE	Organization for Security and Cooperation in Europe
PSO	Peace Support Operation
SEE	South-Eastern Europe
SFOR	Stabilization Force
SIUT	Sind Institute for Urology and Transplantation
SPLA	Sudan People's Liberation Army (Sudan)
TVPA	Trafficking Victims Protection Act
UNDP	United Nations Development Program
UNESCO	United Nations Educational, Scientific and Cultural Organization
UN.GIFT	United Nations Global Initiative to Fight Human Trafficking
UNHCR	United Nations High Commissioner for Refugees
UNICEF	United Nations Children's Fund
UNICRI	United Nations Interregional Crime and Justice Research Institute
UNIFEM	United Nations Development Fund for Women
UNMIBH	United Nations Mission in Bosnia and Herzegovina
UNMIK	United Nations Mission in Kosovo
UNODC	United Nations Office on Drugs and Crime
UNOHCHR	United Nations Office for the High Commission on Human Rights

What Is Human Trafficking?

THIS CHAPTER BEGINS by defining human trafficking and smuggling, discussing the similarities and differences between the two, and examines trafficking as a process rather than a single crime. While trafficking and smuggling are both forms of irregular migration and share some similarities, there are stark differences, particularly for the persons upon arrival at their destination. A distinction will also be made between internal and transborder trafficking, followed by a discussion of "push" and "pull" factors. This is particularly pertinent because the push and pull factors that affect illegal migration and smuggling also affect human trafficking.

TRAFFICKING DEFINED

Since the ratification of the United Nations Trafficking Protocol,[1] there is almost universal agreement on the definition of human trafficking. The United Nations defines human trafficking as follows:

> [T]he recruitment, transportation, transfer, harboring or receipt of persons, by means of the threat or use of force or other forms of coercion, of abduction, of fraud, of deception, of the abuse of power or of a position of vulnerability or of the giving or receiving of payments or benefits to achieve the consent of a person having control over another person, for the purpose of exploitation. Exploitation shall include, at a minimum, the exploitation of the prostitution of others or other forms of sexual exploitation, forced labor or services, slavery or practices similar to slavery, servitude or the removal of organs.

Trafficking must comprise—

1. an action (recruitment, transportation, transfer, harboring, or reception of persons);
2. through means of (threat or use of force, coercion, abduction, fraud, deception, abuse of power or vulnerability, or giving payments or benefits to a person in control of the victim); and
3. goals (for exploitation or the purpose of exploitation, which includes exploiting the prostitution of others, other forms of sexual exploitation, forced labor or services, slavery or similar practices, and the removal of organs).

One element from each of the above must be present for trafficking to occur.

Special protection is extended to children under the age of 18. The recruitment, transportation, transfer, harboring, or receipt of a child for the purpose of exploitation is considered trafficking in persons, even if it does not involve any of the means set forth above.[2]

Coercion and Deception

The U.N. Trafficking Protocol is clear concerning its view toward children. Questions, however, arise with respect to how one interprets the terms coercion and deception when adults are involved. It is a misconception that all trafficked victims have been recruited under false pretenses and that they had no idea what they would be facing upon arrival in the destination country. Just as the source countries and the areas of exploitation differ, so too do the amount and kind of information that victims are given concerning their work and living conditions upon arrival in the destination country. Various promises are made to victims of trafficking to obtain their consent, and the knowledge of what awaits them in the destination country varies from one victim to the other. The nature of victimization can best be understood when it is viewed on a continuum ranging from complete coercion to lesser forms of deception.

Complete coercion exists when victims have been abducted. However, coercion occurs rarely with adults trafficked for labor and sexual exploitation, and seldom in most instances involving child labor. There are exceptions, though, involving cases of kidnapping of children. According to human rights activists, Romanian children are drugged into submission so that they can be forced to beg in metro stations and underground pedestrian walkways of major European cities.[3] Other cases involve the kidnapping of both young boys and girls for use as child soldiers and sex slaves to service the outlawed militias and renegade military units. Children trafficked for labor in other parts of the world, however, are often sold by their parents or freely given to traffickers in the false belief that the children will receive an education or job training.

Deception occurs when individuals have been promised jobs in the legitimate economy as nannies or domestic servants, hotel chamber maids, or unskilled workers only to find themselves forced into sexual slavery. Deception through half-truths occurs when individuals are told they will be working in the "entertainment industry" as dancers or strippers. These women may suspect there will be some sexual contact with customers but are unaware of the fact that they will be forced into prostitution.

A lesser form of deception involves women who are aware before departure that they will be working as prostitutes but are unaware of the extent to which they will be exploited, controlled, intimidated, and indebted.[4] Studies have found that, even in prostitution, some women are willing collaborators.[5] Women are willingly brought to another country to knowingly work in prostitution because they are told their wages will be much higher in the destination country than in the country of origin. This fact was supported by a representative of a Saint Petersburg (the Russian Federation)* human rights organization who reports that, as a rule, victims are informed now about where they are going and what they will be doing. She confirms that the proportion of girls and women who have consented to working in the sex industry is growing, but few realize that when they arrive and begin working, they will be locked behind bars.[6] Even though a woman may willingly agree to working in prostitution, when she is forced to turn over most or all of her wages to her traffickers, or "buy back" her passport at an exorbitant fee, or when she is not free to leave the premises, determine her working conditions, or quit her job, then she, too, is exploited and is a victim of trafficking.

Coercion is a complex issue. Not all victims of trafficking are physically restrained and constantly controlled. For many, the coercion is more psychological than physical. The threat of violence or of being reported to immigration officials as an illegal migrant keeps many trafficked victims in line and prevents them for seeking assistance from the authorities. According to Anti-Slavery International, coercion exists in "any situation in which the person involved has no real and acceptable alternative but to submit to the abuse involved."[7] Conditions in sweatshops or in the agricultural sector may resemble slavery-like practices, but workers may endure these conditions on a voluntary basis, earning more in a wealthy destination country than at home in their countries of origin. The International Labour Organization (ILO) reports that this

> appears to be the case of clandestine Chinese workers in France, who work long hours in heavily indebted circumstances for a number of years, in order to repay the advances they have received in their places of origin. Despite the appalling conditions, the exploited Chinese workers may see the light at the end of the tunnel. They may know that this is a finite period of suffering, a sacrifice that parents are willing to make for their children.[8]

SMUGGLING DEFINED

Smuggling of migrants has been defined by the United Nations as "the procurement, in order to obtain, directly or indirectly, a financial or other material benefit, of the illegal entry of a person into a State Party of which the person is not a national or a permanent resident."[9] Inherent in the definition of smuggling is the crossing of international borders. If an individual pays transportation costs prior to departure and, upon entering the destination country, terminates his or her relationship with the transporter, the individual has been smuggled. The individual then enters the destination country and applies for asylum or, as an illegal migrant, seeks work in the shadow economy.

---

*The Russian Federation and Russia will be used interchangeably throughout the text.

Both illegal migrants and trafficked victims may have been recruited or may have approached someone to assist them in entering another country. Smuggled persons generally pay the entire amount owed prior to departure. Trafficked persons may pay a percentage of the trip prior to departure and incur a debt for the remainder. It is this debt that puts them at the mercy of their traffickers. The difference between smuggled individuals and trafficked persons may be apparent only when the journey has ended. If the person is not able to exercise self-determination and finds him- or herself in a situation of exploitation, what may have begun as a smuggling operation has then turned into a situation of trafficking.

Smuggling is not without its perils. Boatloads of African migrants departing from Libya and Tunisia have attempted to reach the Italian island of Lampedusa or the Spanish Canary Islands. According to data from the Italian Interior Ministry, migrant landings in southern Italy almost doubled between 2004 and 2005, from 13,000 to 23,000—of which at least 10,000 landed in Lampedusa in 2005. Figures had already reached 11,000 in the first seven months of 2006.[10] The Canary Islands witnessed a flood of 30,000 migrants in 2006. Not all survive the dangerous trip, and newspaper accounts and reports by international organizations regularly document their deaths in trying to reach Europe. The Mauritanian Red Crescent estimates that 1,200 migrants died at sea in a five-month period between November 2005 and March 2006.[11] The International Organization for Migration (IOM) estimates that up to 3,000 persons, including women and children, have died attempting to cross by boat to Europe.[12] The United Nations High Commission for Refugees (UNHCR) reported that knife-wielding smugglers forced 450 Somalis and Ethiopian refugees overboard into stormy seas off the coast of the Republic of Yemen. Twenty-nine people died and another 71 were reported missing.[13] The United States faces a similar problem with illegal migrants attempting to cross the Arizona desert. Between October 1, 2005, and September 15, 2006, 426 people died while illegally crossing the border; the death toll since 1994 is reported at about 3,700.[14]

The story of one young Nigerian woman (case 1.1) hoping to find a good job in Italy exemplifies the perils to which smuggled and trafficked persons are exposed in their attempt to illegally enter the European Union in search of work. What began with the promise of a plane trip and a good job, resulted in a two-year-long harrowing trip to Italy filled with violence and death only to be exposed to exploitation upon arrival. This victim's story exemplifies the dangers to which many African victims are exposed on their way to the "promised land."[15]

(IL)LEGAL MIGRATION

Trafficking and smuggling, while different, are in fact intricately intertwined. Migrants may depart their own country legally or illegally and enter the destination country as legal or illegal migrants. The legal status of departure and

Case 1.1. The Story of a Nigerian Woman

A 25-year-old female victim of human trafficking was attracted by the offer to travel abroad because she was from a polygamous family where there was much poverty and suffering. The trip began in 2000. After having been informed that she and the others in her group would travel by air to Italy, she joined five others to leave Nigeria through Kano in the north. From Kano, the group entered the Niger Republic and traveled to Zinde and Tamaraset where they spent 10 days in the Sahara desert; for three of those days, there was no food or water to eat or drink. The group spent a month and half at Tamaraset. From there they proceeded to Regan, Gadaya, and Oran, and eventually arrived in Algeria where they were joined by more Nigerian girls who had arrived there earlier. Together they spent another month waiting. During the trip, which was undertaken by land through North Africa, many in their entourage died in the desert. The group trekked for seven days to get to Morocco from Algeria.

The victim was exposed to violence and death throughout her trip. She reported nearly being shot dead. While in Algeria, a security operative shot at the group and the bullet grazed her body. It hit a pregnant woman who was severely injured and had to be rushed to an Algerian hospital for treatment. While trying to avoid being arrested by the Moroccan police, one of the boys in the group was crushed to death while attempting to jump onto a moving train, while another member of the group lost a leg while trying to jump from a moving train. At a certain stage during the journey, the group had to travel by water and another Nigerian boy drowned.[16] When the group reached a place called Regan, another companion died, and a female member of the group who became pregnant attempted to abort her pregnancy and died in the process. During this part of the journey, 35 people were packed like sardines inside a jeep. One of the girls was stabbed with scissors over a small disagreement, and she also died. Furthermore, a quarrel between the heads of the Yoruba and Ibo trafficking gangs resulted in the latter being stabbed to death.

According to the victim, although only six of the young women left Nigeria together, the group swelled to 106 when they got to Morocco. Out of 106 of the group who set out for the journey from Algeria, only about 100 made it to Spain.

The victim spent two months in Madrid and later proceeded to Italy in 2002. When eventually she arrived in Italy with the expectation that she would get a decent job, she was handed over to a woman, forced into prostitution, and told by the "madam" that she had to refund the sum of $35,000 which was purportedly spent to get her into Italy.

Eight months after having arrived in Italy, she was arrested by a security patrol team while she was on her way to buy something from a nearby shop. By then she had already "reimbursed" $25,000 of the debt imposed on her before she was arrested and deported to Nigeria on September 19, 2002.

---

entry into the destination country may determine whether an individual travels independently or uses the services of a smuggler/trafficker. An individual may depart his or her country with a passport and necessary visa to enter the destination country to visit family members, work, or study. When the visa expires and the individual chooses to remain in the destination country, he then

Table 1.1 Status of Departure from Source and Residence in Destination Country

		Entry into Destination Country	
		Legal	Illegal
Departure from Country of Origin	Legal	All papers are legitimate; if legal status expires, immigration violation; if seeking work in shadow economy there is risk of exploitation	Legal papers destroyed prior to entry; may seek asylum; exit legal but may attempt to enter country illegally; if seeking work in the shadow economy there is risk of exploitation
	Illegal	Departure from source country without papers; forged papers obtained in transit country; is granted legal entry to country (albeit with illegal papers); legal status in destination country (until forgery uncovered); may obtain legal employment	Risk of trafficking or exploitation; may be granted asylum or special permission to reside legally in destination country

Source: Aronowitz (2003a).

becomes an illegal alien. A person may depart his or her country with the necessary legal documents, destroy these while on board an airline, and seek asylum in the destination country (legal departure, illegal entry). A person departing his or her country of origin illegally (without papers or with forged or illegal documents) often uses the service of a smuggler or trafficker to (illegally) enter the destination country. The illegal status can change if the person applies for and is granted asylum. Any time the status of a person in the destination country is that of an "illegal," the person is in danger of being exploited. Table 1.1 shows the status of persons upon departing their country of origin and entering into or remaining in the destination country.

Migrants may enter a country legally or illegally and may have control over their own lives. Table 1.1 shows that once people reside illegally in a country, they are at risk of exploitation. The smuggled person or illegal migrant, however, exercises enough autonomy to leave and seek out a less exploitive situation. The trafficked victim remains exploited until their debt has been paid off (in some cases, this never occurs), or until he or she escapes, is rescued, or dies.

THE MIGRATION-SMUGGLING-TRAFFICKING NEXUS

Both smuggling and trafficking are forms of irregular migration. Although they differ, they do share some common elements. Both smuggled and trafficked individuals often leave a country of origin willingly. Additionally, because their status in the country of destination is that of an illegal alien, both smuggled and trafficked persons are at risk of being exploited. When migrants voluntarily use the services of smugglers only to find themselves in coercive situations, they have then become trafficked victims. Where initial consent is invalidated through the use of deception or coercion, a voluntary trip on the part of the migrant, who may in fact have sought out the services of the smuggler, is easily transformed into a situation of trafficking.[17]

Even if the entire sum of money is paid in full prior to departure, this does not guarantee that a person will not be trafficked and exploited. In a study conducted under the supervision of the United Nations Interregional Crime and Justice Research Institute (UNICRI) in the Philippines, two men paid the entire sum of their journey prior to departure, having been promised work in a factory making paper bags. Upon arrival in Malaysia, they were sold to a plantation owner, imprisoned on the premises, and their salary was withheld.[18] The most important difference between trafficked victims and smuggled persons is that smuggled persons, even if they are living and working under exploitive conditions, are free to leave and look for better opportunities. Trafficked victims are not so fortunate. They are at the mercy of those to whom they must repay a debt or to those who have seized their documentation or are threatening to harm their families back home.

Other differences between trafficked victims and smuggled persons are their legal status in the country of destination once they have come to the attention of nongovernmental organizations (NGOs) or enforcement agencies. Trafficked persons are (or should be considered) victims and entitled in many countries to special protection. Illegal migrants, unless they are granted asylum, are considered violators of immigration law and subject to arrest and deportation. Table 1.2 clarifies the differences between trafficked and smuggled persons.

Internal and Transborder Trafficking

Internal trafficking occurs as well, and possibly to an even greater extent in many countries, than transnational trafficking. It is the subsequent exploitation, and not the crossing of international borders, that defines trafficking of human beings. When trafficking is international, only cooperation between source, transit, and destination countries will ensure success in eradicating the problem.

Some studies have attempted to generate estimates on the degree to which trafficking is a domestic rather than an international problem. In a study by Free the Slaves on child trafficking in Northern India, the organization reports that "[t]he U.S. State Department estimates that 200,000 people are trafficked into, within or through India annually. Within this figure, it is believed that only 10% of human trafficking in India is international, while almost 90% is inter-state."[19] The problem of internal trafficking is also recognized in India and many West African countries in which children and young women are

Table 1.2 Differences between Human Trafficking and Smuggling

Trafficking	Smuggling
Force is used or consent is obtained through fraud, deception, or coercion (actual, perceived, or implied), unless under 18 years of age; the person being trafficked may or may not cooperate	The person being smuggled generally cooperates and consents to the smuggling
Forced labor and/or exploitation	There is generally no actual or implied coercion*
Persons trafficked are victims	Persons smuggled are violating the law; by law they are not victims
Enslaved, subjected to limited movement or isolation, documents may have been confiscated	Persons are free to leave, change jobs, etc.
Need not involve the actual or physical movement of the victim	Facilitates the illegal entry of person(s) from one country into another
No requirement to cross an international border; trafficking can occur within a country	Smuggling always crosses an international border
Persons are exploited in labor/services or commercial sex acts, i.e., must be "working"	Person must be attempting illegal entry or only be in country illegally

Note: *Smuggled persons may be subject to coercion or force during the transportation phase but not upon entry into the destination country and not by the persons who facilitated their journey.
Source: Adapted from U.S. Department of State (2006b).

trafficked for forced labor and prostitution. Internal trafficking of children is documented in a United Nations Children's Fund (UNICEF) report on child trafficking. The Innocenti Research Centre reports that "[k]nowledge of cross-border trafficking in Africa is significantly higher than that concerning movements within countries."[20]

Research in the Netherlands has identified a pattern of internal trafficking whereby young Dutch girls, usually teenagers, are "courted" by older men. The young woman is showered with gifts and after having "fallen in love," her boyfriend then announces to her that he needs money. The "loverboy" convinces the young woman to have sex with other men to help him financially. After having "won her over," the loverboy will use psychological and emotional influence, threats, intimidation, blackmail, and violence to manipulate and control his victim. While this loverboy technique is used to recruit Dutch teenagers into prostitution in the Netherlands,[21] it is a technique also used by men to lure girls and young women from their homes into prostitution in other countries. The IOM in Tirana, Albania, explained that one of the most successful recruitment patterns was for men to "date" young women in small villages, offer to marry them and bring them to a beautiful home in Italy as a new young bride. Instead, the women were subjected to extreme violence and forced into prostitution upon their arrival in Italy.[22]

TRAFFICKING AS A PROCESS

The trafficking of human beings can be viewed as a process rather than a single offense. The first stage involves the abduction or recruitment of a person followed by the transportation and entry of the individual into another country (in the case of transborder trafficking). The third phase is the exploitation phase during which the victim is forced into sexual or labor servitude. An additional phase may occur, one which involves the offender and is common to any large-scale criminal organization: the laundering of criminal proceeds. In studying trafficking from a law enforcement perspective, there may be further links to other criminal offenses, such as the smuggling of weapons or drugs.[23]

During the trafficking process, a number of crimes can be committed. According to Europol (the European Law Enforcement Organization), some of these are instrumental criminal activities that are perpetrated in direct furtherance of the trafficking activity.[24] Examples of these crimes are corruption of government officials, forced prostitution, and violence associated with maintaining control over victims. Other crimes, such as money laundering and tax evasion, are secondary, and occur as a result of the trafficking activity.

As the trafficking process moves along through each of its phases, different crimes are linked to that particular phase. To further refine our understanding of trafficking, it is necessary to understand the "victim" against whom the crime is being perpetrated—that is, the individual victim or the State. The organization of the trafficking operation and sophistication of the criminal groups involved therein will determine the number and types of offenses perpetrated. The operations can be as simple as the smuggling and subsequent trafficking of a single victim by an individual over a border without proper documentation by vehicle or foot, to highly sophisticated operations moving large numbers of persons, using forged documents, corrupting government officials, and generating huge profits that subsequently must be laundered.

Crimes perpetrated against individual victims during the trafficking process include threats, extortion, theft of documents or property, false imprisonment, aggravated or sexual assault, pimping, rape, and even death. Offenses against the State include abuse of immigration laws, document forgery, corruption of government officials, money laundering, and tax evasion.[25] It can be questioned whether or not the State can be viewed as a victim. The unrestrained influx of persons entering a country illegally may result in an increase in vice or criminal activities. Corruption of its government officials leads to the moral and legal deterioration of a government, possibly leading to additional criminal activities on the part of corrupt officials.

Figure 1.1 Trafficking in Human Beings as a Process and Other Related Crimes

Recruitment	Transportation and Entry	Exploitation	Criminal Proceeds

→

Fraudulent promises	*Assault*	*Unlawful coercion*	Money laundering
Kidnapping	*False imprisonment*	*Threat*	Tax evasion
Document forgery	*Rape*	*Extortion*	Corruption of government
	Forced prostitution	*Forced prostitution*	officials
	Corruption of government	*False imprisonment*	
	officials	*Theft of documents*	
	Document forgery	*Sexual assault*	
	Abuse of immigration laws	*Aggravated assault*	
		Rape	
		Manslaughter or murder	
		Corruption of government	
		officials	

Note: *Italics indicate offences perpetrated against the individual victims.
Source: Adapted from Aronowitz (2003a, 29).

Figure 1.1 illustrates the trafficking process and the various offenses per-petrated during different phases, while indicating whether the "victim" is the individual who has been trafficked or the state itself, or both.

The trafficking phases remain the same for all victims. Barring a kidnap-ping, violence is seldom perpetrated against the victim during the recruitment phase. Victims are generally recruited through promises of an education, a good job, or marriage. During the transportation phase, victims of domestic trafficking will be held in the same city or village or will be moved within their country. Victims of international trafficking will be transported across borders, increasing the possibility that forged documents or corruption of gov-ernment officials is necessary to facilitate the activity. Violence may be used during the transportation phase to maintain control over the victims. It is gen-erally not until the arrival at the destination (the exploitation phase) that the trafficker begins the reign of terror against the victim.

Studies carried out by UNICRI in Nigeria and the Philippines show two completely different trafficking practices. The majority of victims traf-ficked from the Philippines traveled by air and arrived at their destination within a few hours. During the transport phase, victims were sometimes housed in (luxury) hotels. Their exploitation began only after arrival in the destination country.[26] The picture that emerges from Nigeria is completely different. In a study of Nigerian women and young girls trafficked to Italy, the author reports that

> The sexual exploitation of victims starts from Nigeria, especially in Lagos where traffickers keep victims for up to two weeks. Some of the victims are raped by traffickers and "groomed" or taught how to service male clients before they com-mence their journey abroad. Along the routes, especially when victims travel by land, victims are also sexually exploited, some of the victims end up becoming

pregnant (one of the victims interviewed was two months' pregnant by the time she arrived in Italy). Many victims have to engage in prostitution during the journey to survive. The survey team was told the story of a Nigerian victim who delivered twins along the route, after spending nearly a year on the road. She lost her life when their boat capsized as they were trying to cross from Morocco to Spain.[27]

A classic case of trafficking involves people working together from the first phase of recruitment to the last phase of exploitation. A woman approaches a person whom she hopes will smuggle her abroad, or is approached by someone who promises her a well-paying job in a restaurant. The trafficker either smuggles the young woman and forces her into prostitution or hands her over to someone else who facilitates her illegal entry into the destination country. At that point, the young woman is sold to a brothel owner who forces her into prostitution and, after having made a profit, may sell her to another brothel owner. The concept of trafficking recognizes the process to which the victim has been subjected "as more than the sum of its parts (deception, abduction, false imprisonment, assault, rape, slavery-like employment practices, etc.), it allows us to identify the man who befriended and betrayed the girl, and all those who colluded with him along the way, as fully implicated in her abuse."[28]

PUSH AND PULL FACTORS

Migration, whether legal or illegal, is driven by "push" and "pull" factors. The reasons why people leave their country of origin (push factors) either through legitimate or illicit channels are the same. Countries of origin are traditionally developing nations or those in a state of transition. Migration takes place from rural to municipal areas, from poorer to wealthier, more stable countries.

Push factors include the following:[29]

- Inadequate employment opportunities, combined with poor living conditions, a lack of basic education and poor health services;
- Political and economic insecurity, which may be caused by mismanagement, nepotism or political corruption, conflict, environmental disaster, or structural adjustment policies resulting in the rising cost of living, in higher unemployment. and a lack of public services;
- Discrimination (ethnic, gender, or caste) excluding certain persons from the employment sector; and
- Dissolution of the family (possibly as the result of sickness, HIV/AIDS, the death of one or both parents) which may compel the remaining family member(s) to migrate or send children away to work and help support the family.

The "pull" of promises of a better future is powerful. The following have been identified as pull factors:[30]

- Increased ease of travel (cheaper and faster travel opportunities, easier access to passports);
- Higher salaries and standard of living in larger cities and countries abroad (greater possibilities for acquiring new skills and education, increased job opportunity, and mobility);
- Established migration routes and ethnic, national communities in destination countries;
- Active demand for migrant workers in destination countries combined with the existence of recruitment agencies and persons willing to facilitate jobs and travel; and
- High expectations of opportunities in other countries boosted by global media and Internet access, and stories of returning migrants or those whose families have profited from the remittances.

The root causes of migration—both licit and illicit—lay in the unstable political, social, and economic conditions in countries or origin. Other causes include rapid growth of the population, high unemployment, abject poverty, internal conflicts resulting in civil disorder and widespread violence, unstable or oppressive political regimes, and grave violations of human rights.[31]

Economic crises have fueled migration from Russia, Central and Eastern Europe, and Asia. Regional conflicts were the cause of migration from areas such as Kosovo, the former Yugoslavia, the Congo, Darfur, and Sudan. Political and religious persecution is the push factor from nations such as China[*] and Russia.[32] Since the beginning of the war in 2003 and the resulting political instability and insecurity in Iraq, the United Nations estimates that 2 million people have fled the country. Over 20,000 Iraqis have entered Sweden, many on forged European passports purchased in Istanbul.[33]

Technological and communications advances, as well as open borders that facilitate the flow of goods also facilitate the flow of people. Closed borders may exacerbate illegal migration, which in turn may facilitate trafficking.

In an exploratory test of a theory of global trafficking, an expert on slavery and human trafficking compiled a number of factors to empirically test which variables are significant predictors of trafficking from (the push factors) and to (the pull factors) a country. The research identified the following "push" predictors, rank ordered, "from" a country: (1) government corruption, (2) high infant mortality, (3) a very young population, (4) low food production (an indication of poverty), and (5) conflict and social unrest.[34]

The "pull" factors predicting trafficking "to" a country were less conclusive. The permeability of the country's border is a strong indicator of a "pull"

---

*China and the People's Republic of China will be used interchangeably throughout the text.

factor, and this may be related to government corruption, particularly within border control or immigration agencies. Other factors, rank ordered, predicting the "pull" of a country were as follows: (1) the male population over the age of 60, (2) (low) governmental corruption, (3) food production, (4) energy consumption, and (5) (low) infant mortality, all of which are indicators of economic well-being of the destination country.[35]

LINK BETWEEN SENDING AND RECEIVING COUNTRY

A link can sometimes be found between sending and receiving countries. These links are influenced by a number of factors, such as the traffickers' use of the local knowledge, key locations, and weaknesses in border or migration control[36] or the ease in crossing borders.[37] This link is apparent in child trafficking in many West African nations. Tribal ties are much stronger than national allegiance. A common language and tribal history (the Yoruba tribe can be found on both sides of the Nigeria-Benin border); the long, unguarded border; and the rural setting of these nations facilitate the trafficking of Beninese children into Nigerian rock quarries. Other determining factors are the presence and tolerance of an extensive sex industry, historical and colonial links between countries,[38] and the existence of a large immigrant population. With respect to Nigeria, destination countries appear to be linked to the recruiting and sending state within Nigeria and are divided up by Nigerian ethnic groups. According to an Interpol officer interviewed in a United Nations study, "[w]hile Edo State citizens monopolize the Schengen states, especially Italy, Spain and the Netherlands, the Yorubas and the Ibos dominate the United Kingdom and the U.S.A. Northern women dominate the Saudi Arabia route."[39]

CONCLUDING REMARKS

This chapter has defined trafficking and has examined a number of issues central to the problem—that of consent, violence, and fraud, as well as push and pull factors. The misconception that trafficking involves the crossing of international borders was discussed, as well as the use that traffickers make of local migrant communities in various countries in which they traffic their victims.

There is often confusion between smuggled persons and trafficked victims. Trafficking and smuggling, while clearly different crimes, are closely related. A person who thinks he or she is paying for safe passage and illegal entry into a country may be tricked into paying off a huge debt and forced into exploitive labor conditions. Alternatively, a person who is being trafficked first may be smuggled into a country before being forced to work under exploitive conditions. With the growth of regional alliances (the European Union, the Association of Southeast Asian Nations) and relaxed visa requirements, it is becoming easier for persons to legally enter a destination country. These individuals still may be trafficked and exploited after having entered a country through legitimate means.

The next chapter will examine what we know about the prevalence of trafficking and the number of persons subjected to this modern-day slavery.

Human Trafficking: How Serious Is the Problem?

IT IS UNDISPUTED that trafficking of persons is a serious problem, but just how serious is it? This section examines what we know, and why what we know may not portray the true numbers. Drawing on research and data obtained from organizations ranging from official government bodies to nongovernmental and international organizations, the following review presents what is known about the magnitude of human trafficking. Numbers of human trafficking victims are notoriously inaccurate and estimates may range to a high 10 times that of the minimum.

DIFFICULTY IN MEASURING THE PROBLEM[1]

Because of its clandestine nature and the hidden economies in which trafficked victims are forced to work, accurate statistics on the magnitude of the problem are elusive and available statistics are notoriously unreliable. A number of reports have documented the difficulty in obtaining accurate statistics on the number of trafficked victims. In a report on sex trafficking in Central America and the Caribbean carried out by the International Human Rights Law Institute, the report states that,

> In view of the clandestine and criminal nature of the phenomenon, the inadequate monitoring by law enforcement agencies, and public confusion about the nature of the problem, accurate quantitative data on the trafficking for sexual exploitation was impossible to obtain. In fact, available quantitative data was purely speculative and based on extrapolations.[2]

The absence of trafficking legislation, or legislation defining human trafficking only in terms of sexual exploitation, or the failure to include internal trafficking of their own citizens under human trafficking violations, further adds to the confusion in trying to compile accurate trafficking statistics.[3] Where good legislation is in place, the lack of political will, inexperience in conducting investigations and prosecutions, and corrupt practices contribute to minimal successes in the identification of victims and the arrest and prosecution of traffickers.[4]

Compounding the problem in obtaining reliable statistics is the fact that victims rarely report their victimization and often are unwilling to cooperate with law enforcement officials if identified and rescued. This is due to a number of reasons. Fear of reprisal from traffickers, lack of trust in the authorities, the belief that the authorities cannot or will not help, rejection by their families, and lack of opportunities in their home countries cause many women to refuse to cooperate with authorities in destination countries. Victims may not see themselves as being exploited, particularly if they are in love with their trafficker/pimp or, in spite of exploitation, if they are earning more than they could in their own country.[5]

Nongovernmental organizations (NGOs), international agencies, and governments provide different kind of data, which often are not comparable.[6] This means that the police may record "presumed" trafficked victims based on the number of "rescues" of those found working in bars, brothels, massage parlors, farms, factories, or as domestic servants. Immigration officials may register cases of trafficking based on interceptions—the number of persons caught trying to leave or enter a country illegally (either without proper documentation or with fraudulent papers). NGOs, international organizations, and embassies often count trafficked persons based on the number of persons to whom they have provided assistance or who have been repatriated.[7]

MAGNITUDE OF THE PROBLEM

Trafficking statistics provided by organizations on the number of trafficked victims are either estimates of trafficking in the country or region, or are made up of statistics based on what is known by governments, NGOs, and international organizations. Estimates vary widely and the methodology used to arrive at these figures is not always explained. The following sections provide estimates on human trafficking and illustrate the difference between estimates and actual numbers.

Estimates of Trafficking

The U.S. Department of State estimates that between around 800,000 children, women, and men are trafficked across international borders each year[8] (some NGOs and international organizations place the number far higher). Other estimates range from 4 to 27 million, and "[e]stimates that include global intra-country trafficking in persons range from two to four million."[9]

Within the United States, figures are much smaller. The U.S. State Department calculated that between 14,500 and 17,500 trafficked victims enter the United States each year.[10] This figure is down from the estimate of 45,000 to 50,000, which included women and children alone, in the year 2000. This reduction in the number of estimated victims in the United States has been attributed to the U.S. government's improvement in the methodology used to calculate the flow of trafficking victims—not to a reduction in the actual number of victims. The methodology used to calculate the figures is not explained.[11]

In a study on labor exploitation in the United States, 131 incidents of trafficking for forced labor between January 1998 and December 2003 were identified. The number of victims involved was reported in 105 of the cases. A total of 19,254 victims were identified. The study goes on to report that experts interviewed revealed that individuals kept in forced labor are held on average for a period of two to five years, suggesting that 10,000 or more individuals are held in forced labor in the United States at any given time.[12]

The International Labour Organization (ILO) estimates that the "minimum number of persons in forced labor at a given time as a result of trafficking is 2.45 million."[13] This figure represents only 20 percent of the estimated total number of persons in forced labor worldwide.[14] There are large geographic differences between regions, with Asia and the Pacific accounting for more than half of the total figure (1.36 million trafficked persons in forced labor). Additionally, in Asia, Latin America, and Sub-Saharan Africa the proportion of trafficked victims is below 20 percent of total forced labor, while in industrial and transition countries, as well as in North Africa and the Middle East, trafficking accounts for 75 percent of the forced labor. In other areas, namely, in the United States, Canada, and Western Europe, trafficking is the main avenue into forced labor. Table 2.1 presents the regional distribution of trafficked forced laborers.

The United Nations Educational, Scientific and Cultural Organization (UNESCO) maintains a Trafficking Statistics Project, which attempts to ascertain the methodology used by other sources to calculate their trafficking statistics with the aim of evaluating their validity.[15] UNESCO provides a data comparison sheet on worldwide trafficking estimates by organizations.[16] The figures vary by year and organization and, in some cases, estimate the total number of persons or disaggregate the data into specific groups (children,

Table 2.1 Number of People in Forced Labor as a Result of Trafficking

Region	People Trafficked
Asia and the Pacific	1,360,000
Industrial Countries	270,000
Latin America and the Caribbean	250,000
Middle East and North Africa	230,000
Transition Countries	200,000
Sub-Saharan Africa	130,000
World	**2,450,000**

Source: ILO (2005, table 1.2, 14).

women, or women and children). Estimates for persons trafficked appear to range from a low of around 2 million to a high of 4 million.

Estimates versus Actual Numbers

Huge discrepancies exist between the number of actual victims identified and estimates projected by government agencies. This was made clear in a paper presented at a United Nations workshop on trafficking in human beings.[17] Estimates placed the number of trafficked women and children in the United States at 45,000–50,000, while the number of documented cases was 38 involving 5,500 women for the year 1999–2000. Both the Netherlands and Belgium estimated between 1,000 and 3,000 victims, while the number of documented cases was 287 in the Netherlands in 1999, and 270 in Belgium in the year 2000.[18] Germany estimated the annual number of victims at 2,000 to 20,000; in the year 2000, 926 victims were registered.[19] According to the Joint Committee on Human Rights in its report to the British Parliament, the U.K. Home Office estimates 4,000 victims of trafficking for prostitution annually. At the same time, the Committee states,

> Referrals from the Poppy Project in some ways provide the most reliable figures on the numbers of identified victims of trafficking for prostitution in the UK, since they relate to the actual women who have been encountered. Between March 2003 and May 2006, 489 referrals were made to the scheme.[20]

The Dutch National Rapporteur on Trafficking in Human Beings estimates that only 5 percent of victims report their victimization or come to the attention of government authorities.[21] In a study of the magnitude of trafficking in the United Kingdom, the researchers, based on 71 known cases, extrapolate the actual figure at between 142 and 1,420 cases annually.[22] In a report for the International Organization for Migration (IOM) on the trafficking of women and children from the Russian Federation, the author states, "[t]he number of women and children who have become victims is unknown, but it is estimated to be in the tens-of-thousands and possibly the hundreds-of-thousands."[23] In general, the proportion of the number of identified victims out of the estimated totals varies considerably between countries, but is somewhere between 5 and 10 percent.[24]

There are a number of criticisms of trafficking estimates. First, the methodology for computing the estimates is rarely given. Reports also often fail to indicate whether estimates are annual figures or cover a period of several years.[25] Furthermore, the ranges are often wide with a high of 10 times that of the low estimate.

There is a danger is using estimates, particularly when it is unclear how an organization arrived at the figure. According to UNESCO,

> Numbers take on a life of their own, gaining acceptance through repetition, often with little inquiry into their derivations. Journalists, bowing to the pressures of

editors, demand numbers, any number. Organizations feel compelled to supply them, lending false precisions and spurious authority to many reports.[26]

To support this argument, UNESCO reported that the widely cited figure of 5,000–7,000 Nepalese girls trafficked each year to India first appeared in 1986, and that this was the figure most often quoted until one organization felt it grossly underestimated the problem. One NGO changed the figure to "5000 to 7000 Nepalese girls are trafficked to India every day."[27]

Overstating the Problem

It is not uncommon for countries to combine statistics on illegal migration, smuggling, migrant sex workers, and trafficking. Statistics collected by police and immigration officials often are not segregated by age or gender.[28] Even when they are separated, it may be difficult to determine whether individuals stopped at a border are being smuggled (in or out of the country) or are being trafficked.[29] Statistics on repatriations—those deported from a country and sent back to their country of origin—often include illegal migrants (and possible traffickers) as well as trafficked victims. The Nigeria Immigration Service for the years 2002–2004 reported 31,277 repatriations (data disaggregated by gender and adults/children).[30] Many of those repatriated were returned from countries known as destination countries for trafficked Nigerian women and children, but it is still impossible, barring the children, to determine the status of those returning to Nigeria. This confusion between illegal migrants and trafficked victims and their inclusion into a single group can increase the number of potential victims.

This problem was documented by the European Commission in a study conducted in 2001 to determine the scale of the problem of child trafficking into the European Union. The United Nations Children's Fund (UNICEF) reported that during the period 1999 to 2000, a total of 33,402 unaccompanied minors came to the attention of authorities. This group included child asylum seekers, minors who had entered the country illegally, as well as a number who were within the protection system of one of the member states. A percentage of these children could have been trafficked, but it is impossible to determine what percentage of those children would have ended up as exploited trafficked victims.[31]

In the Netherlands, 716 unaccompanied minors who had applied for asylum disappeared from reception centers in 2004, almost double the number of children who disappeared from centers in 2003. The independent National Rapporteur on Trafficking in Human Beings believes that some of these children are trafficked through or into the Netherlands and are being exploited in prostitution, as domestic servants, in restaurants, or as drug couriers or thieves forced to work for criminal organizations.[32] It is unclear how many of these children are victims of trafficking.

Understating the Problem

The IOM maintains impeccable statistics on the number of trafficked victims it assists in returning home. While these statistics provide an accurate picture of the number of victims assisted by the organization, statistics measuring the number of victims rescued or repatriated reflect only the tip of the iceberg. IOM statistics and those generated by NGOs often report only those who seek help and thus underrepresent the true nature of the problem.

A study of trafficking in Southeastern Europe sponsored by UNICEF, the United Nations Office for the High Commission on Human Rights (UNOHCHR), and the Organization for Security and Cooperation in Europe (OSCE), highlights the disparity between the number of possible trafficked victims identified during police raids on bars and nightclubs, and those who agree to accept repatriation assistance from the IOM. The number of girls and women referred to the IOM by the International Police Task Force (IPTF) reflects a small percentage of suspected victims found during police raids.

> For example, according to weekly security situation reports from the United Nations Mission in Bosnia and Herzegovina (UNMIBH) for November 2001, the local police and IPTF raided 10 bars and nightclubs, where they found 39 foreign women, of whom only eight requested assistance from IPTF. Moreover, in one week 18-24 February 2002, four bars were raided and 48 women found, out of whom only two requested assistance.[33]

It is impossible to determine whether any of those women identified in the raids but who refused assistance were trafficked victims too frightened to seek help, and if so, how many. Clearly, however, counting victims who accept assistance and who are repatriated does not accurately identify the number of trafficked victims.

Registrations of Trafficked Victims

If we turn our attention away from estimates to the actual number of known cases or victims, these figures are surprisingly and disturbing small. It is possible to examine the number of victims actually identified by organizations providing services to trafficked victims (IOM, ILO, UNICEF, Save the Children, Terre des Hommes, or the myriad of local NGOs involved in victim assistance), to (potential) victims identified by law enforcement agencies or to governments providing legal residency status to trafficked victims.

In the period between 2001 and 2007, the U.S. Office of Refugee Resettlement certified only 1,379 (131 minor and 1248 adult) trafficked victims, providing even fewer with a T-visa.[34] The German Federal Criminal Police identified 689 victims in 2007.[35] This is a sharp decrease from a high of 1,235 in 2003.[36] The United Kingdom identified and referred for services only 489 women between March 2003 and May 2006.

The Dutch National Rapporteur On Trafficking in Human Beings, in its fourth report, identifies two sources of data on trafficked victims in the Netherlands. The Dutch police "victim tracking system" (*slachtoffervolgsysteem*) IKP-S identified 153 possible victims in 2003 (371 in 2002). At the same time, the NGO Foundation against Trafficking in Women (*Stichting Tegen Vrouwenhandel*) registered 257 (potential) trafficked victims (2003), a decline from 343 in 2002.[37]

CONCLUDING REMARKS

An accurate picture of the trafficking problem continues to elude us. Numbers range from estimates of trafficked victims to actual numbers of those identified who have sought help from the police and organizations providing assistance. Governmental and international organizations such as the U.S. Department of State and the United Nations continue to publish and revise estimates of the number of trafficked victims without providing information on how these estimates are reached. The ILO is attempting to provide estimates of worldwide labor exploitation and trafficking while providing information on the methodology used to reach those estimates.

There is a huge disparity between estimates and the actual number of trafficked victims who are identified as such. In spite of the fact that the numbers of victims registered by police and NGOs are small—particularly in comparison to estimates—each number represents a victim with a personal tragic story. Some of these stories will be told in the following chapters when attention is focused on trafficked victims and patterns of trafficking.

The next chapter places human trafficking within a number of contrasting perspectives to better understand how the problem of trafficking should be viewed and solved. This is important because it provides the basis for government and civil society best practices in response to the problem—a topic addressed in the closing chapter.

Contrasting Perspectives on Human Trafficking

TRAFFICKING CAN BE examined and understood from a number of different perspectives. It may be studied within the framework of the globalization, migration, and labor literature. Trafficking also can be studied from a law enforcement and criminal justice perspective focusing on the role of governments in preventing and punishing the trade, or from a human rights perspective, in which the victim takes the center stage. This chapter will briefly outline the different perspectives to provide a more comprehensive understanding of the phenomenon, particularly the implications of viewing trafficking as a unique form of slavery.

TRAFFICKING AS A MIGRATION ISSUE

Human trafficking often occurs within the context of migration—whether it is internal migration from rural to metropolitan areas within a country, or external migration from developing and countries in transition to more industrial nations. As discussed in chapter 1, both documented and undocumented immigrants are at risk of becoming victims of trafficking and being exploited. Irregular migrants are most at risk of being subjected to forced labor and exploitation, but regular migrants are also routinely denied both their human and labor rights.[1]

The dimensions of the crime cannot be accurately measured, but it is a fact that in the United States, and based on U.S. government statistics, trafficking is a crime most often perpetrated against undocumented migrants. Women and children account for a great proportion of undocumented immigrants to the United States and thus are particularly vulnerable to trafficking. High U.S. labor demand, limited country quotas, and the prioritization of family reunification over employment-based immigration make many migrants from less developed countries ineligible for legal entry into the United States. Immigrants trying to enter "Fortress Europe" from Africa meet similar obstacles. Faced with increased border patrols and heightened security at U.S. and European ports of entry, illegal migrants increasingly rely on smugglers to enter the United States and Europe. It is these same smugglers "who are uniquely positioned to engage in both labor and sexual exploitation."[2]

TRAFFICKING AS A DEVELOPMENT ISSUE

Those who fall prey to human trafficking tend to be the most vulnerable—usually the socially deprived characterized by low income, poor education, and lack of employment. These are typically circumstances of the poor—even though available data shows that it is not necessarily the poorest people in a country who are trafficked. Research, however, shows that many of the victims assisted by international organizations and NGOs invariably come from some of the most poverty-stricken countries (for example, Bangladesh, Mali, Moldova, and Nepal).[3]

Extensive research has been undertaken and victim support provided in Southeast Europe. There it is shown that trafficked victims come from the poorer countries of the region—Albania, Bulgaria, Moldova, and Romania. Albania and Moldova are the poorest in the region and are also primary source countries for trafficked persons.[4] In South Asia, Bangladesh and Nepal (two of the region's most poverty-stricken countries) are the major source countries.[5] Poverty is seen as the key factor in human trafficking in West and Central Africa and for rural trafficking in China.[6]

SMUGGLING AND TRAFFICKING AS AN ILLEGAL MARKET

Trafficking is a form of economic activity. Migration, smuggling, and trafficking can be seen as forms of business in which participating institutions aim to make a profit. Trafficking could be viewed as a by-product of migration, from which organizations profit from peoples' mobility. Researchers have argued that trafficking should be studied as a business that acts as the "middleman" in the global movement between origin and destination countries. Thus, trafficking networks can be viewed as business organizations.[7]

Smuggling and trafficking in migrants could not have grown to such proportions if it were not supported by powerful market forces. The increased demand for migrant labor coupled with stricter entry controls or requirements and diminishing legal channels to enter destination countries creates opportunities for unscrupulous offenders to make money while at the same time generates other illicit business opportunities involving the provision of fraudulent documents, safe-houses, guided border crossings, and job brokering.[8]

The crime industry involves the illicit exploitation of business opportunities and is dominated by supply organizations. Criminal organizations provide illicit goods and services to markets where the profits are high.[9] Transnational criminal organizations have become global players in industries such as drug trafficking yielding profits higher than the gross national products of some developing nations. What they share in common is their involvement in theft or smuggling of both licit (for example, cigarettes or persons) and illicit (drugs) products.[10] While lawful enterprises operate within legal parameters, transnational criminal organizations circumvent these legal requirements through deceit, threats, force, corruption, and other evasive tactics.[11]

Smuggling usually involves short-term profit whereas trafficking usually involves long-term exploitation for added economic gain.[12] The profit in smuggling is generated possibly before departure and during the transportation phase. In trafficking, the profit can be made before and during the transportation phase but is made, in particular, through the exploitation, sexual or otherwise, of the trafficked victims upon their arrival in the destination country.

Smuggling and trafficking can be viewed as an illicit market—as the interaction between supply and demand. In countries of origin there are always those who dream of a better life and the ability to support themselves and family members back home. In the receiving countries, there is a demand for cheap sex and labor. There is never a shortage of those who are willing to take risks to satisfy their needs and fulfil their dreams. A complex process links the supply and demand sides of the market.[13]

SUPPLY AND DEMAND

Trafficking, whether for sexual or labor exploitation, cannot be fully understood without looking at the question of supply and demand. If we concentrate on the demand side of the equation, demand has always existed for prostitution and workers in the commercial sex market. As wages increase in highly developed nations, there is a growing demand for cheap labor; as societies progress, there is the demand for cheap, unskilled labor—the agricultural sector, food processing, domestic service, home health care, and construction.[14]

In a multicountry study of the demand side of human trafficking for commercial sexual services and domestic labor, the authors found that demand for such services was "a socially, culturally and historically determined matter ... intimately related to questions concerning supply and vulnerability ... supply generates demand rather than the other way around."[15] The availability of a service, they argue, generates demand—whether it is for live-in domestic workers or lap-dance clubs. It has been argued that it is the market in trafficked women that creates the demand—not the customers. This is the rationale that underlies the Swedish legislation outlawing the purchase of sexual services holding that "[i]t is the market that is the driving force. Demand is defined by the services produced, not vice versa, which contradicts certain popular traditional market theories."[16]

Women are particularly vulnerable. They are in greater demand in many countries, in various legitimate and illicit sectors. In demand countries, there is a booming billion dollar commercial sex and entertainment industry. Women's exploitation in these industries is driven by "the unequal power relations that exist in patriarchal societies, power relations that sexualize women and objectify them for consumption."[17] Prostitution and the sex market aside, women are in high demand, in particular, in the domestic, household and care-providing (nursing) sectors. Other sectors for which there is a high demand for female employees include the fast food, service, and low-wage manufacturing sectors. Migration is often both easier and cheaper for women than for men. Education and skill requirements are lower for women than for men migrating to the Middle East from Indonesia or Bangladesh. Women pay lower fees to migrate than do men, and they are in greater demand in the Middle East as domestic servants.[18]

GLOBALIZATION AND TRAFFICKING

Globalization, market liberalization, and privatization have created an increasing need for cash incomes to purchase the most basic needs, including those once provided by the state. Often this demand cannot be satisfied in the local labor markets, obliging families to send family members out into the global workplace. An increasingly global world, easily accessible through television and the Internet, provides ready access to information about actual or potential opportunities in large cities, neighboring countries or other destinations, such as Australia, Canada, Europe, or the United States[19]

Globalization has resulted in an unprecedented mobilization of unskilled and low-skilled labor to fill labor-deficit markets for domestic work, agriculture, construction, and manufacturing. At an ever-increasing rate, migrant workers from less developed countries in South and East Asia often fill short-term labor contracts in more developed Asian, European, and Near Eastern countries. The International Labour Organization (ILO) estimates the population of migrant laborers to be 120 million. Countries receiving large numbers of migrant workers include Saudi Arabia (7.5 million), the United Arab Emirates (2.3 million), Malaysia (2.3 million), and Kuwait (1.3 million). Supplying countries include the Philippines (7 million), Indonesia (3 million), Bangladesh (3 million), and Sri Lanka (1.5 million). Migrant labor supports the economies in both the sending and receiving countries, and is, in itself, beneficial. It can, however, easily lead to situations of abuse, trafficking, and conditions paramount to slavery.

Globalization goes hand in hand with free trade and the ideology of free markets accompanied by a decline in state intervention and regulation. Those who advocate globalization argue that reducing international regulations and trade barriers will increase investment, trade, and development. The very conditions that promote a global environment, however, aid in the expansion of crime. Crime groups "have exploited the enormous decline in regulations, the lessened border controls, and the resultant greater freedom, to expand their activities across borders and to new regions of the world. These contacts have become more frequent, and the speed at which they occur has accelerated."[20]

TRAFFICKING AS A CRIMINAL JUSTICE ISSUE

From the perspective of the receiving or destination countries, trafficking has traditionally been seen as an illegal migration and security issue[21] often operated by criminal networks or organized criminal groups. From a criminal justice perspective, the focus on human trafficking is upon intelligence gathering, dismantling criminal groups, and arresting and prosecuting traffickers.

Human trafficking seldom occurs in a vacuum. Criminal groups that traffic persons rely to a great extent on existing smuggling routes, border vulnerabilities, and corrupt officials.[22] They may make use of the same persons to supply forged documents and safe-houses. In complex trafficking operations moving large numbers of persons through numerous cities and countries, "[a] major service industry has also developed to serve all forms of transnational criminals. This includes providers of false documents, money launderers, and even high-level professionals who provide legal, financial, and accounting services to ... groups."[23]

The networks that traffic human beings as well as the victims themselves have been linked to other criminal activities. Traffickers have not only forced their victims into prostitution, a criminal offence in most countries, but also have been known to coerce trafficked victims into taking, transporting, or selling drugs; into organized begging and pick pocketing; and to move firearms and stolen vehicles.[24]

Criminal enterprises make use of the skills, existing contacts, corrupt networks, and routes developed in specific markets in certain countries and expand into other illicit markets. Traffickers exploit immigrant smuggling operations to find new victims.[25] According to intelligence sources at Interpol, human trafficking supplements more traditional criminal activities such as vehicle theft, trafficking in arms, and drug trafficking.[26] Albanian groups have been linked to the smuggling of both drugs and aliens across the Adriatic, while Asian crime groups use the same routes to smuggle aliens across the U.S.-Canadian border that were formerly used to smuggle cigarettes. Traffickers have been linked to the use of physical violence, extortion for protection money or loan sharking to victims who must repay their debts, and money laundering.[27]

TRAFFICKING AS A VIOLATION OF HUMAN RIGHTS

Trafficking can be viewed within the framework of historical human rights issues. The exploitation and abuses of victims of trafficking have been addressed by various United Nations and ILO conventions long before the U.N. Trafficking Protocol entered into force.[28] The League of Nations and the ILO worked on the issue of human trafficking in the 1920s and 1930s. The first documented international conference on the trafficking of women

dates back to the previous century and was held in 1895 in Paris. When ana-
lyzing the phenomenon of human trafficking, the human rights paradigm has
the longest history. The emphasis of these international conventions is human
rights: "Human rights are not a separate consideration or an additional
perspective. They are the common thread."[29]

Traffickers in source countries take advantage of the unequal status of
women and girls, which include the misguided and dangerous stereotypes of
women as (sexual) objects, property, and servants of men.[30] Gender discrimination, a risk and push factor associated with trafficking, is recognized as a
fundamental denial of human rights. Among other rights violated are the
rights to health care, life, and liberty, and the right to be free from all forms
of slavery. Children have the right to grow up safe and free from abuse and
exploitation. Violations of human rights have been labeled both "a cause and
a consequence of trafficking in persons."[31]

The trafficking debate continues with attempts by governments to balance
their right to manage illegal migration against those of individuals—that is,
the right of people to leave their country of origin, to be free from political,
religious, or gender oppression, to be able to educate their children and pay
for medical treatment for their families, or to seek asylum in a safer place. To
protect smuggled and trafficked persons from abuses at the hands of those
who profit from their hardships while at the same time enforcing immigration
laws is the greatest challenge facing governments today.

TRAFFICKING AS SLAVERY

Article 4 of the Universal Declaration of Human Rights reads, "No one shall
be held in slavery or servitude. Slavery and the slave trade shall be prohibited
in all their forms."[32] And in spite of its abolition in the contemporary world,
it still exists in various forms in both developing and industrial nations. Debt
bondage occurs on a massive scale in South Asia, while descent slavery[33] can
still be found in countries such as Mauritania and Mali.[34] Child labor is prevalent in Central and West Africa and the trafficking of men for labor exploitation and of women and children for sexual exploitation is a form of slavery
affecting almost every country on the globe.

Kevin Bales, a leading expert on slavery and trafficking, defines slavery as
a state marked by the loss of free will. An enslaved person, forced through violence or the threat of violence, is incapable of freely selling his or her own
labor. Slavery has three key dimensions: the appropriation of labor, control by
another person, and the use or threat of violence.[35] Trafficking is defined by its
end result of the victim arriving in a situation of enslavement. "Trafficking in
persons is one of the means by which people or organizations bring people into,
and maintain them in, slavery and forced labor. Human trafficking is not a condition or result of a process, but the process of enslavement itself."[36]

The traditional slave trade of the sixteenth through the nineteenth centuries depended upon raids, wars, and forced abduction to obtain slaves, whereas trafficking relies to a great extent on false promises and deception. Returning to the definition set forth in the U.N. Trafficking Protocol, victims of trafficking are recruited through means of threat or use of force, coercion, abduction, fraud, and deception; through abuse of power or vulnerability; and through payments or benefits to a person in control of the victim. Studies often show that both children and adults are recruited through means of false promises rather than force. Once they are brought to their interim or final destinations, though, it is force, threat of force, or harm that keeps them prisoners and enslaved. It is at this point within the trafficking process that victims differ little from the seventeenth- and eighteenth-century African slaves who were kidnapped, bought, and sold into slavery and servitude. Unlike traditional slaves of the seventeenth and eighteenth centuries, trafficking victims are often "hidden in plain sight." They, too, however, are openly bought and sold—some in cattle markets, like the Karamojong women and children in Uganda, or like foreign women sold in auctions to sex traffickers in Taiwan[37]—others are bought and sold through hidden means, such as through the Internet, as models, escorts, and brides.

Trafficking violates political and civil rights that include the right to be free from degrading and cruel treatment as well as the right to be free from slavery-like practices.[38]

Slavery had a significant role in the economies of many societies. As Bales observes, "it was one of the first forms of trade to become truly international."[39] In the past, slavery found justification in racial and ethnic differences, but today the common denominator is poverty, not color or religion. It is a special economic institution, able to overcome revolutions, changes in political structures, adapt to a changing world and thrive. It continues to do so today. In this sense, trafficking and modern-day slavery have rapidly adapted to the new global economy.

CONCLUDING REMARKS

While trafficking can be examined from a number of different perspectives, it is virtually impossible to separate any one of these from the other. Just as trafficking must be viewed as a process rather than as a single offense, it must also be understood and examined in relationship to issues of globalization, supply and demand, migration, law enforcement, and human rights. These perspectives must be taken into account when designing effective measures to combat trafficking. Failure to understand the mechanisms that fuel trafficking in source and destination countries means that countries will be ineffective in protecting potential victims before departure and providing safety and services to exploited victims in the destination countries or in their countries of origin after they have been repatriated. Failure to arrest offenders and dismantle criminal networks that operate to exploit people only provides tacit support for traffickers to continue their operations. Failure to acknowledge the human rights abuses in trafficking means that the suffering of victims is not recognized, which then places them in the arena of illegal migrants. Trafficking is one of the most egregious forms of modern-day slavery and as such demands protection of the victims and punishment of those who would exploit and harm them.

Victims of Trafficking

HENRIETTE WAS 15 when she was taken by a friend of the family from Togo to work and attend school in Paris. She ended up working as a domestic servant from early morning until late at night and was forced to eat table scraps and sleep on the floor. At the age of 12, Malik was taken from Niger to Mali under the pretense that he would attend a religious school. Instead he was forced to beg on the streets for long hours. Forty-two-year-old Robert was forced to work eight months' long for sometimes 18 hours a day with limited food and no pay in the construction industry in Armenia. Maria, age 16, was tricked by a friend into traveling from her home town in Romania to Bucharest where she was sold into prostitution and kept in line through the threat of beatings. Two 16-year-old Thai boys, Top and Wirat, were drugged, kidnapped, and forced to work under inhumane conditions on a fishing boat off the coast of Thailand for nine months with little food and no pay. Thirty-nine-year-old Lucy was showered with compliments and gifts in her native Kenya. When she traveled to Germany to be with her German "boyfriend," he forced her into prostitution. These are the stories of real people.[1] They come from different parts of the world. They differ in age and gender. The jobs they are forced to do vary. But they share one thing in common. They were exploited—victims of human trafficking.

The victims of trafficking can be found in any sector in which there is a demand for cheap labor and in which police, aid, human rights, and antitrafficking organizations look to find them. But the victims of trafficking will not always be recognized as such. Their status as trafficked victims to a large extent will depend on whether there is adequate legislation and awareness of the plight of trafficked victims. Countries lacking legislation defining labor exploitation as trafficking will treat persons found in such situations as illegal migrants—that is, as criminals, not victims.

This chapter describes how the different global markets into which persons are trafficked will have a diverse impact on their condition as victims. The chapter provides a more in-depth analysis of child and adult victims of trafficking through the prism of victims' individual stories, and their physical and mental suffering.

MARKETS IN WHICH VICTIMS ARE TRAFFICKED

Trafficking for Forced Labor versus Sexual Exploitation

There exists the belief that trafficking is perpetrated predominantly for the sexual exploitation of the trafficked victim. This is only one form of exploitation and forced labor to which trafficked victims are exposed. The market in which victims are forced to work influences a number of other factors, such as the social stigma attached to the "trade," the visibility of the individual, contact with external sources, and how long the operation can last before being dismantled by the authorities.[2]

Both types of exploitation involve serious human rights abuses. It could be argued, though, that forced sexual exploitation is morally more reprehensible. Because of the social stigma attached to this activity, and the fact that it is illegal in many of the source and destination countries,[3] it is more difficult to gain the cooperation of victims of sexual exploitation and to later reintegrate them back in their original communities.[4] Additionally, these victims require more emotional and psychological support.

Prostitutes, because of their interaction with clients, have contact with those other than their exploiters. This increases the likelihood that they will seek help, escape, or, during police controls or raids, come to the attention of the authorities. Victims trapped in situations of forced labor, particularly in remote areas are more secluded. Victims forced into domestic labor or to work in the agricultural industry are often isolated and lack contact with clients. For these reasons, forced labor operations appear to be able to survive for longer periods of time. According to the U.S. Department of Justice, operations involving trafficking for labor exploitation tend to go unnoticed or are able to operate longer than trafficking for sexual exploitation before being uncovered. On average, trafficking operations for sexual exploitation can last from approximately one to two and a half years, while forced labor operations generally lasted from four and a half to six and a half years before being discovered.[5]

Markets Profiting from Smuggled and Trafficked Persons

Three basic legal and illicit markets profit from smuggled and trafficked persons: (1) the conventional or legitimate market economies (factories, farms, hotels, restaurants, etc.), (2) the legitimate domestic service economy (households that employ maids), and (3) the criminal economies of the sex industry (foremost, prostitution).[6]

Forced labor on farms or plantations often involves deplorable living, working, and sanitary conditions. Haitian workers in the Dominican Republic and Brazilian workers on plantations in Para State in Amazonia (Brazil) were subjected to conditions resembling slavery, kept in virtual debt-bondage, and subjected to the control of armed guards and soldiers who, on the estates in

Para, would beat or shoot workers who tried to escape.[7] In July 2006, Italian police freed 119 Polish workers from forced labor camps in the south of the country. Many of the victims had reportedly been beaten with metal rods, raped, and attacked by dogs. Several committed suicide in the camps in Puglia, southeast Italy.[8] In the United States in 2004, the Ramos brothers were convicted of human trafficking. They employed 700 workers to pick fruit in Lake Placid, Florida. The Federal Bureau of Investigation (FBI) reports that—

> [T]heir workers weren't workers in the traditional sense. They were more like slaves…. They forced these individuals to pick fruit for ten hours a day, six days a week, with no time off. They threatened them at gunpoint, promising torture and death if they tried to escape. And they made them live in filthy, substandard, and overcrowded apartments.[9]

Across Europe, the building trade and textile industries have benefited from smuggled and trafficked persons. In Milan, police uncovered an operation involving a Chinese organized crime group that forced dozens of immigrants, under inhumane conditions, to manufacture handbags, belts, and clothes, which were purchased by major companies operating in the renowned Italian fashion world.[10] The organizations that smuggle and exploit these victims generate a profit. However, the legitimate economy, which subcontracts with these smaller operations, also benefits financially from the use of exploited labor. Thus, a symbiotic relationship exists between the legal and illicit economies in this type of labor market. In 2000, it was estimated that the underground economy accounted for 28 percent of Italy's gross domestic product.[11]

Domestic servants are often the least visible of all trafficked victims. From India to Kuwait to the United States, female domestic workers are subjected to exploitive conditions. Their wages are withheld, they are underpaid, and they are emotionally, psychologically, and physically abused and isolated. Female domestic workers report being beaten and sexually assaulted by male members of the family. Their belongings are searched and their contact with those outside of the family as well as their personal freedom is often limited. They may be denied access to medical or legal services.[12] A Michigan couple, both doctors, imprisoned a woman they had brought from the Philippines as a domestic servant for 19 years. The woman was threatened with deportation, isolated, and psychologically manipulated through fear. She was paid $100 a month for her services.[13]

The practice of keeping children as domestic servants is widespread in Western and Central African countries. The author interviewed a nine-year-old girl in Lagos, Nigeria. Her family had brought her to Lagos when she was six years old to work as a maid in the household from which she escaped three years later. She was forbidden contact with the children in the family and had been made to sleep on the floor and eat leftover table scraps. During a trip to purchase groceries, the police found her wandering the streets. She knew her name but did not know the village or the country from which she came.[14]

The boundaries between these three markets of legitimate labor, domestic service, and the sex industry are not always strictly drawn, and it is not uncommon for those working in the legitimate economy or in domestic service to escape unbearable conditions and find themselves in the illicit sex industry. Research conducted in Germany shows that many domestic servants escape their employee-owner and drift into prostitution.[15]

With respect to the illicit sex industry, Italian researchers have identified three different levels of illicit prostitution. The first level includes those individual entrepreneurs who are involved in small-scale activities, such as running a brothel in a particular area. The second or mid-level prostitution schemes involve women who are controlled by the clandestine operations that imported them. The third and most sophisticated level includes large-scale and international criminal organizations that are linked with domestic criminal organizations. This third group seizes the women's documentation and maintains tight control over the women they have trafficked.[16] Particularly at this last level, profits are high. They are generated for the traffickers as well as for the brothel owners who buy and sell their victims. Money laundering allows the huge profits generated by this industry to be reinvested in the legitimate economy, and thus once again a profit nexus exists between the illicit and legitimate business worlds.

DISTRIBUTION OF TRAFFICKED VICTIMS ACROSS MARKETS

The U.S. Department of State estimated that, worldwide, 80 percent of victims of human trafficking are women and girls, with 70 percent of these the victims of commercial sexual exploitation.[17] These figures vary depending entirely on the region of the world in which trafficking occurs, how national legislation defines trafficking, the awareness of other forms of trafficking for labor exploitation, as well as proactive investigation and enforcement.

With respect to the 14,500–17,500 people estimated trafficked into the United States annually, the U.S. government provides estimates on the age, sex, and type of exploitation to which the victims are exposed. According to these estimates, the largest percentage of victims are adult women (33 percent) followed by girls under the age of 18 (23 percent) who are forced into the commercial sex trade. This is followed by adult women and girls forced into other forms of exploitation. On a smaller scale are boys forced into commercial sex (10 percent) and other forms of exploitation (6 percent) followed by men (4 percent for both forms of exploitation). This information is provided in table 4.1 below.

Research in the United States indicates that these estimates might not reflect reality. In reviewing trafficking cases between 1998 and 2003, 46

Table 4.1 The Distribution of Victims in Exploitative Conditions by Gender and Age

Victim by Gender and Age	Exploitation	Percent
Adult women	Forced or coerced commercial sex	33
Girls (under the age of 18)	Forced or coerced commercial sex	23
Adult women	Other forms of exploitation	14
Girls (under the age of 18)	Other forms of exploitation	11
Boys (under the age of 18)	Forced or coerced commercial sex	10
Boys (under the age of 18)	Other forms of exploitation	6
Adult men	Other forms of exploitation	3
Adult men	Forced or coerced commercial sex	1

Source: U.S. Mission to the European Union (2005b).

percent of 131 reported cases involved forced sexual exploitation, which remained the largest single category, while the remaining 54 percent involved exploitation for forced labor in the domestic service sector (27 percent), agriculture (10 percent), sweatshop/factory (5 percent), service/food care (4 percent), entertainment (3 percent), and mail-order bride (1 percent).[18] Table 4.2 provides information on the number and percentage of cases and the sectors

Table 4.2 Economic Sectors into Which Victims Were Trafficked in the United States Based on Cases Uncovered between 1998 and 2003

Economic Sectors	Frequency of cases (not individuals)	Percent of cases
Prostitution	58	46.4
Domestic Service	34	27.2
Agriculture	13	10.4
Sweatshop/Factory	6	4.8
Service/Food care	5	3.8
Sexual exploitation of children	4	3.1
Entertainment	4	3.1
Mail-order bride	1	0.8
Total	**125**	**100**
No economic sector reported	6	
Total (all cases)	**131**	

Source: Free the Slaves (2004, 14). Courtesy of Dr. Kevin Bales, President, Free the Slaves.

in which victims were discovered. This information says nothing about the number of victims that were identified and rescued in these cases.

Data available on the victims and markets of exploitation may portray a skewed picture of worldwide trafficking patterns. If it even exists, trafficking legislation in many countries only addresses exploitation in the sex market, virtually excluding men as victims of this crime. This has been referred to as the one-dimensional focus of the research.[19] More research exists on trafficking into forced prostitution than into other types of situations, and so it is easy to gather information about this type of trafficking. One trafficking expert argues that trafficking into domestic work may be a more serious problem than trafficking into prostitution, but little attention has been paid to this type of trafficking.

This is the case in the United States and in other parts of the world as well, in particular, in West Africa, where children are often trafficked into domestic service and manual labor. Male victims in the United States are trafficked into forced labor in construction work, agriculture, and street vending. When this same situation occurs in other countries, it is often labeled "slavery" rather than trafficking—for example, this has been seen in situations involving men trafficked from the Brazilian cities into the interior of the country, from Mali to Côte d'Ivoire, or from Cambodia into Thailand's fields and fisheries.[20]

The question then arises whether or not trafficking in women for sexual exploitation occurs more frequently or simply whether it has received more attention and thus greater registration. The United Nations reports that trafficking in persons for forced labor has not been viewed as a serious problem in many countries.[21] Clearly, it can be argued that trafficking for sexual exploitation is more demeaning, robs victims of a basic human right to determine how to use and with whom to share their bodies, and exposes victims to increased danger of infection from sexually transmitted diseases. This fact, and given the limitations of legislation that only defines trafficking in relation to sexual exploitation, may explain why so much attention has been focused on this type of trafficking.

THE VICTIMS: TRAFFICKING IN WOMEN, CHILDREN, AND MEN

The United Nations Office on Drugs and Crime (UNODC) database was established to track global trends in human trafficking. While there are limitations in the data,[22] the database does represent the first attempt, based on research, to provide a global picture of trafficking trends. In an analysis of 113 source institutions providing information on trafficked victims (for trafficking cases involving both sexual exploitation and forced labor) where gender is known, the largest group of persons reported trafficked are minors (consisting of the combined categories girls, boys, and "children"). Adult women account for the second largest group, but the single largest group of victims.

Adult males are reported in only a few sources. This pattern fluctuates from one region to the other. Children are most often mentioned as victims of trafficking in Africa and Asia, whereas women are most frequently reported as trafficked victims in Europe (Western, Central, and Southeastern), the Commonwealth of Independent States, Latin America and the Caribbean, and Oceania.[23]

The International Organization for Migration (IOM) maintains a database on trafficked victims covering more than 80 nationalities and 90 countries of destination. The global database contains 12,750 cases of victims assisted by the IOM through June 1, 2008.[24] In the IOM database, victims are, in general, young, single females: less than 19 percent of the surveyed victims are males, the majority are between 18 and 25 (56.9 percent), and more than 74 percent at or under the age of 25 years. More than half (55 percent) are single, separated, divorced, or widowed; only 8 percent were married.[25]

Trafficking for Sexual and Labor Exploitation

With respect to the nature of the exploitation, the United Nations has divided exploitation into sexual and labor exploitation. While some degree of detail has been lost due to the fact that labor exploitation was not further categorized, this division does provide a picture of the nature of the exploitation and its relation to gender. Where information on the type of exploitation was available, the analysis indicated that 80 percent of the sources cited sexual exploitation, while 19 percent of the sources referred to exploitation for forced labor. Women and children are most often the victims of sexual exploitation, followed by sexual exploitation and forced labor combined. Men, on the other hand, are more frequently the victims of sexual exploitation and forced labor combined, followed by forced labor and then sexual exploitation.[26]

This pattern may be misleading and may cause investigators and researchers, particularly with respect to women and children, to overlook exploitation in the labor sector. The director of the U.S. Office to Monitor and Combat Trafficking in Persons told of a meeting in a shelter in Thailand with a young Burmese woman (see case 4.1).[27]

CHILD VICTIMS[28]

Trafficking cuts across age and gender. The (il)legal displacement and exploitation of persons (within and across borders) affects the most vulnerable—and these are often women and children. Children and women are targeted for the trade because of their powerlessness, innocence, and inability to protect themselves. They are easier to manipulate and less able to claim their rights. Children can be made to work longer hours with less food, poor accommodation, and no benefits allowing employers to keep costs down.[29] Children are taken

Case 4.1. The Story of a Young Burmese Woman

Aye Aye Win was mislead by a recruiter who "painted a beautiful picture" of work in a neighboring country. After having incurred a substantial debt to cover the costs required by the recruiter for the job placement, Aye Aye was taken together with some 800 Burmese migrants, many children, to a shrimp farming and processing factory. She was forced to work in a prison camp. The isolated 10-acre factory was surrounded by 15-foot-tall steel walls, with barbed wire fencing, located in the middle of a coconut plantation far from roads. Workers were forbidden phone contact with anyone on the outside and were not allowed to leave the compound. They lived in run-down wooden huts, with hardly enough to eat.

Aye Aye tried to escape with three other women. Guards at the factory caught them and dragged them back to the camp where they were punished as an example to others, tied to poles in the middle of the courtyard, and refused food or water. As another form of punishment, to stigmatize her, Aye Aye's hair was shaved off. She was beaten for trying to flee.

away from their families and social networks resulting in isolation, which increases their vulnerability to exploitation.

Risk Factors

In some countries, traditional practices contribute to the trafficking of women and girls. There are particular push factors that place girls and young women at a higher risk than boys or young men. Girls in many societies are less valued than boys.

The custom of early and arranged marriage of young girls, particularly to an older man, may be viewed as a manner to relieve the poverty of her family. In other countries, female children are viewed as an economic liability when the family must produce a dowry to the groom upon marriage. Furthermore, there is a demand for young girls, virgins, in many African and South Asian countries, fueled by the false belief that sex with a virgin can cure sexually transmitted diseases or HIV/AIDS.[30]

The "sale" of young girls for early marriage effects 40 percent and 49 percent of young girls in Central and Western Africa, respectively.[31] Pressure for girls to migrate is particularly strong in West Africa, where families are poor and the girls require money for marriage preparations.[32] The same pattern is found in India where the majority of victims—over 60 percent—of both in-country and transborder trafficking are adolescent girls in the 12–16-year age-group. The majority of young girls are trafficked for commercial sex work. The United Nations Development Program (UNDP) reports that in Mumbai and other Indian cities, girl children as young as eight or nine are sold at auctions.[33]

A study of trafficking among Nigerian girls and women in Edo State, conducted by the Nigerian nongovernmental organization (NGO), Girls Power Initiative, attributes the reason why girls are more susceptible to trafficking abroad than boys and young men to a number of factors. First and foremost, there is a demand for their sexual services that makes them marketable commodities. Girls are expected to sacrifice their education and assume domestic responsibilities taking care of their parents and siblings. Because they will leave the family upon marriage, they are regarded as a poor investment and this makes it easier for the parent(s) to send them out to work. Additionally, domestic work is regarded as a preparation for marriage.[34] Because girls are more willing to make a sacrifice to support their families, parents prefer to send their daughters abroad. Low rates of education among young girls—due to the fact that their parents were unwilling to educate them—result in high rates of unemployment. This cultural pattern repeats itself in other countries as well. According to Antonio Maria Costa, director of UNODC, "When families (in Asian villages) sell their daughter, it's not out of poverty necessarily, it may be cultural."[35] All of these factors combined provided a "pool of girls to be trafficked abroad."[36]

The trafficking of young boys into sexual exploitation is a newer pattern that has been identified in countries from Afghanistan to Great Britain, from Pakistan to the Dominican Republic, and beyond. The sexual exploitation is often linked to child sex tourism in countries such as the Dominican Republic, Mexico, Sri Lanka, or Thailand. In Costa Rica, where homosexuality is stigmatized, men prefer to have sexual encounters with male children they have found on the street. In Pakistan, India, and Afghanistan, where boys partake in the cultural practice of "bachabazi" or "launda" dancing (where boys dressed as girls dance at private parties and weddings for men), boys are sometimes forced into prostitution. The U.S. Department of State reports that young boys in prostitution is a growing problem in Ghana and The Gambia, while in the Czech Republic and Great Britain, young "rent boys" are trafficked into prostitution for tourists in cities.[37]

Trafficking of children takes various forms and resembles patterns of recruitment used with adults. In the case of adolescent boys trafficked to Italy from Gabon and Senegal, it appears that Mafia-type organizations are involved. These organizations recruit the boys in their countries of origin through threats or deceit, trafficking them illegally by boat or with false travel documents by plane to Italy. Once in Italy, the young boys are forced into illegal drug dealing on the streets or transporting drugs such as crack, cocaine, and heroin. They are under constant control of the traffickers and are subject to threats of violence. The traffickers have been known to disfigure the victims' fingers with abrasive substances to evade police and immigration investigations based on fingerprint recognition.[38]

A major difference in the recruitment of children in some countries lies in the traffickers' negotiation with the parents of the child to remove the child from the family. While conducting research for the United Nations on trafficking patterns in the West African nations of Benin, Nigeria, and Togo, the author spoke to government officials, representatives from NGOs, and trafficked victims. In one case, the parents had willingly given their two sons to a man who promised to offer them an education and job training skills. Instead, he forced the young boys to work in a factory where they were physically abused, underfed, and denied medical treatment when they became ill. After three years, the boys were reunited with their family, having received no pay for their work. While some children are given away or sold by their parents, others are forcibly abducted or tricked. Other children, eager to travel, gain new experiences, and support their families, willingly leave with their recruiters after being promised some small token such as a radio. Our delegation was told that it is not uncommon for a recruiter to come into the village and promise the children if they work for three years they will be given a bicycle. After three years of hard, physical labor, the children are released and given the promised bicycle. Unaware of the fact that they have been exploited, they return to their villages and, in turn, recruit other unsuspecting victims.

Abject poverty is not the only factor contributing to the trafficking of children in West Africa. The trafficking of children is promoted by historical and cultural patterns of child fosterage, or placing children outside the home. The placement of children outside of the home is based on cultural values and is done to foster extended family solidarity and to further the education and vocational training of the child. This historical practice of child apprenticeship, known as child fosterage or "vidomegon" ("putting a child in a home"), contributes to the internal displacement and trafficking of children that is met with, if not acceptance, then less outrage than the trafficking of children abroad.[39] Children are introduced to work at very young ages and as a result of this are taught social values. It is a common belief that the life and education of a child is the responsibility of the extended family, thus it is not uncommon for children to grow up in the family of relatives, or third persons, particularly if these persons are living in better circumstances and are able to provide the child with better education and work opportunities.[40] The majority of trafficked children in West and Central Africa come from large, poorly educated polygamous families where the children have limited (if any) opportunities for education and training. The voluntary placement of children (which often leads to their trafficking) is the result of poverty and the desire to provide a better life for their children.

The ILO identifies a number of factors that place children at risk of trafficking. These include individual factors (marginalized ethnic minority, orphan or runaway, low self-esteem, naivety); family risk factors (poor, single parent families, large family in poverty, domestic violence or sexual abuse, illness such as HIV/AIDS, alcoholism or drug abuse); external and institutional risk factors (war or armed conflict, natural disaster, weak legal framework of enforcement, corruption, gender discrimination and weak education); community risk factors

Case 4.2. The Story of a Young Woman from Togo

Henriette Akofa was 15 years old and living in Sokodé, Togo, when a friend of her family offered to take her to Paris. In exchange for light housework, Henriette could attend school. Upon arrival in Paris, Henriette was forced to clean the house, shop, cook, and babysit. She was not allowed to eat with the family, was forced to wear rags, and sleep on the kitchen floor. She was taken by a second family as payment for a debt owed the first family. She was not allowed to speak to others and was allowed only limited contact with her family. It took Henriette four years to escape her slavery.[41]

(history of migration, youth unemployment, quality of village and community networks, lack of policing and trained railway staff and border guards); and workplace risk factors (unsupervised hiring of workers, unregulated informal economy of dangerous, dirty and demanding jobs with poor working conditions). These many factors explain why some children from a village or neighborhood are more susceptible to trafficking than others. For a full list of the ILO's risk factors for child trafficking, see Appendix 1.[42]

Poverty drives much of the child sex trafficking in the triple frontier area where Argentina, Paraguay, and Brazil meet. Many of the children most at risk either live on the street or come from impoverished families. In cases of extreme destitution, children are even contracted out by their parents. A blind beggar in Puerto Iguazú, reportedly walks the streets hand-in-hand with a seven-year-old girl—his neighbor's daughter. He makes his living by renting her out for sex.[43]

The ILO's International Program on the Elimination of Child Labour (ILO-IPEC) estimates that 1,200,000 children are trafficked globally. Child trafficking patterns vary by region, although commercial sexual exploitation of children has been identified in all regions of the world. In East Asia and the Pacific, the majority of children trafficked often end up in prostitution, although some are exploited in agricultural and industrial work, sweatshops, begging, and domestic labor. In Africa, children are trafficked into prostitution, domestic labor, mining, and armed conflict.[44] In West Africa, young children are forced to work as car washers, beggars, domestic servants, petty traders, hawkers, and bus conductors, or on farms or in rock quarries.[45] In Europe, children are trafficked for sexual and labor exploitation in agriculture and also into crime.[46] Girls as young as 13, mainly from Eastern Europe and Asia, are trafficked as mail-order brides and are forced to become involved in pornography or prostitution.[47] Children in Southeastern Europe have been trafficked into begging and delinquency.[48] In Central and South America, child victims are trafficked into sexual exploitation, crime, and plantation work. In North America, the pattern is similar, with children also trafficked into agricultural work, crime, and sexual exploitation.[49] The U.S. Department of

---

Case 4.3. Two Boys from Thailand

Two 16-year-old boys from Buriram, Thailand, were kidnapped by a trafficking gang on the first day they arrived in Bangkok. They were drugged, and while unconscious, were transported to a fishing port and imprisoned on a fishing boat with two other kidnapped victims for eight months. At times they were forced to work all day and all night, only being allowed to sleep when they could no longer stand up. They ate two meals a day, but never got paid. They were told stories of individuals on such fishing boats being killed and thrown overboard.

On February 23, 2007, the two boys were eventually released, after begging the captain to be allowed to visit their home. The captain dropped them off at the railway station in Nakornsritamrat and gave them 3,000 baht (less than US$100) each, informing them that the "broker" (i.e., the kidnapper) had already received all his fees from the captain.[50]

Justice has prosecuted cases against traffickers who have exploited children as domestic slaves. Children in the Middle East are exploited in domestic labor and commercial sex.[51]

In China, children are often abducted and forced to work in rock quarries.[52] This pattern differs in the Americas and the Caribbean, where child trafficking is driven by child sex tourism. In South Asia, children are sold into bondage to settle debts.[53] In the Gulf States, children under the age of five from South Asia and Africa have been forced to become camel jockeys while in other parts of the world,[54] young boys are kidnapped or sold by parents to serve as child soldiers.

Those children trafficked into labor exploitation are not necessarily safe from sexual assaults or sexual exploitation. Children hired to work as domestic servants in families have reported being sexually abused by their owners.[55] Children trafficked into one form of labor may be sold into another form of labor. For example, girls from rural Nepal were recruited to work in carpet factories or hotels in the city but are then trafficked into the sex industry over the border in India. The United Nations Children's Fund (UNICEF) reports that in almost all countries, the sex trade is the predominant form of exploitation of trafficked children. This practice results in systematic, long-term physical and emotional abuse.[56]

Debt Bondage: Born into Slavery

Debt bondage is a form of slavery and practiced widely in South Asia. This modern-day slavery results in the exploitation of young children from birth. These unfortunate victims inherit the debts of their family members.

Millions of low-caste laborers are believed to be trapped in debt bondage in South Asia. Bonded labor occurs when victims take loans from

Case 4.4. The Story of One Boy's Debt Bondage

Raman was born at the same brick kiln site where his father and grandfather had worked their entire lives to pay off a debt incurred by his grandfather. For 15 years, Raman and his family earned 3 rupees (2 cents) per 80 kilogram bag of bricks to pay off the US$450 advanced by the brick kiln manager. They were beaten with sticks and hit by the owner if they were not working hard enough or producing enough bricks. They could not leave, because the brick kiln owner threatened to hunt them down and beat them or bribe the police into arresting them.[57]

unscrupulous moneylenders and are coerced into repaying these debts by working in the factories owned by their lenders. Exorbitant interest fees and housing costs are added on to the loan so that it becomes almost impossible to repay the debt. The debt is passed down from one generation to the next and often results in the enslavement of entire families forced to work in rice mills, brick kilns, or other factories owned by the moneylenders. Families may be forced to work 14 to 16 hours a day. Children generally are prohibited from attending school and bonded slave laborers are often subjected to physical abuse (female bonded laborers may be subjected to sexual assaults).[58] According to UNODC, the cultural norms of some countries have not deemed some forms of slavery to be a crime.

WOMEN AS VICTIMS OF TRAFFICKING

The social and economic decline in Southeastern Europe has resulted in inflation, unemployment, poverty, and income differentials. This has had a dramatic impact on women, weakening their position in the labor market and resulting in increased unemployment among women and the feminization of poverty. This has encouraged increased migration, particularly among younger women.[59] Women in many societies face discrimination in the job market, lack of skills training, and the added responsibility of being the sole provider for the family.[60] The feminization of migration has been provided as an explanation for the large number of women exploited in conditions of trafficking.[61] Women from poor countries with little or no education have limited access to the labor market. They are also the first to lose their jobs in times of economic crisis. This unfavorable position strengthens their temptation to seek their fortunes abroad.

In their study of sex trafficking in the Americas, the International Human Rights Law Institute identified "individual" and "outside" risk factors that heighten the likelihood that women may enter the illegal migration market and fall prey to traffickers. Among the individual factors are poverty, lack of economic alternatives, illiteracy or minimal education, physical or sexual abuse, family dissolution, and homelessness. Among the outside factors are gender discrimination, objectification of children (this could apply to women as well), and the demand for prostitution, stripping, and sex tourism.[62]

Because, for years, many countries concentrated only on the sexual exploitation of the victims, more is known about the women victims of the sexual exploitation trafficking dimension. Chapter 1 placed trafficking victims on a continuum from those who are totally unaware of their fate to those who suspect or know that they will be working in the sex industry. It is unclear how many adult women suspect or are aware of what awaits them in the destination country. This understanding may depend on how and under what circumstances they are recruited in their country of origin. A study in the Netherlands on trafficked women from Central and Eastern Europe who were forced to work in prostitution shows that the majority of those interviewed were working as prostitutes in their own countries or at least knew that they would be working as prostitutes abroad.[63] Those working with trafficked victims in Benin City, Nigeria, also report that most victims are aware that they will be working in prostitution upon arrival in Italy.[64]

Others, like Lucy, are caught totally off-guard (see case 4.5).

Case 4.5. Lucy's Story

Lucy Kabanya, 39, left Kenya for Germany in July 2006 for a three-month holiday to join her German boyfriend in Frankfurt. Lucy, who was introduced to the man through a friend, began communicating with him through e-mail early in 2005; in 2006, he came to Kenya to meet her. When he came to Kenya, they stayed together in a hotel for a month before he returned to Germany. He promised to send her an airline ticket to go on holiday and visit him. Before she traveled to Germany, her "boyfriend" sent her gifts and money. "Before I left Kenya, my host had treated me so well; he had lavished me with gifts of all kinds, sent me money whenever I asked for cash. He promised me a life I had never seen before."

Upon her arrival in Germany, instead of a vacation, Lucy had her travel documents confiscated and she was denied food for several days before her "boyfriend" informed her that she would be working as a prostitute. She was raped, viciously beaten, and threatened with death.

Lucy was one of the lucky ones. Although she had been kept incommunicado, denied a telephone, and refused permission to talk to strangers, she was able to convince her captor to allow her to call relatives to inform them that she was all right. Instead, she called a friend who gave her the number of the German police hotline. She was immediately rescued and taken to a hospital, a safe-house, and then to Solwodi, an NGO that provides victim assistance.

The manager of the Kenya branch of German-based Solwodi, said, "We have received more than 25 women who have been returned to Kenya from Europe after falling prey to international crooks who took them there as their boyfriends before they turned them into sex slaves."[65]

Lucy's "hell on earth" in Germany lasted three weeks before she was able to escape. The length of time that women are forced to work in prostitution as trafficked victims depends on a number of factors, perhaps most important, the nationality of the woman and her trafficker, and whether or not the woman has repaid her debt. Research into trafficking patterns in Italy found that Nigerian women were exploited until they repaid the debt incurred. The period usually lasts a couple of years and depends on how quickly the victim can repay the trafficker based on the monthly agreed-on amount. Once they have repaid their debt, they become free agents and may themselves become involved in recruiting and exploiting victims. In contrast, Albanian women are forced to work as prostitutes their entire lives: "The rules imposed upon them and the modes of their recruitment (deceit or abduction) imply unconditional exploitation for an indeterminate period of time."[66]

MALE VICTIMS

Much less is known about male victims of trafficking than about female and child victims. In part this is due to the fact that emphasis has traditionally been placed on trafficking for sexual exploitation.[67] Male victims of trafficking, particularly male children, are represented in victim statistics for sexual exploitation, but adult males tend to be exploited in commercial firms, specifically in the agricultural, construction, and manufacturing sectors. This varies across countries and geographic regions. Florida's citrus industry has been linked to forced labor of predominantly Mexican and Guatemalan men, while foreign men in other states are exploited in sweatshops.[68] In Western Europe, male victims are trafficked into forced labor in restaurants and sweat shops. In Italy, trafficked victims forced to work in the manufacturing industry have been linked to international fashion houses that make use of underpaid labor.[69] Internal trafficking is prevalent in Brazil, where Brazilian men are exploited for forced agricultural labor, while foreign victims are trafficked to Brazil for labor exploitation in factories.[70] In countries that rely heavily on fishing, this industry tends to exploit trafficked victims. Men in China have been trafficked in forced labor, often into brick kilns.[71]

The plight of male victims of trafficking is receiving more notice. Three research projects on male victims of trafficking are being conducted: one examining trafficking patterns from East Africa and the Horn to South Africa; one examining the trafficking of men into maritime, construction, and agriculture in the Philippines; and one examining the trafficking of men in Serbia.[72] In the United States, in 2007, 30 percent of the 303 individuals who received certification letters recognizing them as trafficked victims were male—a significant increase over the 6 percent of male victims certified the previous year.[73]

Case 4.6. A Thai Immigrant Seeks Work in the United States

Sathaporn Pornsrisirisak, a Thai immigrant, thought he was coming to America, the "fairy tale place," to work for a Napa firm as a welder on the San Francisco-Oakland Bay Bridge for wages six times higher than he could earn in his native Thailand. For the privilege of a coveted job in the United States, Pornsrisirisak was required to pay a $12,500 "recruitment fee" from his $200 monthly wage. Desperate to provide for his family, he borrowed the money from a bank and loan shark at exorbitant interest rates. The Napa steel firm agreed to a subcontractor compensation package that amounted to $18.80 per hour for each worker, and that the employment agency, Kota Manpower, was supposed to pay the welders directly.

Instead of providing the 49 Thai nationals with high-paying jobs, the subcontractor/trafficker took away their passports; housed them in a shabby apartment with no gas, electricity, heat, or furniture; and threatened to send the men back to Thailand to face crushing debts if they complained. A Kota employee confiscated workers' passports, drove them to and from the job site, and threatened them with deportation if they complained.

Pornsrisirisak and the others were trapped in near-slavery, working 13-hour days at a Long Beach restaurant. They were kept in safe-houses where they slept on floors and were given scraps of food. For three months of full-time work, Pornsrisirisak was paid a total of $220.

After three months, Pornsrisirisak and the others plotted an escape with a Thai patron of the restaurant who drove them to a Thai temple.[74]

OTHER VULNERABLE VICTIMS

Other vulnerable groups have been known to be trafficked. These include the physically or mentally impaired, the homeless, or drug addicted—individuals who are less capable of protecting or standing up for themselves. In the Commonwealth of Independent States, disabled people are induced into street begging for support and protection,[75] while disabled children are used for begging in Thailand.[76] In New York, two defendants were convicted of smuggling disabled citizens from Romania into the United States to force them to

Case 4.7. Homeless Men Forced to Work on Farms

Ronald Evans recruited homeless men from shelters, forced them to work on his farm, and kept them in debt by selling them beer and overpriced and highly addictive crack cocaine on credit. The men would be lured from Miami with promises of a decent wage, hot meals, and a place to stay. Instead, they were forced to work on one of Ronald Evans' work camps in northeast Florida or North Carolina. When police raided the East Palatka, Florida, camp in June 2005, they found 148 individually wrapped crack cocaine rocks—one night's supply. Evans was sentenced to 30 years in federal prison.[77]

work as beggars.[78] Disabled men were trafficked from the Slovak Republic to Slovenia for the purpose of forced begging in 2007.[79] In Florida, law enforcement officials investigated a case involving U.S. citizens recruited from shelters for the homeless, as well as men who might be suffering from forms of mental illness or who are addicted to drugs and subsequently forced to work in the agricultural sector (see case 4.7).[80]

HARM TO THE VICTIMS

The trauma experienced by victims varies from one individual to the other and may be influenced by the age of the victim upon being trafficked, the nature of the exploitation, the length of time the victim is exploited, and the degree of violence and manipulation to which the victim is exposed. Victims of both sexual exploitation and forced labor are often left with little or no resources to rebuild their lives.[81] Victims of forced prostitution are often stigmatized by their families and communities, making it virtually impossible to return home and receive support. The Nigerian Immigration Service and workers from NGOs in Nigeria reported that the women who were forced into prostitution in Italy and subsequently arrested and deported from Italy are "crazed" when they return home. They are angry and belligerent because of the trauma inflicted on them by the traffickers as well as by the police and immigration officials who arrest and deport them with little more than the clothes they were wearing at the time of arrest. After having spent weeks to months working in prostitution, the women are not even allowed to take the few possessions and clothes that they had been able to accumulate.[82]

Aid workers report that victims suffer from depression and that suicidal thoughts are common. Victims' mental states include withdrawal, disassociation, and feelings of helplessness and self-blame. Trafficked persons experience depressive, psychiatric, and psychotic disorders.[83] Cristina Talens and Joe Murat, workers at the French NGO Committee Against Modern Slavery (*Comité Contre l'Esclavage Moderne*), were involved in the rescue of Henriette Akofa, the Togolese teenager forced into domestic slavery in Paris. Henriette survived her ordeal well. Another trafficked woman from Côte d'Ivoire who they rescued was so traumatized by her ordeal that she was completely withdrawn and incapable of communicating with her rescuers. She had to be committed to a mental institution.[84] The IOM, which often comes into contact with trafficking victims who need assistance in resettling in their home countries, reports that victims "who do escape have been so brutalized that they experience life-long psychological trauma, and, according to psychologists, only 30 percent fully recover to live a normal life."[85]

Trafficking of girls and women for commercial sex places many young victims in situations in which they are not protected by the law, they experience greater social stigma, and they have even less access to health and social

---

Case 4.8. A Wife Is Kidnapped

Coco was kidnapped in Mexico and taken to Canada after her husband double-crossed the men he worked with as a drug money courier. "At the beginning, they wanted all the information about money, properties, bank accounts and everything that my husband stole from them." The drug dealers soon altered their initial plans. Coco was beaten, locked up, and forced to perform sex acts for money. Within three months of working as a prostitute she got pregnant. Her captors took her to a doctor for an abortion. Instead, the doctor helped her escape.[86]

---

services.[87] Trafficking also increases the victims' vulnerability to drug addiction, unwanted pregnancies, and dangerous abortions.

The Link between Trafficking for Prostitution and HIV/AIDS

Forced prostitution and trafficking expose young women and children to sexually transmitted diseases, including HIV/AIDS, during the time that they are exploited. Victims face the risk of unwanted pregnancy, early motherhood, and reproductive illnesses that might affect future reproductive ability. The sometimes-serious health problems experienced by women victims of trafficking for sexual exploitation have been clearly documented.[88]

UNICEF has illuminated a more sublime link between AIDS and child trafficking. According to the organization, studies point to a clear link between the vulnerability of children to trafficking and the spread of HIV/AIDS. According to the latest estimates in Sub-Saharan Africa, the region more heavily affected by HIV/AIDS than any other region in the world, more than 12 million children have been orphaned by AIDS.[89]

Children with families affected by the AIDS pandemic may be abandoned to fend for themselves following the death of one or both parents. Even in instances in which one or both parents is still living, a child may be forced to care for or support a sick parent[90] or the other children or may be pressured to leave a village because of the stigma associated with having a family member with AIDS.[91] All of these factors put children at risk of being trafficked.

NOT ALL VICTIMS ARE THE SAME

A "typical" victim does not exist. Victims are not just young women, nor are victims exploited only in the commercial sex industry. Another quality that differentiates victims is the way in which they cope with their situation. While some victims recognize their victimization and are willing to seek assistance and cooperate with justice authorities in the prosecution of their trafficker, others refuse to relate to the term of trafficking or identify with the victim role and thus refuse assistance. In a study of trafficked women exploited in various sectors of the sex industry (from massage parlors to strip clubs) in Canada, even women brought to Canada under false pretenses, subjected to debt bondage, and forced to work in slavery-like conditions did not consider themselves trafficked victims.[92] One woman, who police believed to be a victim of the Netherlands' largest and most violent trafficking ring, responded to accusations that she was forced into prostitution and subjected to exploitation and violence with the following comment, "This scenario appears to be more like a Hollywood film than reality."[93]

Refusal to recognize that they are victims of trafficking can be caused by a number of reasons, ranging from a failure to realize that they are victims of trafficking or knowing that they can depend on the support of family in their countries of origin, to a desire to protect their exploiter (with whom they may have fallen in love). Some victims fear retaliation or violence against their families, and others may still be in debt to their traffickers or feel they have to continue working to repay the debt. Yet others fear they have failed in their first attempt to go abroad and are determined to "go abroad again."[94] This is often a euphemism for returning to prostitution, but the victims often believe that, once they have "learned the ropes," they can work as freelance sex workers the second time around. Organizations working with children in West Africa have reported that in spite of being exploited at hard labor under deplorable conditions for years at time, children are given their promised bicycle at the end of their term and are allowed to return home, proud of the fact that they are the only ones with a bicycle in their village. Some of these same children return to their village and recruit other children to work abroad. In Chapter 5, we will examine the phenomenon of those who transform from victim into perpetrator.

CONCLUDING REMARKS

Although women and children are most susceptible to human trafficking, even men are not spared this egregious form of modern-day slavery. Trafficking and exploitation will occur in any market in which there is a demand for cheap labor. There is a never-ending supply of potential victims trying to improve their lives and those of their families. Exploitation affects victims in various ways. Whether they are able to psychologically and emotionally survive their situation will depend on their own internal strength, the nature of their abuse, and perhaps the legal, medical, and psychological support and protection they receive upon being rescued. Whether or not victims even recognize that they have been victimized will determine how they process their experience. These issues will be addressed in more depth in Chapter 9. The next chapter will examine the traffickers, their organizations, and how they operate.

5

The Traffickers: Their Methods of Operation and Organization Structure

CHAPTER 5 INTRODUCES the reader to the criminals involved in human trafficking and then discusses the trafficking process and provides an analysis of trafficking organizations—as networks, highly sophisticated criminal enterprises, organized crime groups, and business models. To fully understand the trafficking process, one must understand criminal organizations and the methods they use to recruit, transport, control, and exploit their victims and how they manipulate the system to protect their operations. Only within this context is it possible to formulate enforcement and policy responses to react to the criminal organizations involved in human trafficking and design prevention programs aimed at potential victims—topics that will be covered in more depth in chapter 9.

WHO ARE THE TRAFFICKERS?

Who are the people who so ruthlessly recruit and exploit the victims? What is their national or ethnic background in relationship to the victims? Is it only men who recruit others for exploitation or are women also involved in this insidious trade? The answer to these questions may depend on a number of factors, such as the country of origin of the traffickers and their victims, how the victim was recruited and whether we are examining the recruitment, transportation, or exploitation phase.

Police and court (official) statistics provide us with a good, but limited, picture of people who have been arrested on (suspicion of) human trafficking charges. This is only a limited picture, for it tells us nothing about those traffickers who have not yet come to the attention of the authorities. Trafficked victims and nongovernmental organizations (NGOs) are another source of information on the background of offenders. This is what they tell us.

A number of countries provide annual statistics on traffickers arrested by local or national law enforcement. Germany's Federal Criminal Police Office (*Bundeskriminalamt*) provides the following data: in 2007, 714 suspects (644 in 2006 and 683 in 2005) were identified by the police. More than three-quarters

(78 percent) of those arrested for human trafficking were men. The largest majority, 344 or 48 percent were German (of which 71 [20.7 percent] were not born in Germany). Europeans accounted for 87 percent of those arrested for trafficking with the largest number of traffickers arrested coming from Turkey (49), Bulgaria (42), Hungary (29), Romania (25), and Poland.[1]

The Dutch National Rapporteur on Trafficking in Human Beings provides detailed information on the number of traffickers against whom charges are brought as well as their age, gender, and the country of birth. Between 2002 and 2006, 715 suspects faced charges. The average age of those arrested for trafficking was 32 years old (in 70 percent of the registered cases, the suspects were between the ages of 18 and 41). In 2006, 11 suspects were minors, which represented an increase over the previous years. While the number of suspects with relation to country of birth varied over a five-year period, the countries with the largest number of suspects include the Netherlands, Turkey, Bulgaria, Rumania, and Morocco. The gender distribution is particularly interesting. Of all suspects, males accounted for 81 percent in 2004, 87 percent in 2005, and 83 percent in 2006. This, however, differed among ethnic groups. Among the Turkish traffickers arrested in 2006, there were no females involved in trafficking, and among the Dutch traffickers, there were few females. Among the Russian, Hungarian, Rumanian, and Bulgarian traffickers, the percentage of women was high and varied between 30 percent and 39 percent.[2]

Studies conducted by organizations working with victims may provide information unavailable to the police, because not all victims cooperate with criminal justice authorities. Information gleaned from victims trafficked in Southeastern Europe indicates that recruiters/traffickers from Albania and the province of Kosovo are almost exclusively men, while a large percentage of those trafficking women from Moldova, Macedonia, and Bosnia and Herzegovina are themselves women.[3]

U.K. police provide information on traffickers obtained from cooperative victims and from those arrested during Operation Pentameter (described in more detail in chapter 9). Eastern European groups—including Lithuanians and Czechs—predominate among traffickers; however, Albanian males appear to be the most heavily involved both as pimps and within trafficking. Information was beginning to emerge concerning the involvement in Chinese networks involved in the illicit sex trade. Traffickers are mostly males in their mid-20s. Many of the men are illegal migrants, asylum seekers or those who have overstayed their visas.[4]

WOMEN AS TRAFFICKERS

Women have often been portrayed as the victims of trafficking, although this is not always the case. Women are not only becoming more involved in the trade, but contrary to popular belief, the role of women as traffickers is "significant and increasing."[5] Some of these women have been the victims of trafficking. This may explain the high number of women from the Russian Federation, Bulgaria, and Rumania arrested in the Netherlands as perpetrators—women from these countries are overrepresented among victims of trafficking.

If they play a role in the trafficking process, women are generally involved in the recruitment phase. They may unknowingly be asked to recruit friends to work abroad. They may be sent back to their countries of origins to recruit friends under the watchful eye and threat of the organization that trafficked them. They may knowingly recruit women as a way to buy their freedom or may have become part of the trafficking organization.[6] The United Nations has called this "happy trafficking," although there is nothing happy about it. It has been described as a sort of human pyramid scheme in which a few of the trafficked victims are released, and sometimes provided financial incentives, to return to their home countries and recruit other victims. The term "happy" refers to the illusion that the new recruiters create by pretending that they have had a wonderful experience in a legitimate job abroad. This manipulative method reduces the risk to organizers by putting women in visible positions as recruiters and at the same time increases profits, turning victims into "proxy recruiters" and eventually traffickers.[7]

Law enforcement is noticing an increased involvement of the number of women organizing the business operation and controlling victims. In some cases, the women act as compatriots to male partners, while in others, the women are in control of most of the operation. During an exposé of trafficking in women between the Czech Republic and the United Kingdom, an undercover reporter went to the Czech Republic to allegedly purchase prostitutes for his U.K. brothels. He was shown one of the women who would first be sent to the United Kingdom to work as a prostitute, and at the same time, would verify the legitimacy of the organization for her traffickers back home. According to the reporter, she was being groomed to move up in the trafficking organization.[8] In another case, a San Antonio woman and her two daughters were directly responsible for managing the entire operation trafficking Mexican children to the United States for sexual exploitation. The women allegedly traveled to Nuevo Laredo, Mexico, and recruited and then smuggled girls as young as 15 to work as prostitutes in Texas.[9] This pattern has been found in various countries. Police and justice statistics may provide an indication of the number of women arrested as suspects; individual case files provide more detailed information on the specific role played by the female traffickers.

The role of women in the trafficking of Nigerian girls and women for forced prostitution has been well documented. Young women between the ages of 15 and 25 are recruited for commercial sexual exploitation by an older woman, a Maman or Madam, who acts as facilitator for the women and girls and the organization preparing their migration. When the young women arrive

Case 5.1. Young Women Promised Legitimate Work Are Forced into Prostitution

A sex trafficking ring run by nine illegal migrants smuggled girls and young women from Guatemala into the United States with the promise of legitimate work as babysitters or waitresses. Upon arrival, they were forced to work as street prostitutes to repay an inflated debt. Some of the girls were as young as 13. The children were told to lie about their age if asked. Some of the victims were taken to reputed "witch doctors," who would allegedly place a curse on the victims or their families in Guatemala if the victims tried to escape. All victims were told that if they did not repay their debt or tried to escape, they, their children, or their families back home would be beaten or killed.

The majority of those arrested for trafficking were women. The nine defendants included a family of six, among them, five women. Other traffickers were the son of a trafficker and his live-in girlfriend, and two live-in boyfriends of the same women.[10]

in the destination country, another Maman[11] supervises, controls, organizes the groups (comprising 10 to 15 girls or women), coordinates their activities, and collects their profits. Most Mamans were themselves prostitutes. Once they repaid their debt to their Maman, they, in turn, use the same method to make money.[12]

A study of Nigerian women involved in trafficking of Nigerians to the Netherlands revealed that the women were on average 45 years old, had legal residence in the Netherlands, or were awaiting a residence permit based on a relationship or marriage to a Dutch partner. All had worked in prostitution in Nigeria and the Netherlands and had worked their way up to the role of madam. The women play a key if not the main role in the trafficking organization, planning and controlling the entire process.[13] The Dutch National Rapporteur reports that among Nigerian trafficking suspects arrested between 2002 and 2006, the numbers are small, yet 78 percent are women.[14]

Limited statistics are available on the number of females suspected of or convicted for their involvement in human trafficking. The International Organization for Migration's (IOM's) Counter-Trafficking Module (CTM) database (data obtained from 78 countries between 1999 and 2006) indicates that 42 percent of the 9,646 sex recruiters were women (an additional 6 percent of the cases involved recruitment by both women and men).[15] Statistics from the Dutch National Rapporteur on Human Trafficking indicates that 32 (17 percent) of the suspects arrested in 2006 were females from Bulgaria, Romania, and the former Soviet Union (five suspects each), the Netherlands (four), Morocco (three), and one each from Brazil; Hong Kong, China; Hungary; India; the Islamic Republic of Iran; the former Yugoslavia; Lithuania; Nigeria; Poland; and the former Czechoslovakia. Thirty-eight percent of the Bulgarian and 36 percent of the Romanian suspects are women.[16] The

German Federal Criminal Police reported that almost one-quarter (22 percent) of the 714 suspects arrested in 2007 were women.[17]

Other statistics provided by the United Nations Office on Drugs and Crime indicate that, in Nigeria, 60 percent of those prosecuted (and 50 percent of those convicted) for trafficking are women, while in the Slovak Republic, a quarter of those prosecuted in trafficking cases are women. Furthermore, the United Nations. reports that the percentage of women involved in trafficking in Italy varies tremendously from one country to the next. Data collected between 1996 and 2003 show the percentage of women traffickers: Albania (7 percent), the former Yugoslavia Republic (11 percent), Italy (12 percent), Romania (25 percent), and Ukraine (79 percent).[18]

RELATIONSHIP BETWEEN TRAFFICKERS AND THEIR VICTIMS

Law enforcement agencies and studies reveal that (sex) traffickers, particularly those operating in source countries, recruit victims of their own ethnic background or nationality.[19] The relationship may determine the method used to recruit the individual victims. Victims may be recruited by strangers through formal advertisements, Internet ads, word of mouth, or family members or friends. In Albania, young women from rural areas are reported to be "courted" with expensive gifts and recruited with false promises marriage. Almost one-third of the women (738) repatriated to Albania were found to have been recruited through fraudulent promises of marriage.[20] Kidnapping, while an uncommon recruitment practice among traffickers in other countries, appears to occur with some regularity in Albania. Within this same sample, 7 percent of the repatriated women reported having been kidnapped. Children in West Africa are often placed in the trust of traffickers—often family members or friends—who promise the parents to provide education or work opportunities. Organizations working with trafficked children report that they are at times sold outright or traded for items. One NGO told of an Albanian child who was traded for a second-hand television set.[21]

THE TRAFFICKING PROCESS

Recruitment and Preparation for Travel

Recruitment very often involves promises of marriage (or of employment, education opportunities, or a better life). The U.S. government identified this same pattern in Taiwan, China, where the demand for young Vietnamese women as brides and concubines has resulted in a record number of these young women being brought into Taiwan. After being married and becoming legal citizens, many are sold into prostitution.[22] Believing that they will be happily married, all women willingly depart their native countries.

This is also true for women who believe that they will be working abroad. A study in the Philippines found that all victims left the Philippines willingly. The majority of respondents in the study said they were sought out by recruiters, while less than a quarter of the 85 victims interviewed sought out the recruiters themselves. A large majority of the victims were contacted through word of mouth by intermediaries that included family members, friends, or acquaintances known to the respondent or the family.[23]

Traffickers use various methods to bring trafficked persons into a destination country. They may, under false pretenses, attempt to secure legal visas into a desired country, or use this country as a point of entry into Western Europe. Once in the European Union, they are subject to no or minimal border controls. During a mission to Nigeria in 2000 to assess the problem of trafficking in women, our U.N. delegation[24] was told by embassy personnel of EU Member States, that Nigerian traffickers used to "visa shop" for the embassy, which imposed the fewest restrictions on the issuance of visas. Consular officers told of individuals who sought to obtain travel visas for women's study groups or tours. One consular official told of a Nigerian who sought visas for members of his young women's badminton team. When embassy personnel invited the young women in individually to interview them and test their knowledge of the sport, the women had no idea what a badminton shuttlecock looked like. When embassies began coordinating their efforts and made it more difficult to obtain visas from EU countries, Nigerian traffickers began moving their victims to Benin to attempt to secure visas from the embassies of EU Member States in that country. When this failed, they began moving victims overland to Northern Africa.

Customs and immigration officials report other ruses as well. Picture substitution in passports or passport rental from young women to smuggle look-alikes into a country have also been reported by law enforcement officials. While more and more passports contain bio-information printed on chips, this clearly is not the case in many developing nations where funds are scare and the verification of a person's identity is difficult—birth records in rural villages are often nonexistent.

Transportation

The transportation phase varies per trip and client. Some victims are unaware of what awaits them at their destination due, in part, to the fact that they are treated so well during the transportation phase. The exploitation or victimization of persons in transit may depend in part upon whether they are transported by plane or through other modes of transportation prolonging the journey. In a U.N. study of Filipinos who were trafficked to Japan, the Republic of Korea*, and other destinations, many reported residing in four- to five-star hotels in transit.[25] Others are not so lucky.

---

*Republic of Korea and South Korea will be used interchangeably throughout the text.

Stories of children trafficked from and within West African countries portray a harsher reality. Togolese child victims reported varying degrees of hardship and exposure to uncomfortable and dangerous situations during their travels. Children reported being transported without documents across national borders and being forced to walk long distances. Child victims interviewed told of being subjected to physical and psychological violence once they were on the journey. Children transported by boat reported that other child victims had succumbed to thirst or drowned.[26] Likewise, Nigerian women reported being raped while in transit overland to Northern Africa to "groom and prepare" them for what awaits them in their destination country in Western Europe or to force them to pay for their upkeep during the transport phase.[27]

Exploitation

Creation of debt is one of the main mechanisms used by traffickers to maintain control over victims. Debt can be incurred as a result of the cost of the trip of having been smuggled into the destination country. Trafficking, however, occurs also in situations in which no debt was incurred—either the victim paid all costs before departure, or there was never any discussion of repayment for expenses, in cases, for example, when women are unsuspectingly brought to a country as the "girlfriend" of the traffickers.

Even when the initial debt has been repaid, victims are not always free to leave. Some victims continue to be financially exploited—by having to pay for food, rent, and other services, often at exorbitant prices. In the case of Turkish traffickers in Amsterdam, women were forced to turn over €1,000[28] per day to the traffickers and also had to pay for the rental of their rooms and an additional €100 to €150 a week for their "security guards."[29]

Nigerian women are generally exploited until they repay the debt incurred.[30] This means that they are forced to remain in prostitution for a couple of years depending on how much money they repay their "madams" each month. The conditions in which the women work and live is reported to be abominable and results in a short life expectancy, "which sometimes does not extend much beyond the time needed to extinguish the debt."[31] Once the women are successful in repaying their debt, they often themselves become madams, join the criminal organizations, and recruit their own victims who they force or trick into prostitution.

In contrast to the Nigerian victims, Albanian women are forced to work in prostitution their entire lives. They are subjected to "unconditional exploitation and for an indeterminate period of time."[32] Their only chance of being saved is to escape or be caught by police, report their victimization, and testify against their traffickers. The situation is similar for Eastern European women who are forced to work in prostitution in Italy.

This pattern of exploitation and debt bondage extends to trafficked victims in situations of labor exploitation as well. Bangladeshi workers responded to an advertisement to work in a garment factory in Jordan promising them a salary of US$125 a month to work eight hours a day, six days a week. The three-year contact also offered paid overtime, free accommodation, free food, and medical care in addition to no advance fees. Upon their arrival in the United States, workers' passports were confiscated, and they were prohibited from leaving the factory and forced to pay exorbitant fees. No salary was forthcoming, food was inadequate, and sick workers were tortured. Workers were forced to stay to repay the debt they had incurred in having borrowed money to pay for their trip.[33]

MAINTAINING CONTROL OVER VICTIMS

Traffickers resort to a number of psychological and physical means to manipulate and control their victims.

Use of Violence and Threats to Control Victims

Violence or threats of violence are often used to intimidate or punish noncompliant victims. The degree to which traffickers exercise control over their victims has been well documented in victims' accounts. Seizure of documents and threats of violence (to beat the victims or to harm the victim's family in the country of origin) have been reported to police and NGOs. In one case in the United Kingdom, a trafficker threatened to use a young Czech mother's children in pornographic videos if she did not cooperate and work for him as a prostitute.[34] Violence or the threat of violence is used routinely to "keep women in line" or prevent future transgressions.

Violence is also used as punishment for rule-violating behavior. Women who have tried to escape, communicate with customers, or cooperate with police are often severely beaten. A Human Rights Watch study on Nepalese girls and women trafficked to brothels in India reported that "trafficking victims in India are subjected to conditions tantamount to slavery and to serious physical abuse. Held in debt bondage for years at a time, they are raped and subjected to other forms of torture, to severe beatings, exposure to AIDS, and arbitrary imprisonment."[35] Numerous studies report that between a quarter to more than half of trafficked women seeking assistance from organizations working with migrants or those repatriated have been severely beaten and or raped by their pimps and traffickers.[36]

Another instance in which violence is used by traffickers is as a warning to keep other trafficked victims "in line." Punishment is extreme and occurs publicly. In a murder in Istanbul, Turkey, two Ukrainian women were thrown to their deaths from a balcony while six of their Russian friends watched. In another incident in Serbia, a woman who refused to work as a prostitute was beheaded in public.[37]

Case 5.2. Latvian Women Forced to Strip

Alex Mishulovich, a naturalized U.S. citizen from Russia, posed as a nightclub owner and contacted Latvian women whom he and his wife approached on the streets of Riga, Latvia. He told them they could earn up to $60,000 a year in a nightclub and that the men would not be allowed to touch them. At least five Latvian women were trafficked to Chicago and held in slavery-like conditions and forced to strip at Chicago nightclubs. The women would earn as much as $600 a night but were forced to give all but $20 to the traffickers.

Mishulovich, who claimed allegiance with the Chechnyan mafia, helped the women obtain immigration papers, but as soon as they arrived in Chicago he took their papers, locked them in apartments or hotel rooms, beat them, and threatened to kill them. He told the women his mobster associates would kill their families in Latvia if they refused to obey him. At times, he held a gun to a woman's head or put a knife to her throat.[38]

The large-scale and highly sophisticated trafficking-prostitution ring run by two Turkish-German brothers (Hasan and Saban B.) in the Netherlands was described as one of the most brutal. Women who spoke to police were beaten with baseball bats and then submerged in cold water to prevent or reduce the visibility of bruises. They were forced to undergo abortions and breast implants. A number of victims were also tattooed with the name or initials of one of the two brothers. The message: the girls were not for sale.[39]

While seizure of documents and beatings are a common method to exert control, other forms are more psychological, nuanced, and less visible. The Turkish-German brothers Hasan and Saban, in addition to beating and constantly supervising the women they forced into prostitution, manipulated them to ensure their compliance. Women were complimented, made jealous, belittled, and abused.[40] This same pattern is found in the practices of "loverboys" (a modus operandi) in the Netherlands. After having convinced their young Dutch victims that they are in love, these older men (usually of Moroccan and Antillean descent) ease these girls into prostitution. This creation of emotional dependence facilitates the long-term exploitation of young women who may not even realize that they are being exploited.[41]

The deputy director at the Washington-based Polaris Project describes the same pattern in the United States. Runaway girls are targeted by pimps and showered with a mixture of affection and violence, gifts, and degradation. The girl may be required to tattoo her pimp's name on her thigh as a sign of ownership. In exchange, she may be given jewelry or clothing as presents. It is the emotional bond and fear that keeps the victim tied to the trafficker. This "trauma bonding" occurs when the trafficker wields the power to kill the victim, but does not do so.[42]

Unique to a number of West African countries, in particular, Nigeria and Ghana, is the use of voodoo practices or "juju" to instill fear into young women and prevent them from escaping or cooperating with police. Traffickers practice voodoo rights on the girls prior to departure from Nigeria. Young women are forced to swear an oath, and a piece of (intimate) clothing, a fingernail clipping, or lock of hair is used in a voodoo ritual that binds the victims to their traffickers. Failure to respect the oath results in misfortune befalling the girls or their families.[43] Allegedly, the trafficked women are so fearful of these oaths that Italian police note that, compared with other foreign women trafficked into prostitution into Italy, Nigerian women are subjected to much less physical supervision and control.[44]

The situation may be changing in some countries. According to organizations working with or conducting research on trafficked victims, trafficking is increasing but fewer victims are coming to the attention of these or other official agencies. The patterns of exploitation and abuse are changing. The use of physical abuse and overt violence is decreasing, while psychological abuse and manipulation is increasing.[45] Exploitation is becoming more subtle and control over victims is more relaxed. Victims are being given small payments and are even being moved into their own apartments in an attempt on the part of traffickers to buy the victim's silence and ensure that victims to do not denounce their traffickers.[46] This diffuses the sharp line drawn between trafficked victims and freelance sex workers and makes it difficult for agencies providing assistance and law enforcement to identify who is a trafficked victim entitled to help and who is an illegal migrant and freelance sex worker subject to deportation.

Rotation of Victims and Provision of Sex Services to Illegal Migrants

Traffickers and brothel owners treat women as commodities. A typical pattern that emerged in case studies of police files conducted in the Netherlands revealed the buying and selling of women to brothel owners and pimps after they had spent a certain amount of time in particular brothels. These "prostitution carrousels" meant new faces that in turn ensured new clients. The manner in which brothel owners and pimps acquired trafficked victims for forced prostitution varied from those who went to the countries of origin (often from the former Eastern Bloc) to bring back their women, to others who simply bought women from known pimps and recruiters.[47]

Organizations protect their operation through the rotation of prostitutes between clubs, massage parlors, or brothels in a city, between cities, and even between different countries. The prosecutor's office of Ascoli Piceno, Italy, reported that Eastern European women are rotated every six to seven months both within Italy and to other countries as a result of the need to protect the criminal organization from arrest and market forces (clients want new girls).[48] In the United States, Asian trafficking networks rotate trafficked victims forced into prostitution between "hostess clubs" or "room salons," massage parlors, and brothels hiding behind legitimate businesses. According to the deputy director of the Polaris Project, workers are shared by all three kinds of sex operations, all sell sex, and all are linked to organized crime.[49]

At an IOM shelter in Tirana, Albania, many of the young victims of sex trafficking spoke Italian, German, Dutch, and English. They learned these different languages while "working" in those countries. Some of the girls were in as many as four different countries during their time as sex slaves. That was disturbing, but more shocking was the realization that the majority of the girls were under the age of 21. This same pattern was revealed in a police and prosecutorial investigation into the trafficking of women from Lithuania to the Netherlands for forced prostitution. Victims were being moved or sold to brothels in Austria, Denmark, the Netherlands, and Spain.[50]

Rotation provides new faces to the male clientele but also ensures that male customers do not establish a relationship with the trafficked women. This situation may result in a customer reporting the woman's situation to the police.

While this rotation is a protective mechanism used by trafficking organizations to prevent the establishment of a bond between the customer and victim, other traffickers exploit this situation for further financial gain. Trafficking gangs in Dubi, Czech Republic, reportedly do not sell their victims, rather they rent them out to other traffickers and brothel owners. One young 21-year-old woman had worked as a prostitute in different cities in the Czech Republic, Germany, the Netherlands, and the United Kingdom.[51]

Women and children also may be rotated out of the commercial sex market if they are "sold" to a customer. In a U.N. study of Filipinos trafficked to Malaysia, four cases were uncovered of women being "bought" by men to become "wives" or mistresses. It cannot be determined whether the men, in buying them, freed these women from sexual slavery and improved their position, or whether the women then became domestic and sex slaves to these men.[52]

Another way in which criminals avoid detection is to keep their business within the illegal circuit. The Mexican Cadena family created a market for sexual services among illegal migrant workers in Florida and then supplied the men with often-underage women from Mexico. They protected their enterprise by beating and threatening the young women and by providing services to illegal migrants who, themselves, were hardly in a position to report any criminal practices. Their silence was guaranteed by the migrant workers' fear of arrest and deportation.[53]

MANIPULATION OF THE SYSTEM

To avoid detection, trafficking networks often rely on corruption of government officials in source, transit, or destination countries or exploit laws in destination countries.

Corruption

Trafficking does not exist in a vacuum and corruption of government officials is central to many trafficking operations. Data from the Council of Europe suggest that corruption is one of the most important cost factors for traffickers.[54] Without corrupt law enforcement, border guards, police, consular officials, diplomats, lawyers, security, and transport sectors, this trade could not exist. These and other officials such as personnel in the airports and railroad industry, or border agents turn a blind eye, often after the payment of a significant sum, and allow traffickers to proceed and trafficking networks to prosper. Human Rights Watch found evidence of Bosnian officials facilitating human trafficking by creating or ignoring false documents produced by traffickers to facilitate transport through the country, visiting brothels to partake of free sexual services in exchange for ignoring trafficking and sometimes engaging in trafficking directly by operating bars in which trafficked women were forced to work as prostitutes.[55]

Corruption can be either (or both) proactive (such as actively assisting traffickers in procuring travel documents) or passive (a failure to react by turning a blind eye). A study of corruption and human trafficking in Southeastern Europe suggests that organized trafficking requires systematic corruption entailing corrupt relationships and networks, as well as corruption at high levels. Bribes do not remain with lower-ranking officials who take them, but flow up the chain of command.[56] The Albanian prime minister accused the judicial system and government of widespread corruption that exacerbated the country's human trafficking problem.[57]

A U.N. study in Malaysia looking at trafficking of Filipinos to that country also found corruption at different levels. Senior police officers in collusion with trafficking syndicates were provided with regular financial payments and free access to drinks as well as sexual services of the (trafficked) women in the entertainment centers. Lower-ranking law enforcement personnel who were not party to those arrangements attempted to get their share through direct extortion of the women themselves using harassment with the threat of arrest and detention. Three different incidents were reported where women were told by club owners to provide sexual services to men identified as "police officers."[58]

Within the course of this same study, victims identified corrupt practices on the part of immigration officers at the airport in Manila, claiming that traffickers would notify immigration officials by beeper of when and where escorts would be coming through immigration checks with a number of people and that officers had escorted them through immigration checkpoints with false or no documentation. The Philippines Bureau of Immigration took prompt steps to thwart these practices, including removing numbers from immigration counters; prohibiting the use of pagers, beepers, or cellular phones; banning escorts from bringing groups of persons through immigration; and assigning restaurants near the airport known to be contact places for smugglers and traffickers "off limits" to immigration personnel.

Police corruption in Indonesia also reportedly facilitates trafficking in that country. Individual members of the security forces were accused of engaging in or facilitating trafficking by providing protection to brothels and prostitution fronts in karaoke bars, discos, and hotels, or by receiving bribes to ignore the practice.[59]

Exploitation of the Laws in Destination Countries

Traffickers are often good entrepreneurs and adapt to the laws and regulations in destination countries. As embassies, customs, and law enforcement officers make it more difficult for traffickers to secure visas or smuggle their victims into destination countries, traffickers have become more creative in their methods. They are familiar with laws and exploit these laws to maximize the number of victims that can be brought into a country and at the same time reduce the chances of getting caught. Over a two-year-period, Nigerian traffickers brought more than 140 Nigerian minors to the Netherlands under false pretenses and had the minors claim asylum upon entering the Netherlands. Traffickers supplied the young women with false passports and instructions on how to apply for asylum upon landing at Schiphol airport. Dutch law prohibits asylum seekers from being deported until their case has been investigated. Unaccompanied minors are housed in an "open" reception center—meaning that they are free to come and go as they please—while they are awaiting a decision on their case. According to Dutch law, asylum seekers cannot be incarcerated; they are viewed as victims rather than offenders. These young victims remained for a period of weeks or months in these receptions centers before being contacted by traffickers. Shortly thereafter, they disappeared into street prostitution in a number of southern European countries. Those victims found in France, Italy, and Spain were returned to the Netherlands and offered assistance. As a result of this practice, high-risk groups of unaccompanied minors are now being housed in a closed institution at a secret location. In connection with this case, police and justice officials arrested more than 20 suspects in Belgium, England, France, Germany, the Netherlands, Spain, the United Kingdom, and the United States.[60]

CRIMINAL EARNINGS

Experts perhaps know the least about criminal earnings. Few trafficking operations are uncovered and, when they are, it is difficult to get the victims to testify against their traffickers. Even when traffickers are arrested, it is a technical and time-consuming task to uncover the criminal earnings of these organizations. Much of the money has been laundered and sent back to the traffickers' home country or invested in (il)legitimate businesses.

In the case of trafficking for sexual exploitation, the earnings per victim and the number of clients per day serviced by a victim will determine the profit earned by traffickers. A number of studies based on interviews with victims indicate that women are forced to have sexual relations with as many as 15 to 30 customers a day.[61] The women are generally allowed to keep very little, if any, of the money they earn.

In the case of trafficking for forced prostitution, traffickers earn money on the women they exploit and then sell them to other traffickers. An undercover report by ITN news on the trade of Czech women to the United Kingdom found, however, that women are not sold but "rented" to brothel owners or other traffickers. Reporter Chris Rogers established an Internet cover operation, EUrotica, in the United Kingdom and then traveled to the Czech Republic to discuss with traffickers the possibility of securing women for his U.K. brothels. The girls, he was told, were for rent for a period of six months. The rental price for a woman, who would be delivered to the United Kingdom, was £5,000—£3,000 of which was to be paid upfront and the remainder upon delivery of the woman. Half of her earnings would be paid to the brothel owner in the United Kingdom, the other half to the traffickers in the Czech Republic. To provide an idea of the huge amount of money generated by prostitution, Rogers told CNN that within two hours of launching his Web site, the Internet company had received 400 bookings for prostitutes. If only half of the bookings were realized, his "organization" would have made £20,000 pounds in a two-week period.[62]

Police in the United Kingdom found that the services of prostitutes cost between £25 to £40 for half an hour of sex. An hour of unprotected sex could bring as much as £70. Some trafficked victims reported being forced to work 16 hours a day, possibly earning their traffickers in excess of £1,000 a day. Prices paid by pimps for purchasing trafficked victims in the United Kingdom varied from £3,000 to £8,000.[63] Police found a Lithuanian girl had been sold for £8,000 on arrival in the United Kingdom because she was a virgin.[64]

Concrete sums of money found during police raids provide only a limited picture of the trafficking operation. Spanish police arrested 60 people involved in a trafficking operation suspected of having forced 2,000 Russian women into prostitution in Spain. Alerted to large transactions with Russian money through foreign currency exchange outlets, police began an investigation. Police found the equivalent of $28,350 in cash, gold, nine cars, five computers, passports, and plane tickets and estimate that traffickers sent more than $74,000 back to Russia.[65] The Dutch police estimate that the prostitutes working for the Turkish-German brothers in the Sneep case generated €400,000 a month.[66] Two university professors from Uzbekistan living in Texas victimized two young Uzbek girls and in 18 months made $400,000 off the services of their victims.[67]

Europol reports that trafficked Lithuanian women are traded for between €2,200 and €6,000. Women may be resold numerous times, and in the case of Lithuanian women, up to seven times during the course of their exploitation. A bar owner from the former Yugoslav Republic of Macedonia generated a profit of between €10,000 and €15,000 from one trafficked victim. Recent research in Italy estimates that approximately 5,000 trafficked victims generate annual profits for the traffickers at between €380 and €950 million.[68]

The International Labour Organization (ILO) attempted to calculate the profits generated by criminal agents and organizations trafficking humans. Based on an estimate of 1.1 million victims of human trafficking for forced economic exploitation, the ILO found that total profits[69] amounted to US$3.8 billion—most of it generated in industrial countries. Profits in other regions varied between US$40 million in Sub-Saharan Africa and US$776 million in Latin America. When restricting the assessment to profits from forced commercial sexual exploitation as a result of trafficking,

> [T]he ILO found that the global profits made from trafficking into forced commercial sexual exploitation amounted to US$27.8 billion. Almost half of all profits— US$13.3 billion—are made with people trafficked into or within industrial countries. Second highest profits are in Asia (US$9.5 billion), followed by transition economies (US$3.2 billion), Middle-East and North Africa (US$1.0 billion), Latin America (US$0.6 billion) and Sub-Saharan Africa (US$0.1 billion).[70]

The study estimated that each woman in forced sexual servitude generates approximately US$100,000 per year.

The ILO study examined a number of cases to test their estimates. Profits varied. In a case in Finland, police seized accounts showing that prostitutes generated between €75,000 and €120,000 per year per woman. A case in the United Kingdom (the so-called *Plakici* case) generated earnings of about US$276,000 by forcing a 16-year-old girl into prostitution over a period of two years (representing earnings of about US$140,000 per year). An investigation by the Canadian police into a prostitution network revealed that brothel keepers made about US$5 million annual profits with 100 trafficked women— amounting to annual profits of US$50,000 per women.[71]

GENERAL OVERVIEW OF TRAFFICKING ORGANIZATIONS

The degree to which traffickers and networks are organized varies from one incident, operation, and country to the next. Trafficking can range from something as simple as a single individual recruiting and exploiting single victim in the same city or country of origin, to highly sophisticated operations moving large numbers of victims across numerous borders. The operation can be solely in the hands of criminals who arrange everything from recruitment to the production of false documents, transportation, and exploitation, or it can be a segmented business involving an interaction between a criminal network and, for instance, a legitimate transportation company, which may knowingly or unknowingly transport victims (as was the case involving the tragic death of almost 300 illegal Pakistani migrants in 1996).[72] Trafficking can involve numerous people who provide the entire range of services[73] and be as sophisticated and complex as the international operation that smuggled 60 Chinese persons from Fujian province, China, to Serbia, Hungary, Austria, France, Belgium, the Netherlands, and finally to the United Kingdom. The journey, which included travel on airline flights, by high speed train, and being smuggled in the back of a truck, ended in death by suffocation of 58 of the 60 passengers.[74]

Operations moving large numbers of persons through numerous countries over a longer period of time are, by nature, highly organized. There is, however, little evidence of highly structured, hierarchical organized crime enterprises involved in human trafficking. Instead, human trafficking "tends to be the domain of more loosely organized, entrepreneurial organized crime networks that work together and flexibly move along, dealing with numerous partners and have a wide range of players that are not part of the 'group' but a part of a network that provides criminal services."[75] This concept has been supported by research in the Netherlands that found that offenders trafficking Central and Eastern European women to the Netherlands were organized in trafficking networks.[76]

Trafficking organizations fall on a continuum ranging from (and broadly grouped into) individuals, or amateur traffickers, to small groups of organized criminals, to international trafficking networks.[77] Individual traffickers who maintain control of the entire operation recruit, transport, and exploit their victims. The Albanian men who "court" their young victims with promises of marriage, smuggle them into Italy, and then force the girls into prostitution are examples of individual traffickers. The family who brought Henriette Akofa from Togo to France (see chapter 4) and forced her into domestic slavery, or the foreign diplomats in the United States who have been accused of holding their nationals as domestic helpers in virtual slave-like conditions are also examples of individual traffickers.[78] Freelance criminals may have ties to organized crime overseas, as is the case with Russians smuggling women into the United States to work in the sex industry.[79]

Case 5.3. Forced Prostitution in Philadelphia

In Philadelphia, a Ukrainian national, Yelena Telichenko, met a Russian woman who she convinced to move down to Orlando with her. Shortly after arriving in Florida, Ms. Telichenko forced the young woman to serve as a mistress for a series of men so the men would support the two women through gifts. If the victim objected in any way, Telichinko repeatedly and brutally beat her. Telichenko was caught and plead guilty to violation of 18 U.S.C., Section1589 (forced labor) for holding the Russian victim in servitude.[80]

The second type of trafficking organization is characterized by small groups of organized criminals. They may be involved in trafficking within a country's borders or small-scale international trafficking. These loose confederations of organized criminal entrepreneurs or enterprises were seen among the Asian gangs who control the trafficking of women to and in the United States.[81] In the United Kingdom, police characterized this group as "market traders" who seize opportunities in the most profitable markets. They rotate their victims around the United Kingdom and sell them to other traffickers.[82] There is some degree of specialization and sophistication, but not to the degree witnessed in the third group—those of international trafficking networks.

At the end of the continuum are the highly structured, criminal organizations controlling the trafficking process and providing the full set of services (from recruitment, documentation forgery, transportation, corruption of police officials, where necessary, and exploitation) from start to finish. These complex networks are characterized as flexible, horizontal, and decentralized. This flexible structure allows cooperation with other criminal groups. Increased flexibility facilitates a rapid response to changes in legislation and law enforcement activity as well as fluctuating supply and demand in different markets. Members of these organizations may be located in origin, transit and destination countries providing transportation and safe-houses along the route. Larger organizations are divided into smaller subunits that make use of criminal specialists, who provide particular services and expertise that otherwise might be outside of the scope of the criminal organization itself. This enables the organization to rapidly adjust to new market opportunities.[83]

The Bureau of the Dutch National Rapporteur on Trafficking in Human Beings conducted an in-depth analysis of 156 trafficking case files from the police over the period 1998–2002. Researchers identified three organizational forms and examined the distribution of these criminal organizations. In 41 cases (26 percent), the criminal organization form was classified as a soloist operation. The soloist is generally a single person who exploits one or more girls. Slightly fewer cases (35 or 22 percent) involved isolated criminal groups. The isolated criminal group with a minimum of two and a maximum of five members is responsible for the entire range of activities from recruitment to forcing women into prostitution. Members of the groups travel to foreign countries to bring the women into the Netherlands. More than half of the cases (51 percent) were classified as criminal networks—an undefined criminal infrastructure, in which members are bound together and in which membership and clear clusters are based on geographic proximity, family relationships, friendships, trade relations, and related activities.[84]

The Sophistication of Large Trafficking Organizations

Larger, more sophisticated trafficking units have been described as horizontal designs divided into several subunits that specialize in a particular part or sequence of the operation.[85] Subunits may provide the same services to smuggled and trafficked persons initially—recruitment, provision of false identity papers or passports, transportation, safe-houses, and entry into the destination country. In situations in which persons are trafficked, the exploiting unit and re-escort unit (for the purpose of rotation to other destinations) provide "services" to networks dealing with trafficked persons. The management unit maintains a vertical structure and has knowledge of and controls the other subunits. All other subunits are organized horizontally and have limited knowledge of the other subunits.[86] Migrant trafficking enterprises are characterized by a number of specific roles that individuals take on within the organization to provide specific services.[87]

- **Investors:** put forward funding for the operation, and oversee the entire operation; these people are unlikely to be known by the everyday employees of the operation, as they are sheltered by an organizational pyramid structure that protects their anonymity
- **Recruiters:** seek out potential migrants and secure their financial commitment. These people may be members of the culture and the community from which migrants are drawn
- **Transporters:** assist the migrants in leaving their country of origin, either by land, sea, or air
- **Corrupt public officials or protectors:** may assist in obtaining travel documents, or accept bribes to enable migrants to enter/exit illegally
- **Informers:** gather information on matters such as border surveillance, immigration, and transit procedures, asylum systems, law enforcement activities[88]
- **Guides and crew members:** are responsible for moving illegal migrants from one transit point to the other or helping the migrants to enter the destination country
- **Enforcers:** are primarily responsible for policing staff and migrants, and for maintaining order
- **Debt collectors:** are in the destination country to collect fees
- **Money launderers:** launder the proceeds of crime, disguising their origin through a series of transactions or investing them in legitimate businesses
- **Supporting personnel and specialists:** may include local people at transit points who might provide accommodation and other assistance

Significant evidence points toward a high degree of organization and sophistication in trafficking operations. The European Police Agency, Europol, characterized a highly organized operation as one that (1) smuggles large numbers of persons over great distances, (2) is able to smuggle different nationalities on the same transport, (3) moves large amounts of money, and (4) when things go wrong, has immediate legal assistance. A study of illegal migrants intercepted in Lithuania found that the migrants had passed through an average of 3.6 transit countries and that their journey had been multimodal with an average of four modes of transport used. No migrant had covered the entire journey by the same means of transport.[89]

Case 5.4 describes a large and highly sophisticated trafficking organization. This case, dubbed Sneep, was described by Dutch police as "significant" in terms of violence and degree of organization.

Open border and technological advances have facilitated criminal activities (smuggling, counterfeiting, and fraud) that require less specialization than was previously necessary and that have allowed criminals to diversify their activities. The criminal groups have been known to make use of existing contacts, routes, corrupt government officials, and networks to expand their operations.[90] Intelligence sources at Interpol reveal that trafficking in human beings supplements more traditional criminal activities, such as drug trafficking, trafficking in arms vehicle theft, and money laundering. Traffickers have been linked to money lending to repay debts, extortion for protection money, and physical violence. Furthermore, traffickers have been known to coerce their victims into smuggling and selling drugs. Belgian investigators, confirming reports by Europol and Interpol, found that organized criminal groups rarely limit themselves to one activity but are involved in people smuggling, drug and human trafficking, theft, and fraud.[91]

Europol reports that these criminal groups reach informal agreements to work together, and the organization has seen an increase in multinational criminal groups active in the European Union. In July 2000, the Dutch police apprehended an international criminal group, including 54 Iranians, three

---

Case 5.4. The Dutch Case: Sneep

In 1998 two Turkish-German brothers arrived in Amsterdam forcing two young women to work as prostitutes from a hotel in the city's Red Light district. They began bringing more women, mainly from Eastern Europe, who were then forced to work behind the windows in the Red Light district. Over the years, they expanded their operation to two other Dutch cities, Utrecht and Alkmaar. The police suspect that as many as 90 women from Bulgaria, Germany, Ireland, the Netherlands, Poland, and Rumania were forced into prostitution by the brothers.

They had established an enterprise, with themselves as the directors of the organization. Working under them were pimps, all of whom were responsible for a specific operational branch. One was responsible for the bodyguards; a second oversaw the production and management of false documents, while the third pimp coordinated prostitution services in Germany. Under this "mid-level management" (the pimps) were guards (assigned to protect the women if clients became aggressive). Lower on the scale were chauffeurs and others who provided peripheral services. According to the police, approximately 30 people were working for the organization.[92]

Case 5.5. A European Prostitution Ring

Adult women and juvenile females were recruited from countries in Eastern and Central Europe. They were brought via diverse routes to a central meeting place in Hungary, provided with false documents and handed over to chauffeurs who organized their transportation to the Netherlands. Once in the Netherlands, victims were distributed among various individuals. Transportation was arranged to bring the young women to their place of employment where they were forced to work in prostitution from 12 to 15 hours a day.

The police arrested 22 suspects mainly from the former Yugoslavia. Three suspects played an executive role in the trafficking network, while the remainder fulfilled such tasks as recruiters, transporters or chauffeurs, guards, debt collectors, or providers of a safe-house. In addition to these suspects, the police identified a large number of people providing supportive services to the network; 11 others were involved in a false marriage scam.[93]

Iraqis, two Algerians, and one Romanian. They were charged with drug trafficking and falsification of documents. The criminal group, in possession of 265 passports, Schengen visas, and other identification papers were believed to also be involved in the smuggling of migrants.[94] Researchers in organized crime find that criminals of different ethnic backgrounds "seem able to find each other."[95]

ORGANIZED CRIME AND TRAFFICKING

There is a considerable body of research concerning organized crime, and there have been many attempts to link organized crime to trafficking, particularly as organized crime has a long history of exploiting opportunities in regard to vice, police corruption, and drug dealing.

Organized crime groups involved in trafficking humans can be studied from a number of different approaches. One of these approaches looks at traditional organized crime with its hierarchical structure and central authority. Another approach examines trafficking operations from the perspective of network analysis, while a third position analyzes trafficking organizations as business models. The role of organized crime groups will be dealt with briefly, while more emphasis will be paid to the last two structures.

A definition or organized crime that has gained widespread recognition is the definition put forth in the U.N. Convention against Transnational Organized Crime and is considered to be "the most important attempt to date to arrive at a globally agreed upon concept of organized crime."[96] Article 2 of the Convention defines organized crime as follows:

(a) "Organized criminal group" shall mean a structured group of three or more persons, existing for a period of time and acting in concert with the aim of committing one or more crimes or offences established in accordance with this Convention, in order to obtain, directly or indirectly, a financial or other material benefit;

(b) "Serious crime" shall mean conduct constituting an offence punishable by maximum deprivation of liberty of at least four years or a more serious penalty;

(c) "Structured group" shall mean a group that is not randomly formed for the immediate commission of an offence and that does not need to have formally defined roles for it's members, continuity of its membership or a developed structure.

This widely accepted definition of organized crime provides a sharp contrast to the traditional, hierarchical organized crime structures most closely associated with organizations such as the Italian mafia. Organized crime groups matching all of these models have been identified as being involved in the trafficking and exploitation of persons.

Traditional Organized Crime Groups and Sex Trafficking

Older, traditional organized crime groups such as the Russian mafia, Japanese Yakuza, and Chinese triads have long been involved in the prostitution and sex industry.[97] With the disintegration of the Soviet Union, destabilization in the Balkans, globalization, economic instability, and more supple border controls, new opportunities and crime groups have sprung up to fill the demand for smuggling and trafficking, labor and sexual exploitation.[98] Albanian crime groups control the flow of drugs, arms, and people into Italy and are responsible for the "traffic [of] thousands of women and girls into Italy for prostitution every year ... they are known for their ruthlessness and retaliation against anyone interfering with their trafficking business."[99] Similar organized crime groups operate in other parts of the world. In India, organized prostitution is reported to be in the hands of the Dawood Ibrahim group, while Nigerian organized crime groups traffic drugs and force young Nigerian women into prostitution in Western European countries. These groups and practices have expanded into other West African countries such as Ghana and Benin. Law enforcement in Great Britain refers to a West African rather than a Nigerian crime problem.[100] In Mexico and Latin America, organized crime groups smuggle drugs and people and use these same routes to traffic humans.[101]

Trafficking as a Network

Network analysis is a more formal way of giving structure to much of what was reviewed in the overview of smuggling and trafficking operations presented in the beginning of this chapter. The approach generally identifies two important dimensions of networks involved in organized crime: the degree of dominance or influence exercised by some members of the network over others, and the degree to which there is explicit coordination among members of the organization.[102] With respect to this second dimension, characteristics such as the degree of specialization or division of tasks within the organization are the focus. Are there a limited number of persons responsible for carrying out a large number of tasks, or is the organization highly specialized with numerous individuals only responsible for a limited number of assigned tasks? Network analysis of trafficking organizations also studies the nature of underlying social relationships—or the degree to which members of the organization are related to one another—through friendship, familial, or ethnic ties. Can the organizations be described as ethnically homogenous or heterogeneous? Are members of the organization related to one another through family or tribal ties?

Clearly, the relationship between members and the division of tasks within trafficking organizations varies. The Sneep case (see case 5.4) was run by two Turkish brothers, who were assisted by their mother and sister. Other members in the criminal organization were Dutch, German, and Polish. In another case in the Netherlands, three suspects came from Azerbaijan, two each from Lithuania, Morocco, and the Netherlands, and one each from Latvia and Russia. Police in another case in the Netherlands identified seven Estonian suspects, five of whom were related. They were assisted by two Dutch members of the organization.[103]

Trafficking as a Business Model

Human trafficking is "driven by profit." Similar to legitimate businesses, traffickers look at market forces and adapt their methodology according to the environments in which they work and the markets that exist for forced labor.[104] Louise Shelley, an expert on international organized crime, has compared trafficking with business models, arguing that certain ethnic or national groups are more closely associated with a particular type of business model. Each of the five models reflects the market forces, geographic positions and limitations, and historical and cultural influences of the group.[105] These groups can be characterized by the types of people they transport, the reasons for transportation (smuggling versus trafficking), use of force or violence, human rights abuses, and the investment of profits generated from trafficking. The regions represented include Africa, China, Latin America, and the former Soviet Union and Eastern Bloc.

Natural Resource Model: Post–Soviet Organized Crime

The Natural Resource model is involved almost solely in the trafficking of women. Rather than functioning as an integrated business, criminals involved in post-Soviet organized crime focus on short-term profits rather than long-term durability of the business. The emphasis is not on the maximization of profits. Women are sold as commodities—as if they were a readily available natural resource (such as timber). The business focuses on the recruitment of women who are then sold into prostitution to intermediaries who deliver them to the markets to "serve clients." The women are frequently sold off to nearby trade partners (usually the most proximate crime group). Profits made are not repatriated or used for development but generally are disposed of through conspicuous consumption or are sometimes used to purchase other commodities with a rapid turnover. British law enforcement, for instance, found that the profits from trafficking women were used to buy cars for sale in the Baltics or rubber boots for sale in Ukraine.

Trade and Development Model: Chinese and Chinese–Thai Traffickers

The Trade and Development model is designed for maximum, long-term profit and operates as a structured business that is integrated from start to finish, controlling the process from recruitment to transportation and exploitation. Chinese and Chinese-Thai trafficking is most applicable to the smuggling of men; however, confiscated ship logs show that as much as 10 percent of the human trade includes women who may be forced to work in brothels. The Chinese smuggling and trafficking operations differ based on the destination country to which individuals are brought. The vast majority is smuggled to the United States and after having paid off enormous debts, individuals are free to leave. Prosecutors in Italy, however, report that individuals remain enslaved in that country because they cannot be absorbed into the legitimate Italian economy and repay their debt. It appears that operations to the United States are smuggling operations, whereas those to Italy (and perhaps other European destinations) involve trafficking.

Supermarket Model: Low–Cost and High–Volume U.S.–Mexican Trade

This Supermarket model, based on large-scale supply and existing demand, aims at maximizing profits by moving the largest number of people. In order to do this, the price for the trip must be kept low. U.S.-Mexican smugglers may charge as little as several hundred dollars for the trip to entice large numbers of people to make use of their services. In most cases the smuggler releases the illegal migrants after having gotten them (safely) across the U.S.-Mexican border—sometimes with fatal results.[106] While this low-cost, high-volume model is most applicable to the smuggling of illegal migrants, it is also applicable to the trafficking of persons. The low cost of the transportation gives the impression that a debt can be easily repaid and increases the number of willing participants. Trafficked women can be brought across the border in the same transport as smuggled men.

The trade in women is part of a much larger trade that involves moving large numbers of people across the border at low cost. This trade may require multiple attempts because 1.8 million individuals were arrested on the border in 2000. There have been cases reported of Mexican traffickers forcing a group of deaf individuals to peddle goods and, in the Cadena case,[107] young Mexican girls were forced into brothels. Because there is little profit to be made in each individual transported, smugglers and traffickers are not necessarily interested in the safe delivery of their passengers, which often results in violations of human rights, inhumane practices, and fatalities in crossing the desert.

Corruption and payoffs of local border officials facilitate smuggling and trafficking operations. In the Cadena case of young women trafficked to the southeastern United States, millions of dollars of profits were invested in land and farms in Mexico.

Violent Entrepreneur Model: Balkan Crime Groups

The Violent Entrepreneur model is opportunistic and highly profitable. Balkan crime groups, which trade in women, run an integrated business and serve as middlemen for the groups from Eastern Europe. Crime groups from the former Eastern Europe and Soviet Union sell women to Balkan traders who force these women into prostitution in destination countries, predominantly in Western Europe. These groups control women from their base in the Balkans through their exploitation in Western European brothels. This is an opportunistic model in both the source and destination countries.

Violence and force is an underlying and integral aspect of this model. Balkan criminals are involved in significant violations of human rights and high levels of violence against trafficked women. Women suffer terrible physical abuse at the hands of their traffickers and threats are made to harm family members at home. Violence is used against law enforcement officials who seek to investigate these crimes. Force is also used by the Balkan crime groups against established crime groups to conquer the sex markets in Great Britain and continental Europe. The Balkan crime groups have been known to have links with top-level law enforcement personnel in the home country, which hinders a successful international investigation.

The control of many victims in the highly profitable Western European sex markets generates high levels of profits for the traffickers. These profits appear to be used to finance investments in property and trade businesses overseas and at home, as well as to invest in other illicit activities at home.

Traditional Slavery with Modern Technology Model: Trafficking Out of Nigeria and West Africa

Since the late 1990s, there has been an increased awareness of trafficking of young women and girls from Nigeria and other West African nations for the purpose of exploitation in the Western European sex industry. By combining traditional slavery with modern technology, Nigerian organized crime groups have emerged as multifaceted crime groups. The trade in women for forced prostitution is just one of numerous criminal activities in which these crime

Table 5.1 Characteristics of Trafficking Crime Groups as Businesses

Business Model and Crime Group	Victims	Modus Operandi	Violence	Human Rights Violations	Profit
Natural Resource Model: Post-Soviet Organized Crime	Women recruited and trafficked for prostitution	Women are recruited in source country and then sold off to intermediaries	Violence occurs	Very significant violations of human rights	Short term
Trade and Development Model: Chinese and Chinese-Thai Traffickers	Smuggling and trafficking of men for labor exploitation and to a lesser extent trafficking women for prostitution	Structured business integrated from start to finish	Violence is known to occur when debts have not been paid	Less significant violations of human rights	Maximum, long-term profit
Supermarket Model: Low-Cost and High-Volume U.S.–Mexican Trade	Smuggling of both men and women; trafficking of women for forced prostitution	Move large numbers of persons while keeping costs low	Not characteristic of this group; although human rights violations are reported	Significant violations of human rights	Maximizes profit
Violent Entrepreneur Model: Balkan Crime Groups	Women trafficked for prostitution	Serve as middlemen for crime groups from Eastern Europe; control women from base in Balkans through exploitation in brothels in Western Europe	High level of violence used against victims	Very significant violations of human rights; reliance on violence at all stages of operation makes it the most significant violator of human rights	Opportunistic and highly profitable
Traditional Slavery with Modern Technology Model: Trafficking Out of Nigeria and West Africa	Trafficking of young women and girls for prostitution to destinations in Western Europe; regional trafficking of children for labor exploitation	Use of contracts and voodoo practices to bind victims to traffickers and force compliance	Willing to use physical violence against victims	Significant violations of human rights	Multifaceted crime groups; trade in women and girls generates significant profits

Source: Information taken from Shelley (2003).

groups are involved. In addition to their willingness to use physical violence against their victims, traffickers often use voodoo practices as a form of psychological violence to frighten victims into compliance.

Human rights violations are significant. Children (young women) are often transported to Western European countries and abandoned. Women who are forced to work in prostitution are forced into the most dangerous type of prostitution as streetwalkers. The trade resembles traditional slavery that has been modernized to meet the needs and challenges of the global age. "Using the modern transport links of present-day Nigeria, they are very effective because they 'combine the best of both modern and older worlds by allying sophisticated forms of modern technology to tribal customs.'"[108]

This activity generates significant financial profits. Small amounts of the profits are occasionally returned to family members of the girls and women, while some profits are passed on to the local operations of the crime groups. It is believed that much of the profits are invested in other illicit activities and are laundered.

If we compare the crime groups as business models, we see that they differ in terms of the victims they recruit and exploit, their modus operandi or method of operation, the willingness to use violence, human rights abuses, and the profits generated from the trafficking practice. This comparison is portrayed in table 5.1.

CONCLUDING REMARKS

Traffickers, their organizations, and methods of operation differ as much as the victims and the markets in which they are exploited. It is important to identify recruiters and how they work in order to design successful prevention programs. The notion that recruiters are dark, swarthy men in dingy rooms promising young women successful jobs in foreign countries must be exposed for the myth that it is. A trafficker can (knowingly or unknowingly) be a person's neighbor, relative, or high school friend.

The exposure of international trafficking networks demands that governments and law enforcement agencies initiate international cooperative relationships to unmask trafficking practices in source, transit, and destination countries. Chapter 9 deals more fully with the issue of measures—including international legal instruments, law enforcement cooperation, and civil society programs. For now, we turn our attention to trafficking patterns around the world.

Regional Trafficking Patterns

GLOBALIZATION AND HUMAN trafficking have resulted in many different patterns of movement and exploitation. In 2006–2007, Dominican women were trafficked to Montenegro for commercial sexual exploitation, while Russian students were trafficked to the United States for labor exploitation and forced to sell ice cream. Zambian girls were trafficked to Ireland and Kenyan women were trafficked to Mexico for commercial sexual exploitation. Vietnamese children were trafficked to the United Kingdom for forced involvement in drug smuggling and Filipino women were trafficked to Côte d'Ivoire for commercial sexual exploitation. While Thai men were trafficked to the United States for labor exploitation and debt bondage, Chinese women were trafficked to Afghanistan for commercial sexual exploitation. Children in Burma* were trafficked into armed conflict.[1]

Traditional destination countries such as Australia, Canada, Japan, the United States, and countries in Western Europe receive much attention and frequently link the practice of human trafficking to the exploitation of women and children in the sex industry. A closer study of human trafficking in these and other parts of the world indicates a more nuanced picture.

International trafficking has received widespread coverage, in part, because destination countries have recognized the need to work together with source and transit countries to stem the tide of current and future victims, while at the same time working together to repatriate those exploited and to aid in their reintegration. The problem of internal trafficking, however, is one that is often overlooked and possibly more difficult to identify. This practice may be completely underestimated and deserves attention if countries are to offer the most basic human rights protection to their citizens.

According to the United Nations Office on Drugs and Crime (UNODC), trafficking is reported *from* 127 countries with exploitation occurring *in* 137 countries.[2] The latest U.S. annual *Trafficking in Persons Report* describes trafficking practices from, to, or through 170 countries.[3] Using their own database, the International Organization for Migration (IOM) examined data and research on human trafficking around the world. The majority of studies were

---

*Burma, officially the Union of Myanmar, will be referred to in this report as both Burma and Myanmar.

conducted in European countries (44 percent), followed by the Asia-Pacific (25 percent), Africa (13 percent), the Americas (7 percent), and the Middle East (1 percent).[4] More information is known or made publicly available on certain regions, which says nothing about the level of trafficking in other parts of the world. It could simply be a lack of awareness or neglect of the problem in those countries.[5] The IOM's global case management trafficking database, which at the time contained information on 5,233 individual trafficking victims from more than 50 source and 78 destination countries, showed that the largest source countries are Moldova, Romania, Mali, Ukraine, Belarus, Bulgaria, Uzbekistan, Colombia, and the Kyrgyz Republic.[6] UNODC adds to this list Albania, China, Lithuania, Nigeria, the Russian Federation, and Thailand as source countries with a serious trafficking problem. Countries identified by the United Nations as major destination countries are Belgium, Germany, Greece, Israel, Italy, Japan, the Netherlands, Thailand, Turkey, and the United States.[7]

The UNODC study, *Trafficking in Persons, Global Patterns,* identified the regions of Central and Southeastern Europe, the Commonwealth of Independent States, Western Africa, and Southeast Asia as the most commonly reported regions of origin for human trafficking. Destination regions are countries in Western Europe, North America, and Asia, in particular in Western Asia and Turkey.[8]

This chapter takes a closer look at differing trafficking patterns in various regions and subregions of the world, highlighting subregions that are particularly prone to trafficking as well as specific countries that have been identified as either important sources or destinations for trafficking. Beginning with trafficking patterns in Africa, chapter 6 continues with patterns of trafficking in Asia and the Pacific, the Commonwealth of Independent States, Europe, Latin America and the Caribbean, the Middle East, North America, and Oceania. Within each region, there are subregional difference in terms of the seriousness of the problem as well as the victims and markets of exploitation. Countries within subregions that are particularly problematic may be given special attention. For a complete list of countries and the patterns of trafficking linked to these countries, see appendix 2. Individual stories provide a human side to the statistics and trafficking patterns that form the basis for this chapter.

AFRICA

Within Africa there are subregional differences in human trafficking. Africa can be seen as comprising Western Africa, Eastern Africa, Central Africa, Southern Africa, and Northern Africa. Within these subregions, Western and Central Africa have received the most attention as a major source and destination area (to include intraregional trafficking), while Southern Africa serves predominantly as a destination subregion. Northern Africa is an origin and transit area for persons from Sub-Saharan Africa on their way to Western Europe.[9]

Western and Central Africa

Trafficking patterns of Western and Central Africa are similar. Western Africa comprises the following countries: Benin, Burkina Faso, Côte d'Ivoire, The Gambia, Ghana, Guinea, Guinea-Bissau, Liberia, Mali, Mauritania, Niger, Nigeria, Senegal, Sierra Leone, and Togo. Countries in Central Africa are Angola, Cameroon, Central African Republic, Chad, Congo, the Democratic Republic of Congo, Equatorial Guinea, and Gabon. The figure for child trafficking in these two subregions is estimated at between 200,000 and 300,000 children.[10] The number of countries reporting trafficking in children is twice the number of countries reporting trafficking in women.[11] Furthermore, trafficking is recognized as a problem in more than 70 percent of the countries in Central and Western Africa and almost 90 percent of the countries in Africa.[12] Countries in the region most heavily affected by trafficking are Benin, Burkina Faso, Cameroon, Côte d'Ivoire, Gabon, Ghana, Guinea, Mali, Niger, Nigeria, and Togo. Internal trafficking from rural areas to metropolitan areas occurs in almost all of the countries.[13] The second major trafficking pattern involves transborder trafficking flows with respect to the exploitation of children for (predominantly) the labor market. While this pattern of trafficking is largely intraregional, children have been sent as far away as Europe and the Middle East. Male children are trafficked predominantly for labor on coffee or cocoa plantations, into mines, or in the fishing industry, while female children are trafficked for work as market vendors or domestic servants.[14] In countries torn by conflict, children are abducted by militias[15] and forced to either fight or provide sexual services to soldiers. Children are also forced into soliciting and begging.[16] Intraregional trafficking appears to be the most dominant trafficking pattern in Africa, with large scale flows in the Western and Central African region.[17] The third trafficking pattern in Western and Central Africa involves the trafficking of adult women for exploitation in two different sectors. The first entails trafficking for the purpose of forced domestic service; the second example involves the trafficking and sexual exploitation of young women, as is seen in the trafficking of Nigerians to destinations in Western Europe and the Middle East.[18] The following figures, the "tip of the iceberg," are an indication of trafficking of persons in West Africa (see table 6.1). The repatriated children were identified, rescued, and returned home. Many others are not so fortunate.

In Western and Central Africa children are trafficked not only into commercial labor exploitation and domestic servitude, but also as beggars and to labor in rock quarries and mines (in Côte d'Ivoire, the Democratic Republic of Congo, Niger, and Nigeria), and on farms (Côte d'Ivoire, Ghana, Mali, and Nigeria).[19] In 2002, a study of child labor on cocoa farms in West Africa (in Cameroon, Côte d'Ivoire, Ghana, and Nigeria) estimated that 284,000 children had been either trafficked to work on the farms, or were working in unprotected, hazardous conditions.[20]

Table 6.1 Statistics on Trafficking in Persons in West Africa

Country	Number of Repatriated Persons
Benin	200 children repatriated from Nigeria between September and October 2003
Mali	More than 600 child trafficked victims repatriated from Côte d'Ivoire (2000–2003)
Mauritania	256 camel-riding children reintegrated into their family in 2004
Togo	2,458 children victims of trafficking repatriated (2002–2004)
Nigeria	10,703 victims of trafficking repatriated (2003)
Nigeria	50,000 girls as sex workers in Italy (NAPTIP 2005)

Note: NAPTIP = National Agency for the Prohibition of Traffic in Persons and Other Related Matters (Nigeria).
Source: UNODC (2008d, box 1, 17).

African children have been reportedly trafficked and exploited in situations of armed conflict, in Angola, Burundi, Côte d'Ivoire, the Democratic Republic of Congo, Liberia, Somalia, Sudan, and Uganda.[21] In 2006, children were still trafficked into armed conflict areas in the Democratic Republic of Congo.[22]

Case 6.1. An Orphan Is Promised a Bicycle

Sélom S., 13 years old, became an orphan but continued living with his older and two younger brothers. Sélom was approached by an older man and asked if he wanted to go to Nigeria, promised that he would learn a trade, be given a bicycle, a radio, and batteries. Sélom met the man at night at Balanka, a village near the Benin border. There were many other boys waiting, like Sélom, to go to Nigeria. The children traveled by truck and at the Togo-Benin border they had to get out and cross the border by foot. The three-day journey proceeded with the children packed into the truck and without enough food to go around.

Sélom was forced to work on a farm from 5:00 A.M. to 6:00 P.M. every day and all wages that he would have made were kept by the trafficker to pay for the trip to Nigeria. He worked and slept outside in makeshift huts and was injured while using a machete.

After 11 months, Sélom was allowed to leave Nigeria. For his work, he was given the amount of $9.00—which he had to share with five other boys—and a bicycle. He was told to ride the bike back to Togo. The money earned was spent paying bribes to soldiers and bandits. Sélom made it back to Togo after a four-day trip where he continued living and working with his older brother.[23]

Eastern Africa

This region, comprising the countries of Burundi, Djibouti, Eritrea, Ethiopia, Kenya, Madagascar, Malawi, Mauritius, Mozambique, Rwanda, Somalia, Uganda, Tanzania, Zambia, and Zimbabwe, experiences intraregional as well as transnational trafficking. Internal trafficking has been described as "endemic" and affects mainly women and children, and to a lesser extent, men.[24]

Children, usually between the ages of 13 and 18 (many of which are HIV orphans), fall victim to trafficking by relatives or persons they know. Internal trafficking—from rural to urban areas—affects children and women who are forced into commercial sex work and exploitative domestic service. The markets into which victims in this region are forced to work varies. In addition to domestic service and prostitution, girls are also trafficked for forced marriage, while young boys are forced to work in agriculture (fishing, livestock, farming, and plantations). Adult men are trafficked into criminal activities, manual and agricultural labor, and construction.[25] Victims trafficked abroad are usually sent to other African countries, Europe, and the Middle East mainly for sexual exploitation and domestic work.

Thousands of Ethiopian girls were said to be trafficked as domestic servants to Lebanon and other destinations in the Middle East.[26] In Sierra Leone, the United Nations Children's Fund (UNICEF) found that trafficking of both young female and male children was an issue of concern. Trafficking occurred both internally (from rural to urban areas) and abroad for the purpose of labor (domestic work, fishing, agriculture, trading, and mining), sexual exploitation (marriage and prostitution), and for petty crime (begging) and child soldiering. Adults, too, were trafficked for various reasons within and outside of the country.[27] This pattern repeats itself across Eastern Africa.

International organizations estimate that between 25,000 and 30,000 children, both boys and girls, have been abducted or recruited by rebel forces and forced to work as child soldiers in the Democratic Republic of Congo, Kenya, Rwanda, Sudan, and Tanzania.[28] Uganda has witnessed an increasing number of passport applications, mostly by foreigners for fostered children.

In Kenya, evidence exists of child trafficking for exploitation in the sex industry, particularly in the coastal areas of the country. A report by UNICEF indicates that 30 percent of 12- to 18-year-old girls—approximately 15,000 children—are involved in the child sex tourism business. There is evidence that these children have been trafficked internally. Children have reportedly been trafficked in Kenya for domestic service.[29] IOM cites a study of human trafficking in Kenya that found 43 percent of the victims interviewed were men.[30]

Southern Africa

Southern Africa comprises the countries of Botswana, Lesotho, South Africa, and Swaziland, but only South Africa has gained attention in this region with respect to human trafficking. South Africa serves as a destination for children and women trafficked from more than 10 countries in Africa, predominantly from Eastern and Southern Africa.[31] Women are trafficked for commercial sexual exploitation to South Africa from countries in Africa and as far away as Europe and Southeast Asia.[32] IOM identified nine different trafficking patterns in, to, and from South Africa. Some of these included the trafficking of women for commercial sexual exploitation from as far away as South Asia and Eastern Europe. Women were trafficked from refugee-producing countries to South Africa; children were trafficked from Lesotho to towns in the eastern Free State of South Africa; women and girls were trafficked from Mozambique to Gauteng and Kwa-Zulu Natal; women were trafficked from Malawi to Northern Europe; male and female children were trafficked from Malawi to Northern Europe; women and girls were trafficked overland from Malawi to South Africa; and women were trafficked to South Africa from Thailand, China, and countries in Eastern Europe.[33]

Anecdotal evidence exists of the trafficking of men within Africa, in particular in Eastern and Southern Africa. Trafficking flows from the countries in Eastern Africa and the Horn of Africa to South Africa. IOM has documented cases of men having been trafficked from Tanzania to South Africa and forced into criminal activities.

Northern Africa

This region comprises the countries of Algeria, the Arab Republic of Egypt, Libya, Morocco, Sudan, and Tunisia. Less research has been conducted on Northern Africa than on other regions of the continent. In spite of the geographic obstacle—the Sahara Desert—cases of trafficking are reported from other subregions in Africa to the north. Victims are moved by boat along the western Africa coast or overland across the desert.[34] The region serves predominantly as a transit region for both trafficked and smuggled persons.

ASIA AND THE PACIFIC

Although it is not possible to provide exact figures, a number of studies on trafficking in the region point to Asia as one of the geographic areas most heavily affected by trafficking. UNICEF reports that in the last 30 years, trafficking in women and children for sexual exploitation alone has victimized more than 30 million people in Asia.[35] IOM estimates that 200,000 to 250,000 women and children are trafficked every year in Asia,[36] while the U.S. Department of State suggests that 150,000 South Asians are trafficked every year.[37]

Trafficking patterns differ within Asian subregions. Trafficking, particularly in South Asia (Southeastern and South-Central Asia) appears to be an intraregional phenomenon. The United Nations reports that trafficking within countries in the region is even more prevalent than trafficking between countries. Exploitation takes on various forms, but trafficking for sexual exploitation appears to be the most common form of trafficking.[38]

Southern Asia (Southeastern and South-Central Asia)

Southeastern Asia comprises the countries Brunei Darussalam, Cambodia, East Timor, Indonesia, Laos, Malaysia, Myanmar, the Philippines, Singapore, Thailand, and Vietnam. South-Central Asian nations are Afghanistan, Bangladesh, Bhutan, India, the Islamic Republic of Iran, Maldives, Nepal, Pakistan, and Sri Lanka.

An expert from IOM estimated that nearly one-third of the global trade in women and children are trafficked from Southeastern Asia, stating that about 50,000 women and children were trafficked annually to the United States from other countries, approximately 60 percent of which originate from South Asia.[39] Estimates based on data or reports provided by law enforcement agencies or nongovernmental organizations (NGOs) indicate that "hundreds of thousands of women and children have been or are vulnerable to being trafficked from South Asia."[40] Within South Asia, (China), India, Pakistan, and Thailand are considered major countries of origin for trafficking. Other source countries within the region are Bangladesh, Cambodia, India, Laos, Myanmar, Nepal, Pakistan, the Philippines, and Vietnam. When victims are trafficked out of the region, they are often trafficked to Israel, Japan, and Turkey. The region also serves as a destination for victims from the Commonwealth of Independent States.[41]

Southeastern Asia: The Mekong Subregion

The Mekong subregion, a subregion within Southeastern Asia (comprising Cambodia, China, Laos, Myanmar, Thailand, and Vietnam) is an area heavily affected by human trafficking, with extensive intraregional trafficking occurring around Thailand. Thailand serves as a source, transit, and destination country for trafficking in the subregion. Thailand attracts children trafficked from Cambodia and forced to sell flowers on the streets, as well as children and adults trafficked from Cambodia, Laos, and Myanmar who are forced to work in brothels, factories, and homes, or on fishing boats. It is estimated that thousands of Uzbek women have been trafficked into Thailand's sex industry.[42] Vietnamese women who marry Taiwanese men have found themselves trafficked into brothels, while Vietnamese, Myanmar, and Chinese boys are sold for adoption within China to couples looking for a son.[43] Cambodia's sex trade, while difficult to quantify, often involves young children, with a third of the sex workers in Phnom Penh estimated to be under the age of 18. International organizations such as End Child Prostitution, Child Pornography and the Trafficking of Children (ECPAT), Save the Children, and UNICEF estimate that between 50,000 to 100,000 women and children are involved.[44]

With respect to child trafficking in the region, UNICEF reports that most trafficking in Southeastern Asia and the Pacific involves child trafficking for

---

Case 6.2. A Girl Is Sold by Her Parents to a Brothel

In Cambodia, five-year-old Srey was sold by her parents to a brothel. She was probably sold for somewhere between $10 and $100. The child was drugged to gain her compliance and passed from one customer to the next. This small child suffered months of abuse from pimps and sex tourists. At the age of six, Srey was rescued from the life of a sex slave by a former prostitute who runs victim shelters for Cambodia's rescued children. Somaly Mam, who runs the shelter, describes Srey as "timid, quiet and damaged." The child was diagnosed as HIV positive and suffering from pneumonia and tuberculosis. Other children at the shelter with Srey may be even more traumatized. One child who had been imprisoned for two years in a cage where she was repeatedly raped is suffering from profound psychological trauma.[45]

---

prostitution.[46] Girls are also recruited as domestic servants and mail-order brides, while other children are trafficked into the agricultural and industrial sectors. Research on the trafficking of women and children in and from Indonesia found that they were trafficked for domestic and sex work; migrant work in restaurants, plantations, and factories; servile marriage; and child labor.[47]

South-Central Asia

Within South-Central Asia, India and Pakistan serve as the major destination points for children and women trafficked from Bangladesh and Nepal, the major countries of origin in South-Central Asia. India and Pakistan also serve as transit countries for trafficking to the Middle East.[48] Exploitation occurs in the sex industry as well as other labor markets.[49] An alarming trend is reported in South-Central Asia: girls trafficked into the sex trade are increasingly younger. The average age of girls trafficked into India from Nepal has decreased from 14–16 years to 10–14 years, with girls as young as 8–9 years being sold at auctions in Mumbai and other Indian cities. It is estimated by police that more than 15,000 children and women are taken out of Bangladesh every year; NGOs estimate that between 160,000 and 250,000 Nepalese girls and women are forced to work in India's brothels.[50] Young girls from Pakistan and Sri Lanka are also trafficked into Indian brothels.[51]

Internal trafficking is a problem in India. According to a 2005 report of the Indian National Human Rights Commission, trafficking from neighboring countries such as Nepal and Bangladesh accounts for about 10 percent of India's trafficking into brothels, while 89 percent of the crime "takes place internally."[52] Trafficking for the purpose of forced marriage and organ transplant has also been reported in India.[53]

Trafficking is only a part of the extensive child labor problem in the region of South Asia. Children are often "sold" to pay off a debt and thus are placed in debt bondage. Children are trafficked into sex work, but also into garment and carpet factories, construction projects, and begging.[54]

While the trafficking of women and girls for commercial exploitation in Nepal occurs both within the country and to Indian brothels, there are signs that men and boys are being trafficked to work in households, factories, and agriculture, and also for the purpose of organ transplants.[55] In Sri Lanka, children are trafficked for the purpose of commercial sex and domestic work, and also as child soldiers. Between the beginning of 2002 and the end of 2007, UNICEF reported the 6,248 cases of child recruitment by the Liberation Tigers of Tamil Eelam (LTTE).[56]

Eastern Asia

The countries of China, the Hong Kong Special Administrative Region of China, the Macau Special Administrative Region of China, Taiwan, North Korea, Japan, Mongolia, and South Korea together form the region of Eastern Asia. Within this region, China and Japan serve as countries deserving special attention.

Japan serves as a destination country not only for victims trafficked from the region (China, Korea, Thailand, and the Philippines), but also in increasing numbers from Colombia[57] and other Latin American countries. Women are trafficked predominantly for sex work in the entertainment industry in Japan.[58] Japan's sex industry—hostess bars, strip clubs, sex shops, mail-order video services, and escort services—also exploits trafficked women from China, South Korea, and countries in Southeast Asia and Eastern Europe. Internal trafficking of women and girls occurs for the purpose of sexual exploitation.[59]

The People's Republic of China is plagued by internal trafficking of men, women, and children for labor and sexual exploitation. Trafficking occurs from poor provinces to the more prosperous ones along the east coast.[60] It is estimated that between 10,000 and 20,000 victims are trafficked within China each year. The U.S. Department of State reports that in poor rural areas, women are sold as wives to unmarried men and kidnapped children have been sold illegally to childless couples. NGOs in China have reported that children in rural areas have been trafficked and forced to work in factories or under the control of local gangs where they have been forced to work as petty thieves, beggars, and prostitutes.[61] Men, too have been trafficked into labor exploitation in factories and mines.

COMMONWEALTH OF INDEPENDENT STATES

With the dissolution of the Soviet Union, the Commonwealth of Independent States (CIS) was formed in 1991. Countries in this region are Armenia, Azerbaijan, Belarus, Georgia, Kazakhstan, Kyrgyzstan, Moldova, Russia, Tajikistan, Turkmenistan, Ukraine, and Uzbekistan. A number of countries in the CIS have been identified as high-trafficking source areas. According to the United

Case 6.3. Teenagers and Men Are Forced to Work in Kilns

China was shaken by a scandal involving the imprisonment and forced labor of teenagers and men forced to work in "brutal, furnace-like brick kilns." Heng Tinghan was accused of exploiting workers in a kiln in a county in the northern province of Shanxi. One worker, a mentally handicapped man, died after being beaten by one of Heng's helpers. Heng had cheated or coerced the workers to the site from March 2006 (until their rescue in June 2007), forcing them to work 16-hour days and live mostly off steamed bread.

Heng was one of a number of persons accused of exploitation and mistreatment of workers. Police in Shanxi and Henan freed 568 people, including 22 minors, from kilns and other work sites. Chinese state television reported that owners of the primitive brick-making operations used fierce dogs and beatings to deter escape from the prison-like setting. When interviewed, the kiln owner denied having anything to do with the death of his disabled employee and remarked, "I felt it was a fairly small thing, just hitting and swearing at the workers and not giving them wages."[62]

Nations, victims of CIS countries are trafficked out of the region, mainly into countries in North America and Western Europe, but also to countries in Central and Southeastern Europe, Western Asia, and Turkey. The same study identified Belarus, Moldova, the Russian Federation, and Ukraine as countries with a particularly serious trafficking problem.[63] While most of the research on trafficked victims from the CIS, in particular the Russian Federation, Moldova, and Ukraine, focus on transnational trafficking for sexual exploitation, Russian experts argue that the extent of intraregional trafficking is "many times greater than the trafficking of CIS citizens outside the region." There are indications that intraregional human trafficking for the purpose of labor exploitation dwarfs trafficking for sexual exploitation, although the latter also occurs.[64] Russia, which had long served as a source country for the recruitment of trafficked women into the European Union, now serves as a destination country for persons trafficked from other CIS countries and as a transit for those on their way to Western Europe.[65] Increasing numbers of women from poor neighboring countries, in particular, Belarus, Moldova, and Ukraine, but also from Kyrgyzstan, Tajikistan, and Uzbekistan, are trafficked to Russia and forced into prostitution in Moscow and other cities.[66] Armenia, Azerbaijan, and Georgia serve as a major source and transit area for the trafficking of women to North America, Europe, and the Middle East.

Internal trafficking in Russia occurs and affects both men and women. While women are trafficked throughout the country and forced into domestic labor or prostitution, men are trafficked into construction work and agriculture. Destination countries for trafficked persons include Germany, Greece, Israel, Portugal, and the United States. Anti-Slavery International reports that

Case 6.4. A Young Woman Is Forced into Prostitution

Maryam, a 17-year old from Kazakhstan, left home to seek employment as a shop assistant in a store in a Russian city. Her parents were paid $300, she was given a false passport, and she was taken by a man to Samara in central Russia. Instead of a shop, Maryam was placed in a guarded and locked cell with barred windows and a metal door. Refusing to work as a prostitute, she was starved, raped, and beaten into submission. It took five days to break her down and force her to comply.[67]

in the far-eastern part of the country, Russian women are trafficked to China, Japan, and Thailand.[68] Children trafficked internally and from Moldova and the Ukraine often are brought to Moscow or St. Petersburg and forced into begging or prostitution.[69]

The trafficking of victims from Moldova focuses mainly on children and young women trafficked for sexual exploitation. Moldovan victims are trafficked predominantly to the Balkans (Albania, Bosnia and Herzegovina, the Autonomous Province of Kosovo, and the Former Yugoslav Republic of Macedonia), Western Europe, Israel, Russia, Turkey, and the United Arab Emirates.[70] Moldovan men have been trafficked for their kidneys.[71] In Tajikistan, women are trafficked for the purpose of commercial sexual exploitation to the Middle East (Kuwait, Iran, Turkey, and the United Arab Emirates). Male victims are trafficked to Russia and are exploited primarily in the agricultural and construction industries. Internal trafficking of both male and female children occurs for forced labor, including begging.[72]

Case 6.5. A Young Man Is Exploited in Portugal

In 2001, 27-year-old Sergey from Perm in Russia responded to an advertisement in a local newspaper for a job in construction work in Spain. The job agency promised a salary of US$1,200 per month, six times more than Sergey's monthly salary of $200 in Perm. Sergey's application was accepted and the agency paid for his plane ticket to Madrid on the condition that the money would be paid back when Sergey started work. Upon arrival, Sergey was met by someone from the agency who took his passport, brought him to Portugal, and forced him to work on a construction site for several months without pay. Sergey was held captive behind a barbed-wire fence. He finally managed to escape and "begged his way to Germany." Because he had no passport, Sergey was arrested by the German authorities who, according to Sergey, "beat him and took away what little money he had before deporting him to Russia." Sergey is back home but traumatized by his experience. He reportedly is suffering from psychological problems and was unable to work for several months.[73]

EUROPE

Much of the trafficking in Europe has focused on the trafficking of women and children for commercial sexual exploitation. Trafficking occurs in an east-to-west and south-to-north direction. Much attention has been give to the sub-regions of Central (Czech Republic, Hungary, Poland, Slovakia, and Slovenia) and Southeastern Europe (comprising the countries of Albania, Bosnia and Herzegovina, Bulgaria, Croatia, Kosovo, FYR Macedonia, Moldova,[74] Monte-negro, Romania, and Serbia). These two subregions have been identified as origin, transit, and destination areas, with intraregional trafficking occurring as well. When women outside of the region are trafficked to Central and South-eastern Europe, they are generally reported to be trafficked from the former Commonwealth of Independent States. Central Europe serves as a major transit (for victims from the Balkans and Eastern Europe on their way to Western Europe) area and secondary destination area. The sex markets in Western and Southern Europe (predominantly in Belgium, Germany, Greece, Italy, and the Netherlands) serve largely as a trafficking destination for women from Central and Southeastern Europe and from destinations as far away as the Commonwealth of Independent States, Africa, Latin America and the Caribbean,[75] and South-Eastern Asia. The Southern European countries (Andorra, Italy, Malta, Portugal, San Marino, and Spain) serve as a major transit and destination area for victims coming mainly from the Balkans,[76] Latin America, and Western Africa. Trafficking flows to countries in Northern Europe (Denmark, Norway, and Sweden) indicate that trafficking is mainly intraregional with the Nordic countries serving as a destination area and the Baltic countries (Estonia, Latvia, and Lithuania) and Northwestern Russia serving as source and secondary destination areas.[77]

The United Kingdom's "Threat Assessment of Serious Organised Crime" has, over the years, identified a number of different routes into Europe. While the routes appear to fluctuate, the organization has identified a number of different "nexus points" and broad routes into the European Union. There are six main routes—used for both trafficking and the smuggling of migrants into the Europe. These are (1) from Russia (nexus point: Moscow) through the Baltic States to the Czech Republic and Poland; (2) from Ukraine (nexus point: Kiev) to Poland, the Czech Republic, Hungary, Slovakia, and Slovenia; (3) from Turkey (nexus point: Istanbul) to the Balkans (Belgrade and Sara-jevo are nexus points) and on to either Greece or Italy (nexus point: Rome); (4) from Turkey to northern Cyprus, then on to the European Union via Romania and Bulgaria; (5) from Libya (nexus point: Tripoli) to Greece or Italy; or from Somalia via the Suez Canal to Greece or Italy; and (6) from West Africa to Spain.[78]

Estimates of trafficked victims vary by region. The variance in the estimates is huge, ranging from 5,000 to 150,000 victims trafficked to Western Europe; a few thousand up to 100,000 in Central Europe; from tens of thousands to more than 100,000 in Eastern Europe; and from tens of thousands to 200,000 in the Balkans and Eastern Mediterranean. Other ranges for the estimates are smaller (from 10,000 to up to 50,000 in Southern Europe).[79] Yet other sources place the numbers much higher at 500,000 women and children trafficked annually *to* Western Europe from the following regions: from 200,000 women and children *from* Eastern Europe; 120,000 *from and through* the Balkans; and 80,000 *from* the CIS countries. Approximately 200,000 children and women are trafficked through the Balkans each year. [80]

According to the European police organization, Europol, the European Union has witnessed an increase in the number of victims trafficked into the European Union over the last five years. Victims come predominantly from the Russian Federation, Ukraine, Central and Southeastern Europe (Bulgaria, Moldova, and Romania) and to a lesser extent from the far East, West Africa (in particular, Nigeria), and Latin America. Germany, Lithuania, and Poland have been identified as emerging source countries with victims trafficked into Austria, Belgium, France, Germany, Italy, Spain, the Netherlands, and the United Kingdom.[81]

The following sections will provide a more detailed picture of trafficking patterns within various subregions throughout Europe.

Northern Europe

Trafficking in Northern Europe (Denmark, Estonia, Finland, Latvia, Lithuania, Norway, and Sweden) tends to be intraregional with the Baltic countries of Estonia, Latvia, and Lithuania serving as sources, and the Scandinavian countries serving as destinations for women trafficked into prostitution. Women from Latvia and Lithuania are trafficked predominantly to Denmark, Germany, and Sweden, while women from northwestern Russia and Estonia are trafficked to Finland, Norway, and Western Europe. The Baltic countries themselves are destinations for persons trafficked from the CIS countries, Russia, and Ukraine.[82] While researchers report that the number of foreign women in prostitution has increased since the Baltic countries joined the European Union, "the number of cases of coerced prostitution reported to the police remained almost nonexistent.… Most of the prostitutes working in the Nordic countries work at the same time as prostitutes in their home countries."[83] The number of minors trafficked into prostitution in the Baltic countries is considerable and is almost nonexistent in the Nordic countries. UNICEF reports that 20 percent to 50 percent of the prostitutes in Lithuania are believed to be minors. Children as young as 10 have been used to make pornographic movies and 11 year olds have been known to work in prostitution.[84]

Southeastern Europe

This region comprises the countries of Albania, Bosnia and Herzegovina, Bulgaria, Croatia, FYR Macedonia, Montenegro, Romania, Serbia, and the

Autonomous Region of Kosovo. Three patterns emerge: one comprises intraregional trafficking; the second involves the trafficking of women from Southeastern Europe (SEE) to destinations in Western Europe and beyond; the third pattern involves the trafficking of women from Moldova, Russia, and Ukraine into the region. The major source countries in the region are Albania, Bulgaria, and Romania; the major destinations are Bosnia and Herzegovina, Croatia, FYR Macedonia, Serbia and Montenegro, and the Autonomous Region of Kosovo. Trafficking occurs almost exclusively for the purpose of prostitution. Women trafficked out of the region are sent to Greece and Turkey,[85] while Albanians are often trafficked to Italy and destinations in Western Europe.[86] Between January 2000 and June 2003, the IOM assisted 4,072 victims, the majority of whom (70 percent) were from this region. The largest single group was Albanians (43 percent), followed by Moldavians (22 percent), Romanians (15 percent), Bulgarians (7 percent), Ukrainians (6 percent), and Kosovars (5 percent).[87]

While SEE was previously a major center of human trafficking, a follow-up study conducted by three international organizations found that the number of those identified as victims—either through immigration services, bar raids, or those returning home and seeking assistance—has been in decline.[88] A study of trafficking in the region suggested that while the number of identified trafficked victims may be in decline, in reality, the number is increasing but has become less visible. Rather than finding trafficked women in bars and public brothels, traffickers have changed their modus operandi and have brought women into the private domain, where they work out of apartments or via the Internet and phone. Furthermore, new trends were identified involving the emergence of organ trafficking in the region as well as corruption of diplomatic and government officials to facilitate the crime.[89] Trafficking routes throughout the region are in constant flux adapting to changes by law enforcement. In Albania, for instance, when the police clamped down on smuggling routes to Italy, new routes opened to fill the void. Victims of trafficking increasingly are using valid documents to travel directly to their destination country, which is due, in part, to the relaxation of visa regulations for EU Member States and candidate countries for accession to the European Union.[90]

Central Europe

The Central European countries of the Czech Republic, Hungary, Poland, Slovakia, and Slovenia serve as an important transit area for trafficked victims from the East into Western Europe. The area also serves as a destination region for women trafficked into prostitution from Southeastern Europe and the CIS countries. Women from Central Europe are trafficked into prostitution in Austria, Belgium, Germany, and the Netherlands. The number of women from this region being trafficked into Western Europe has been declining over the past years; however, the number of women trafficked through and into the area has not decreased.[91]

The Czech Republic serves mainly as a transit point for women trafficked into prostitution in Western European countries. It is a destination country for women and men trafficked from Belarus, China, Moldova, Ukraine, and Vietnam for labor exploitation. Roma women are trafficked internally and internationally for the purpose of sexual exploitation.[92]

Southern Europe

This region, comprising the countries of Andora, Greece, Italy, Malta, Portugal, San Marino, and Spain, is a major transit and destination area for trafficked victims. Italy, in particular, is one of the foremost destinations for young women trafficked from West Africa, especially from Nigeria. Women are brought to Spain and Portugal from Latin America (in particular Brazil, Colombia, and the Dominican Republic) and are forced into prostitution.[93] A similar pattern of exploitation can be seen in Greece, Italy, Portugal, and Spain where women from Latin America, Eastern Europe, and West Africa are trafficked into commercial prostitution and men are trafficked into labor exploitation in the agricultural industry (Spain) and the construction industry (Portugal). In Greece, most Albanian children are trafficked for forced labor, forced begging, and petty crimes, although some are trafficked for sexual exploitation. In Italy, the country has witnessed an increase in Romanian minors forced into sexual exploitation and in Roma children forced to beg.[94]

Western Europe

The countries in Western Europe (Austria, Belgium, France, Germany, Iceland, Ireland, Luxembourg, the Netherlands, Switzerland, and the United Kingdom) serve as transit or destinations for trafficked victims from around the globe. It has been designated "the most important destination area in Europe for prostitution-related trafficking," where most victims come from Central and Southeastern Europe, the CIS countries, and the Baltic countries (Estonia, Latvia, and Lithuania), as well as from Latin America, Africa, and Southeastern Asia.[95] Almost all of the countries in Western Europe have taken significant action to combat trafficking.[96]

Case 6.6. An Italian Work Camp

After having paid up to €900 to recruiters who advertised in local newspapers, 119 Poles were brought and forced to work in labor camps near Puglia in the south of Italy. Many were reportedly attacked by dogs, beaten with metal rods, and raped. Several people committed suicide in the camps. Italian police report that hundreds of Polish citizens had been exploited over a two-year period. Twenty-seven arrest warrants were issued in Italy and Poland and more were expected.[97]

Before 2005, trafficking in human beings was viewed by many countries in Western Europe as an offense involving exploitation only in the commercial sex industry. In spite of changes to legislation providing for a broader definition of human trafficking, most statistics involving trafficked victims still describe women or children exploited in the sex industry, although a growing number of organizations are dealing with male victims being exploited in various industries. Belgium, Germany, and the Netherlands issue annual reports on the state of trafficking in their respective countries.[98]

Austria is a transit and destination country for women trafficked from Eastern and Southeastern Europe, the Dominican Republic, and Nigeria for forced labor and commercial sexual exploitation. Roma girls are trafficked to Austria from Bulgaria for sexual exploitation and forced petty theft. Approximately two-thirds of those assisted were victims of sexual exploitation and one-third were victims of forced labor.[99]

In Belgium, girls and women are trafficked for sexual exploitation primarily from Albania, Bulgaria, Romania, Nigeria, and the People's Republic of China. Male victims are trafficked to Belgium for exploitative labor in bars, construction sites, restaurants, and sweatshops. Traffickers also force victims to beg in Belgium.[100] In 2006, shelters providing assistance to victims reported an increase in male victims and victims trafficked for forced labor "almost solely due to the significant increase in the number of Brazilian men being exploited in the construction business."[101]

Women and girls are trafficked to France for forced labor and commercial sexual exploitation. Source countries are Albania, Bulgaria, Romania, and the African nations of Cameroon, Nigeria, and Sierra Leone. Women and girls from China are also trafficked to France. In 2006, the percentage of women trafficked from Eastern Europe declined, whereas the percentage of women from Africa, South America, and Asia increased. It is estimated that one-fifth of involuntary domestic servitude cases in France involve abusive employers who are diplomats. They enjoy diplomatic immunity.[102]

Germany has witnessed internal trafficking of women forced into prostitution and German victims represent the largest victim group. The number of registered victims increased between 2005 (642) and 2006 (775) but decreased in 2007 (689) with the largest number of victims coming from Europe (Germany, Bulgaria, Romania, the Czech Republic and Poland, Russia, and Hungary), followed by a much smaller percentage from Asia, Africa, and the Americas.[103]

The Netherlands serves as a source, transit, and destination country. The number of victims who were registered in the Netherlands continued to increase over the past three years. The majority of victims are girls and women forced into commercial sexual exploitation, while men are exploited in restaurants and in the agricultural sector. Dutch victims represent the largest group, followed by Nigerians, Bulgarians, Romanians, and Chinese. Of the 579 registered victims, 30 were male, mainly from India, China, Bangladesh,

Case 6.7. A Girl Is Sold by Her Sister

Maria grew up in the countryside of an Eastern European country. She was the product of an alcoholic father who constantly beat the children. Poorly educated, Maria was sold to an unknown man by her sister when she was only 13 years old. She was taken by boat to Italy and there was sold again to another man who raped and beat her. The police rescued Maria and she was eventually returned to her family, only to be sold four days later—this time by her father. Again she was taken to Italy, imprisoned for seven months and made to drink vinegar. After being smuggled into the United Kingdom, she was forced to work for five years as a prostitute, seeing 65 to 70 customers a day. Maria, 24 years old, has been "raped, beaten, sold, cut with knives and threatened." She was finally able to escape and went to the police who brought her to a shelter. "My traffickers threatened to kill me, and they threatened to take my sister too and do the same to her.... I was beaten often, very badly. I have scars from it now, especially from my broken arm. I have been raped many times.... I will never forget what they did to me."[104]

Nigeria, Turkey, and the Congo.[105] Belgium, France, and the Netherlands, while serving as destination countries, are also transit areas for people being moved to the United Kingdom.

The United Kingdom is primarily a destination country for trafficked victims originating from Eastern Europe (in particular, Russia and Ukraine), the Baltic States (Lithuania), the Balkans (Albania), or from the far East, especially China, Malaysia, and Thailand.[106] Victims from Eastern and Central Africa, Nigeria, and Ghana have also been identified. Women, children, and men are trafficked into the country for sexual exploitation and for forced labor in agriculture, construction, domestic servitude, food processing, and restaurants. Trafficking for illicit activities such as street theft has been reported. Children, particularly from West Africa, have reportedly been trafficked to the United Kingdom for forced labor in cannabis factories. Afghan minors may be trafficked for forced manual labor.[107]

LATIN AMERICA AND THE CARIBBEAN

Latin America is one of the most under-researched and underfunded regions in the world when it comes to people trafficking.[108] Reports from the region indicate that women and children make up the largest group of victims of trafficking for sexual and labor exploitation. Within the region, trafficking occurs from poor nations to more affluent ones. The International Labour Organization (ILO) estimates that 1.3 million people suffer in situations of forced labor in Latin America—20 percent (250,000) of these are trafficked.[109]

Latin America and the Caribbean countries serve mainly as an origin and destination for intraregional trafficking and as a source region for trafficking to the United States, Western Europe, and Japan. Both intraregional and trafficking to other parts of the world involve trafficking for the purpose of labor and sexual exploitation. Women and children are reportedly trafficked within Latin America and the Caribbean countries as well as between cities that serve as tourism sites within individual countries in the region.[110]

While the majority of studies focus on trafficking for commercial sexual exploitation and child sex tourism, the United Nations reports that exploitation in forced labor is becoming more of a problem and that, in some countries of the region, child soldiers increasingly are used in armed conflicts. Drug gangs are also known to traffic children into urban warfare and forced begging. Slave labor in the mining sectors and agriculture often involves men; when women are trafficked into slave labor it is often as sex slaves or domestic servants in the cities.[111]

A literature review of trafficking in persons in Latin America and the Caribbean found that trafficking for prostitution and domestic servitude was a problem in Argentina, Brazil, El Salvador, Guatemala, Guyana, Jamaica, Mexico, and Paraguay. The use of children for child soldiers was reported in Colombia, but also documented in El Salvador, Ecuador, Honduras, Paraguay, Guatemala, Mexico, and Peru.[112]

Much of the research in the region into child trafficking has focused on the abuse of children in the commercial sex industry; however, child trafficking takes on other forms of exploitation as well. Whereas adult women are often trafficked internationally, children tend to be trafficked and exploited within their cities or countries of origin, often by child sex tourists.

The region can be further divided into three subregions—South America, Central America, and the Caribbean. Brazil and Colombia (South America), Guatemala and Mexico (Central America), and the Dominican Republic (the Caribbean) are seen to have a significant trafficking problem.[113]

Central America

In a study of trafficking in women and children for sexual exploitation in Belize, Costa Rica, the Dominican Republic, El Salvador, Guatemala, Honduras, Nicaragua, and Panama, extensive intraregional trafficking with trafficking of Central American and Caribbean women was reported to destinations as far away as the United States, Europe, and Israel. A large number of women from the region work in the sex industries in the United States, Europe, and Japan—although the percentage of trafficked victims is not known.

A report to the U.S. Congress found that border crossings throughout Central America and Mexico, in particular, the Mexico-Guatemala border, have become the newest trafficking focal points. Women who are unable to enter the United States end up being forced into prostitution in Mexico.

Mexico serves as a source, transit, and destination country for persons trafficked in the Central America subregion or on to the United States. Victims are trafficked internally and are lured from rural areas to urban, tourist, and border areas for forced prostitution. Children are used by sex tourists in border towns and tourist destinations in the country.[114]

Costa Rica was reported to be a destination country for women trafficked from Eastern Europe and Thailand.[115] Trafficking of women for domestic labor has been reported in Argentina, the Dominican Republic, El Salvador, Guatemala, Haiti, Nicaragua, and Paraguay.[116]

Child sexual exploitation is linked to the sex tourism industry often found in coastal resorts.[117] The NGO Casa Alianza estimates that 2,000 girls are prostituted in San Jose, Costa Rica, which serves as a sex tourist destination country for children and young adults trafficked from Colombia, the Dominican Republic, and the Philippines.[118] Police in Guatemala City report that the city's 600 brothels are home to 2,000 children from El Salvador, Guatemala, and Honduras.[119]

South America

Major recruitment and source countries within the region are Brazil, Colombia, Surinam, Uruguay, and Venezuela. Latin America and Caribbean women are often trafficked to the United States, Germany, the Netherlands, Portugal, and Spain.[120] Early estimates placed 45,000–50,000 Colombians and 75,000 Brazilian women working in the sex industry in Europe. Another estimate placed 1,700 trafficked women from primarily Brazil, Colombia, and Peru in Japan.[121] International trafficking may be more visible than intraregional trafficking, which also occurs. Women trafficked from the Andes or countries in the Caribbean, in particular the Dominican Republic, are trafficked to Argentina and Brazil. Many trafficked Colombian women are forced to work in prostitution in Panama.

Countries that stand out in the region as particularly serious are Brazil and Colombia. Brazil accounts for 15 percent of women trafficked in South America. A large majority come from the northern part of the country, which shares borders with seven countries.[122] Colombia is one the region's major countries of origin for girls and women trafficked for the purpose of sexual exploitation. Colombian girls and women are trafficked throughout Latin America and the Caribbean to the United States, Western Europe, East Asia, and the Middle East. Internal trafficking, in particular from rural to urban areas, involves the sexual exploitation of children and women. Colombian men are trafficked for forced labor.[123]

Labor exploitation, while receiving less attention than the trafficking of women and children for sexual exploitation, is also a serious problem in South America. The U.S. government estimates that 25,000 Brazilian victims, the majority of whom are men, are trafficked within the country for forced labor

and the United Arab Emirates. These small children from Sudan, Bangladesh, Pakistan, and India were at times abducted or sold by their parents and forced to work as jockeys in camel races. This occurred as late as 2005.[143]

NORTH AMERICA (THE UNITED STATES AND CANADA)

Evidence of trafficking has been found in numerous states in the United States.[144] Between 1990 and 2000, at least 38 separate instances of trafficking into the United States were documented that together involved at least 5,500 women.[145] Trafficking occurs for the purpose of sexual exploitation as well as for labor exploitation. Cases in the United States document persons trafficked for sweatshop labor and domestic servitude, while young children are also kidnapped and sold for adoption. Law enforcement in the United States documents a significant domestic problem involving trafficking in children for the purpose of commercial sexual exploitation.[146]

The U.S. Department of State suggests that a relatively equal number of trafficked women come from four main areas: Asia, Central and South America, Russia and the newly independent states, and Eastern Europe.[147] Cases of trafficking have been documented from Russia and Ukraine; from Malaysia, the Philippines, and Thailand; from Brazil, Costa Rica, and Puerto Rico; and from Cameroon, China, the Czech Republic, and India. In Los Angeles alone, trafficking instances have involved women from Burma, Cambodia, Canada, China, the Czech Republic, El Salvador, Guatemala, Indonesia, Korea, Laos, Malaysia, Mexico, Peru, the Philippines, Romania, Russia, Thailand, and Vietnam.[148]

The Federal Bureau of Investigation reports that the majority of victims of human trafficking in the United States are young girls and women from Asian and Central American countries who are forced into domestic servitude or service in the commercial sex industry. When boys and men are trafficked, they are found to be exploited in the restaurant, migrant farming, and other service-related industries. An increasing number of young men are being forced into the commercial sex industry as well.[149]

Not all trafficked victims in the United States are foreign nationals. American citizens and legal resident aliens are also trafficked. At the time (2008), the U.S. State Department estimated between 14,500 and 17,500 foreign nationals being trafficked *into* the United States each year, the number of U.S. citizens trafficked *within* the United States was estimated at between 100,000 and 300,000, and according to a trafficking expert, most of these young sex workers were teenage runaways.[150] These American children are at risk of becoming victims of commercial sexual exploitation.[151] According to one organization, "[e]vidence suggests that children under the age of 18 now constitute the largest group of trafficking victims in the United States."[152] In what has been the largest nationwide operation ever to rescue children trafficked into prostitution and identify the networks that traffic them, Operation Cross-Country was a five-day action involving 350 local, state, and federal enforcement agencies in 16 cities, resulting in the recovery of 21 children and the arrest of 389 people. [153] To date, the Innocence Lost National Initiative has rescued more than 575 child victims of prostitution.[154]

Underage girls and women—mostly runaways, homeless, or those in low-paying jobs—were "invited" to work in Don Arthur Webster's Anchorage, Alaska, alleged escort services. They were, in fact, forced into prostitution. His youngest victim was 13 at the time that she was recruited and worked for Webster for two years. Webster controlled the women by first getting them addicted to crack cocaine, then confining them to a small closet for days at a time and subjecting them to beatings, threats of severe bodily harm, and other forms of violence.[155]

It is impossible to determine the actual number of persons trafficked into the United States, or the number of U.S. citizens trafficked within the United States, but in fiscal year 2007, the U.S. government did supply 303 certification letters[156] to victims in 29 states, as well as Washington, D.C., and Saipan, Northern Mariana Islands.[157] Between 2001 and 2007, 1,379 certification letters were issued (1,248 to adults and 131 to children). Certified victims came from more than fifty countries from the Americas (41 percent of the victims were from Latin America and the Caribbean), Asia (41 percent of the victims originated in Asia), Africa, and Europe. The top five countries of origin were Thailand, Mexico, Guatemala, the Philippines, and China—constituting slightly more than half (52.7 percent) of all victims certified.

Cases range from those involving individual victims to caseloads involving numerous victims in a single setting.[158]

Case 6.10. Small and Large Trafficking Operations

A couple in Texas smuggled a 12-year-old girl from Mexico under the pretense of using her as a babysitter. She ended up becoming their domestic slave, deprived of school and having to sleep on the floor. The child was told she could not return to Mexico and was physically abused by the wife. Only after the local sheriff responded to a call involving a drug overdose was the child found and rescued. After pleading guilty, the couple were sentenced to 33 and 84 months in prison and ordered to pay $28,822 restitution to the victim.[159]

In another case, defendants running karaoke bars in Saipan worked with recruiters and brokers to bring Chinese women to the Northern Mariana Islands under the pretense of working in restaurants. Instead, the women were saddled with large debts, forced into prostitution, physically threatened, and subjected to violence. The two defendants were sentenced to 33 and 78 months in prison, ordered to pay restitution of $22,200 and $25,200 to two victims, and fined an additional $55,000.[160]

The U.S.-Canada border is increasingly becoming an entry point for criminal networks involved in sex trafficking.[161] Canada serves predominantly as a destination country for foreign-born women and children. Children and women are mostly trafficked from Asia (the Republic of Korea, Thailand, Cambodia, Malaysia, and Vietnam) and Eastern Europe (Romania, Hungary, and Russia), although victims from Latin America and the Caribbean, Africa, and the Middle East have also been identified. Vancouver and Western Canada are the destination points for Asian victims; Latin American and Eastern European victims are trafficked more often to Toronto and Eastern Canada.[162] Toronto and Vancouver are emerging as hubs for trafficked persons in the international sex industry. Girls from the former Czechoslovakia, Hungary, Romania, and countries in South America, and Asia are brought to Toronto to work in clubs as exotic dancers.[163]

National Royal Canadian Mounted Police investigators estimated as many as 800 to 1,200 trafficking victims in Canada, while some activists have put the number as high as 15,000. In addition to foreign victims, Canadian women are also trafficked within the country and exploited in the commercial sex industry. Aboriginal girls and women living in poverty are high-risk persons. According to the president of the Union of British Colombia Indian Chiefs, 3,000 or more aboriginal women are missing in Canada who may have fallen victim to trafficking either in or outside of the country.[164]

The U.S. Department of State has also identified Canada as a transit country for South Korean women brought into the United States, where they are exploited in the sex industry.[165]

OCEANIA

The major destination countries in the region are Australia and New Zealand. Victims trafficked into Oceania, are reported to be trafficked predominantly from Southeastern Asia. Australia is a destination country for women trafficked predominantly into commercial sexual exploitation from Indonesia, Malaysia, Thailand, Vietnam, China, Hong Kong, Taiwan, and the Philippines.[166] The U.S. Department of State also reports that many trafficked women end up in forced prostitution in Australia after having traveled freely to the country to work in both legal and illegal brothels. Reports have also surfaced of men and women from China, India, Ireland, the Republic of Korea, and the Philippines migrating temporarily to work in Australia, but then these individuals are exploited.[167]

In New Zealand, internal trafficking of women for commercial sexual exploitation has been reported. It also serves as a destination country for women from China, Hong Kong, Malaysia, and other Asian countries.[168]

CONCLUDING REMARKS

Human trafficking occurs within every region of the world and affects men, women, and children. The prior emphasis in Western Europe on human trafficking for sexual exploitation is slowly changing to include investigations into labor exploitation—something that has been at the forefront of human trafficking studies in other parts of the world. Studies in Southeastern Europe and the United Kingdom indicate that trafficking patterns alter when the necessity arises to establish new routes. Reports emerging from Germany and the Netherlands with respect to trafficked victims show that, from year to year, the number and percentage of victims of different nationalities increases or decreases. Trafficking patterns, like the criminals and the organizations with which they are involved, are in a constant state of flux.

Trafficking patterns and markets of exploitation will change based on the demand for labor in the destination countries and the availability of potential victims in a given place in a source country. New opportunities or situations will arise that create a market for trafficked persons—the subject of the next two chapters.

Hidden Forms of Human Trafficking

SO MUCH ATTENTION has been directed toward international trafficking of women and children for the purpose of sexual exploitation and other forms of forced labor that additional forms of trafficking, although they do occur, have been overlooked. It is unclear whether they occur less frequently than other forms of trafficking, or whether they simply have received less attention. This chapter begins with an exploration of child trafficking in armed conflicts, followed by organ trafficking, trafficking for forced marriages, and illegal adoptions.

CHILD SOLDIERS

The United Nations Children's Fund (UNICEF) defines a "child soldier" as

> [A]ny child—boy or girl—under 18 years of age, who is part of any kind of regular or irregular armed force or armed group in any capacity ... and anyone accompanying such groups other than family members. It includes girls and boys recruited for forced sexual purposes and/or forced marriage.[1]

Kidnapping and forced or illicit recruitment of children for use in armed conflicts are estimated to affect around 300,000 children in conflicts throughout the world. The trafficking of children for use in armed conflicts can take place within a country or transborder. According to the United Nations, there are indications that cross-border trafficking of child soldiers is increasing in West and Central Africa "as a result of elaborate international organized criminal networks."[2]

The problem of trafficking of child soldiers is most extreme in Africa (Angola, Burundi, Central African Republic, Chad, Côte d'Ivoire, Democratic Republic of the Congo, Guinea-Bissau, Liberia, Mozambique, Rwanda, Sierra Leone, Somalia, Sudan, and Uganda), but countries in Asia (Afghanistan, India, Indonesia, Myanmar, Nepal, the Philippines, Sri Lanka, and Thailand) the Middle East (Iraq and the Occupied Palestinian Territories), and Latin America (Colombia) also have been affected.[3] The use of children in government, paramilitary, or rebel armies extends beyond the task of carrying weapons and fighting and includes use in other services. Children serve not only as soldiers but also as spies, cooks, porters, sexual slaves, and human land mine detectors.[4] Children have been reported to fight on the front lines, have been sent into minefields ahead of adult soldiers, and have even been used for suicide missions.[5] Young children, ages seven and eight, are recruited or kidnapped to begin serving their military apprenticeships as messengers or carrying food or ammunition as porters.[6] Most child soldiers are between the ages of 14 and 18; however, children as young as nine have been used in combat.

Geographic Distribution of Child Soldiers

Africa

In Africa, 100,000 child soldiers are currently active in Burundi, Chad, the Democratic Republic of Congo, Guinea, Rwanda, Sudan, Somalia, and Uganda.[7] The 20-year war in Uganda between the Ugandan government and the Lord's Resistance Army (LRA) claimed more than 20,000 child soldiers,[8] many of whom were kidnapped. In the first half of 2007, the LRA forcibly recruited children from Southern Sudan. Up to 2,000 women and children are believed to remain in LRA camps.[9]

Thousands of young child refugees who have survived the war in Darfur are being abducted and sold as child soldiers to militias operating in the vicinity of the refugee camps. Boys, mostly between the ages of 9 and 15 have been taken forcibly from their families in refugee camps in Chad and are being trafficked to militias. The rebel group, the Justice and Equality Movement, which is fighting the Khartoum government, is the main offender, but opposing rebels and the Chadian army are also involved.[10]

Asia

Children are serving in armies in Afghanistan, India, Nepal, Myanmar, Sri Lanka, Indonesia, and the Philippines.[11] Some of the most egregious offenses involved the government of Myanmar whose army regularly uses children to fight ethnic armed groups and regularly recruits children ages 12 to 18. The Myanmar army is believed to be using thousands of children.[12]

In Sri Lanka, the Liberation Tigers of Tamil Eelam (LTTE) or Tamil Tigers reportedly recruited 6,248 children (including 2,469 girls) between January 2002 and December 2007. The TMVP/Karuna faction, allegedly supported by the government of Sri Lanka, is suspected of having recruited 453 children (including one girl), between April 2004 and December 2007. The United Nations Children's Fund (UNICEF) suspects the numbers to be significantly higher. Between January 2006 and June 2007, more than 1,100 mainly Tamil civilians, including children, have "disappeared" or been abducted.[13] The Tamil Tiger rebels are believed to have thousands of children in their ranks.[14]

The United Nations reports the recruitment of children in Pakistan from religious schools ("madrassas"), by militant groups to carry out suicide bombings. The district coordinator of Pakistan's Child Rights Committee (CRC) reports that about 25 to 30 madrassa students, between the ages of 7 and 15, have been used by leaders of extremist outfits in the district of Swat to carry out attacks. Six others students from another madrassa were apprehended by the police for their alleged involvement in an attempted suicide attack. A 12-year-old child was forced to wear a suicide bomb jacket with instructions to blow up the district court. He, along with the other children arrested, are now being held in jail.[15]

The Taliban is reported to have used child soldiers in Afghanistan as suicide bombers. They have further forcibly and voluntarily recruited children in the southern provinces and parts of Pakistan.[16]

Latin America

In one of the longest-running battles between government and armed opposition forces, lasting 50 years, children in Colombia have been driven by rural poverty to voluntarily join and have been forcibly recruited and used by both the rebel National Liberation Army (ELN) and the Revolutionary Armed Forces of Colombia (FARC). The children were forced to lay mines, carry explosives, work as guides and messengers, and fight in combat. Female children were subjected to rape, abortion, and other forms of sexual abuse. The children were further exploited by government forces that used surrendered and captured child soldiers to gather intelligence for opposition forces.[17]

Middle East

Child soldiers are reportedly deployed in Israel, Iraq, and the Occupied Palestinian Territories. The NGO War Child reports that "children in these areas are encouraged to commit suicide attacks or are used as a human shield."[18]

Voluntary or Coerced Recruitment of Child Soldiers

While large numbers of children have been forcibly abducted in some countries, not all children have been kidnapped or fraudulently recruited. Some children join rebel forces voluntarily as a means of survival in a country or region affected by poverty and lack of education or job prospects. Children may voluntarily join armed groups because of social or economic pressure, or in the belief that the group will provide them with security or food.[19] Children may voluntarily join rebel forces to avenge the death of their family members killed by armed groups or government forces.[20]

A study of child soldiers in Chad found that some children join the rebel FUC (United Front for Change) voluntarily, but Human Rights Watch questions whether the decision was made freely given the lack of options. Most children come from villages characterized by poverty; they are uneducated and voluntarily join the army to escape difficult home environments. Their country was characterized by violence, which led the children to believe that they were safer with the rebel forces than remaining unarmed in their villages. A brigadier general of the Chadian National Army reported that boys between the ages of 12 and 15 were obliged to join.

> They are called *bandios* and their job is to make tea, find water, collect firewood, mind the goats. It is forced recruitment. They don't want to join, but they are obliged to. Their parents don't want their children to join the army, because they know they are going to die. But they have no choice.[21]

A study of child soldiers carried out in Colombia by the NGO War Child identified a number of reasons why children voluntarily join militias, which include cultural, ideological, socioeconomic, protection, and revenge. A love of weapons and the status and power that carrying a weapon brings in a culture that values manliness drives some children into the ranks of armed groups. For others, their ideological convictions are the driving force. Joining a militia may mean they believe they are fighting against social injustice or for the rights of a minority group. Poverty and lack of education or job perspectives forces some children to join armed groups. The final motivations were protection and revenge. The study found that less than 15 percent of child soldiers were forcefully recruited to the FARC, ELN, or paramilitary troops, although this number differed for the various armed militias. Fourteen percent of the children who had worked with the paramilitaries had been abducted, while for the FARC it was 12.5 percent and for the ELN it was only 8 percent. The main reason for joining the groups differed: children joined paramilitary groups (25 percent) because they provided work opportunities (socioeconomic reasons) and joined both the FARC (24 percent) and the ELN (40 percent) out of ideological conviction. The second most important reason for joining the FARC and ELN was a love of weapons (cultural reasons) followed closely by lack of options and availability of work, while for the paramilitaries, the second most important reason was lack of options (socioeconomic reasons).[22]

Psychological Manipulation of Children

Human Rights Watch, which has interviewed child soldiers in Angola, Burma, Burundi, Chad, Colombia, the Democratic Republic of Congo, Lebanon, Liberia, Nepal, Sierra Leone, Sri Lanka, Sudan, and Uganda reports that children typically make obedient soldiers. They are physically vulnerable and easily intimidated. To prove their allegiance to the armed forces, children are sometimes forced to commit atrocities against their own family or neighbors. These practices help ensure that the child is stigmatized and unable to return to his or her home community.[23]

Stories have surfaced of the manipulation of children by supplying them with drugs, some of which reportedly make them fearless. The United Nations reports that others are given drugs and alcohol to agitate them, notating that this "make[s] it easier to break down their psychological barriers to fighting or committing atrocities."[24] At the same time, children are trained to obey orders to kill and maim. Failure to do so may result in their own death.[25] One 16-year-old child soldier described his experience:

> The first time I went into battle I was afraid. But after two or three days they forced us to start using cocaine, and then I lost my fear. When I was taking drugs, I never felt bad on the front. Human blood was the first thing I would have every morning. It was my coffee in the morning ... every morning.[26]

Ishmael Beah, the former child soldier from Sierra Leone, was a 12-year-old boy when rebels killed his parents and brother and most of the residents of his village. He was forced to fight with rebels as a child soldier until he was "rescued" by government soldiers who fed him, protected him, and gave him an AK47. Ishmael was told to fight for the army or be killed by the rebels. He was then 13 years old. Ishmael and other child soldiers were given marijuana and a drug known as "brown-brown"[27]—a mixture of cocaine and gun powder used to enhance the effect of the marijuana. Under the influence of the drug, Ishmael reports that he was "not afraid to kill or be killed." In addition to the drugs, the children were shown movies praising the use of violence, such as Rambo, while being told that they were fighting for their country.[28]

Female Victims

According to UNICEF, the risk of exploitation, abuse, and sexual violence of women and children increases during armed conflicts. Girls have reported voluntarily enlisting in armies to escape domestic servitude, sexual abuse, and violence at home.[29] The role of female children used in armies is particularly grim. According to one expert, nearly one-third of child soldiers are girls who face danger from sexually transmitted diseases (including HIV/AIDS), unwanted pregnancies, and complications or death during childbirth. If they are able to survive with their child, the child is often rejected or faces discrimination in their local villages.[30] Girls are further subjected to social stigmatization, human trafficking, and prostitution.[31]

Girls reportedly have been abducted and served in armed conflicts in El Salvador, Ethiopia, and Uganda. Almost a third of the child soldiers in these countries are girls who are enslaved, raped, and "given" to military commanders as "wives."[32] Unlike boys, who may join rebel armies willingly, most girls in armed conflicts are abducted or recruited by coercion. This was particularly true in Angola, Sierra Leone, and Uganda. Girls predominantly serve in rebel or government-opposition armies.[33]

Given the nature of their systematic sexual abuse and possible health problems, female child soldiers require special care, which is not always provided during their reintegration phase.

The Psychological and Physical Impact on Child Soldiers

Child soldiers are subjected to brutal initiation, cruel training regimes, hard labor, punishment rituals, and torture. In addition to ill treatment and sexual abuse, child soldiers have often been traumatized by the violence they have seen or in which they have been forced to partake, sometimes against their own families or community. They are threatened with violence or killed if they attempt to escape.[34] Child soldiers are often wounded or suffer from "multiple traumas and psychological scarring. Their personal development is often irreparably damaged."[35]

During and even after their involvement as child soldiers, many children report psychosocial disturbances. These range from nightmares, anger, and aggression that is difficult to control, to substance abuse and antisocial behavior.[36] As a result of this behavior, many former child soldiers are rejected by their families and communities and have difficulties adjusting to civilian life. Even after having been removed from the armed forces, ex-child soldiers are more at risk of abuse, in particular sexual abuse.[37]

A study of 301 child soldiers in Uganda who had been kidnapped by the LRA found that almost all the children had experienced several traumatic events: 233 children (77 percent) saw someone being killed, 118 children (39 percent) were forced to kill someone, 190 (63 percent) had to loot and burn the houses of civilians, 193 (64 percent) were forced to fight, 21 of the 53 girls (39% percent) interviewed were sexually abused or given to one or more

---

Case 7.1. A Teenage Girl Is Abducted and Exposed to Violence

Sixteen-year-old Susan, abducted by the Lord's Resistance Army in Uganda, reported the following:[38]

> One boy tried to escape, but he was caught. They made him eat a mouthful of red pepper, and five people were beating him. His hands were tied, and then they made us, the other new captives, kill him with a stick. I felt sick. I knew this boy from before. We were from the same village. I refused to kill him and they told me they would shoot me. They pointed a gun at me, so I had to do it. The boy was asking me, "Why are you doing this?" I said I had no choice. After we killed him, they made us smear his blood on our arms. I felt dizzy. There was another dead body nearby, and I could smell the body. I felt so sick. They said we had to do this so we would not fear death and so we would not try to escape.
>
> I feel so bad about the things that I did.... It disturbs me so much—that I inflicted death on other people.... When I go home I must do some traditional rites because I have killed. I must perform these rites and cleanse myself. I still dream about the boy from my village who I killed. I see him in my dreams, and he is talking to me and saying I killed him for nothing, and I am crying.

---

soldiers as a wife, and half of those girls gave birth to one or more children in captivity. The children were diagnosed with showing "a high rate of post-traumatic stress reactions."[39]

Former child soldiers are at high risk of contracting HIV/AIDS. The children have been taught to be disinhibited to violent and sexual behavior while serving in the army and they have difficulties adjusting once released. The United Nations reports that once demobilized, former child soldiers are often poor, lack family ties, and find themselves in a new world—one in which they find it difficult to adjust. Their coping mechanisms put them at high risk. In Sierra Leone, former child soldiers turned increasingly to illegal intravenous drugs. Former child soldiers from Uganda have been found to resort to brewing or abusing alcohol and turning to sex work to support themselves.[40]

The Fate of Child Soldiers

With the end of conflicts in the countries of Burundi, Côte d'Ivoire, Guinea, and Liberia, the large-scale recruitment and deployment of children into government armies ceased. So, too, did the use of child soldiers in Indonesia and Nepal.[41] Between 2004 and 2007, the world has witnessed a decrease in the number of conflicts involving children from 27 in 2004 to 17 in 2007.[42]

Whether children join armies voluntarily or not, the U.N. Trafficking Protocol views this as trafficking regardless of the conditions under which the children were recruited—even where there is no use of fraud or deception. Children fail to understand the consequences of their actions and their rights to health, safety, free movement, and association. All children under the age of 18, regardless of why or how they joined the armed forces with which they worked or fought, are victims of trafficking.

Because child soldiers have often committed such atrocities, questions arise in their villages and countries concerning their degree of responsibility. They are often treated as criminals rather than victims of trafficking, and the U.N. Trafficking Protocol calls for special protection for trafficked victims. Campaigns[43] to *disarm, demobilize,* and *reintegrate* child soldiers are under way in many postconflict countries. Once a child has escaped or been discharged from an armed group, the child's identity has to be established. The child's needs are determined and future plans of action for the child are mapped out (demobilization). The reintegration phase is a long-term and most difficult process involving assistance in helping the children resume life in their community, or in an alternative community if the child soldiers are rejected by their communities. If reunification with the parents is desirable and possible, this occurs. UNICEF and other organizations that work with demobilized child soldiers provide education, training, and in some cases, psychosocial support. The needs, often medical, of female child soldiers are different and these children require special care.

Between 2001 and 2006, UNICEF disarmed and demobilized 20,000 children from the former rebel forces of the Sudan People's Liberation Army (SPLA) and returned them to their families. At the time, UNICEF reported approximately 2,000 more children involved in the armed conflict, of which, a significant minority were girls.[44] During the demobilization of Maoist soldiers in Nepal in January 2007, the U.N. team found 2,973 minors.[45] The United Nations also reports the successful demobilization of child soldiers from Côte d'Ivoire.[46]

ORGAN TRAFFICKING

Organ trafficking is perhaps the least-profiled form of human trafficking. There has been almost no empirical research, but individual stories and investigations of illegally harvested organs surface on a regular basis. Urban legends exist of children being kidnapped and killed for their organs, but there is little empirical evidence to support these claims. In 2006, the United Nations came to the conclusion that it was impossible to provide any estimation on the scope of organ trafficking. The topic was not a priority nor had it received close scrutiny from the United Nation's member states. Most cases included in the report involved the illegal removal and trafficking of organs or tissue from deceased persons.[47]

With the improvement of health care in many parts of the industrial world, life expectancy has increased resulting in a larger population of older people. At the same time, medical and technological developments have facilitated the transplantation of organs, which has become a rather routine procedure. This would normally not present a problem, except for the fact that demand far exceeds the supply, and the shortage is acute. Between 1990 and 2003, kidney donations in the United States increased only 33 percent, but people awaiting a kidney for transplant increased by 236 percent.[48] The chronic shortage in Europe means that between 15 percent and 30 percent of European patients will die while waiting for a kidney transplant, which averages about three years. By 2010, the wait for a new kidney is expected to increase to 10 years.[49]

The shortage in organs is due, in part, to religious beliefs that the body should be buried intact and in part to a fear of hospitals intentionally allowing patients to die to harvest their organs for paying patients. Waiting times for an organ from a cadaver, usually a kidney (which accounts for the most sales of organs throughout the world), varies from one country to the next. In Britain and the United States, the average wait is two to three years. In Singapore, the wait is six to eight years. In the Gulf States and Asia, the wait is even longer. This long wait has led many in need of a kidney to try to obtain one from a live donor.[50]

While organs harvested from deceased donors are packed on ice and transported around the world by plane, the harvesting of organs from live donors generally involves the travel of both donor and recipient to the place where the transplant will occur. The discussion around the phenomenon is not about the trafficking of organs per se, but the trafficking of human beings for the purpose of organ removal. This is considered human trafficking even when donors often agree to voluntarily sell their organs. Both deceit concerning payment and the medical risks involved in the operation often occur, so donors are unable to make an informed decision.

Patterns of Organ Trafficking

In the 1990s, most recipients of kidneys were Asians who traveled to China or India to purchase an organ or were residents of the Gulf States who traveled to India. The market has expanded, and while India remains a popular destination for both purchase and transplant, buyers come from India's middle class and from around the world and now include the United States, Canada, England, and the countries in the Middle East.[51] One of the world's leading experts on human trafficking for organ transplant, Dr. Nancy Scheper-Hughes, describes it as a trade that can bring together parties from three of more

Table 7.1 Organ Donor and Recipient Nations

Common Countries of Origin for Those Selling Kidneys	Common Countries of Origin for Those Buying Kidneys
Bolivia	Australia
Brazil	Canada
China	Hong Kong, China
Colombia	Israel
Arab Republic of Egypt	Italy
India	Japan
Islamic Republic of Iran	Malaysia
Iraq	Oman
Israel	Saudi Arabia
Moldova	Republic of Korea
Nigeria	Taiwan, China
Pakistan	United States
Peru	
Philippines	
Romania	
Turkey	

Source: Information taken from Scheper-Hughes (2003, 2005a) and modified with data from Saletan (2007) and Shimazono (2007).

countries—the donors and recipients often come from different countries, while the transplantation may occur in yet a third country. The trade in kidneys from live donors generally flows from poor, underdeveloped countries to rich, developed ones, creating both organ-donor and organ-recipient nations.[52]

Regional Patterns

The Middle East

For the past two decades, organized programs have taken wealthy patients from the Middle East (Israel, Kuwait, Oman, and Saudi Arabia) first to India and then to Turkey, the Islamic Republic of Iran, and later Iraq for transplants. This pattern was later followed by trips to the Russian Federation, Romania, Moldova, and Georgia, and within the last decade to Brazil and South Africa. Another popular route brought Israeli kidney recipients by plane to Turkey where kidney sellers from rural Romania or Moldova were matched. The operation was performed by Israeli and Turkish doctors.[53] Wealthy Palestinians travel to Iraq where poor Arabs coming from Jordan sell their kidneys.[54] Donors sell their kidneys in Iran, Iraq, and India.[55]

East and Southeast Asia

In the People's Republic of China, organs of executed prisoners have been removed by the state and used for transplant. Reports have surfaced of cases in which organs have been sold abroad for the profit of illegal brokers. An independent investigation into organ harvesting of Falun Gong members in China came to the conclusion that

> [T]he government of China and its agencies in numerous parts of the country, in particular hospitals but also detention centers and "people's courts," since 1999 have put to death a large but unknown number of Falun Gong prisoners of conscience. Their vital organs, including kidneys, livers, corneas and hearts, were seized involuntarily for sale at high prices, sometimes to foreigners.[56]

Organs harvested in China are used by wealthy recipients from Hong Kong, China; the Republic of Korea; Japan; Malaysia; Singapore; and Taiwan, China. This practice of using organs of executed prisoners also occurs in Singapore.

Organ transplants have surged in the Philippines with foreign recipients coming from Japan, Europe, and the Middle East to purchase kidneys from poor Philippine donors. In 2007, about half of the transplant operations in the Philippines involved foreign recipients.[57] Donors have had kidneys removed and they were not paid.[58] According to the International Organization for Migration (IOM), organ trafficking is on the rise in Southeast Asia, particularly in China and other impoverished countries such as Cambodia, Indonesia, Laos, the Philippines, and Vietnam.[59]

South Asia

Research has shown that India is the place for kidney and cornea transplants. Those looking to purchase a kidney come from the Middle East (Bahrain, Kuwait, Oman, Saudi Arabia, and the United Arab Emirates), Malaysia, Singapore, Canada, and the United States. Donors tend to be concentrated in the states of Andhar Pradesh, Karnataka, Tamil Nadu, and Punjab. There are accounts of laborers in Punjab who have been deceived and even forced into selling a kidney. According to the Voluntary Health Association of India, it is estimated that about 2,000 Indians sell a kidney every year.[60]

Forty percent of people in some villages in Pakistan are turning up with only one kidney. According to the World Health Organization, the number of donations from unrelated Pakistanis is increasing dramatically. The majority of those receiving the organs are foreigners. In 2003, the Sind Institute for Urology and Transplantation (SIUT), in Karachi estimated that around 2,000 kidney transplants were performed each year in Pakistan. Almost two-thirds of these were performed on foreign patients and 80 percent were from unrelated donors.[61]

In Nepal, laborers have had kidneys removed and the promised payment was withheld.[62] The same pattern is occurring in the Philippines.[63] The Philippines National Bureau of Investigation reports that organ trafficking now involves children who are kidnapped or sold by their parents for their organs, which are purchased by Middle Eastern nationals.[64]

North America: The United States

Organ donors and sellers meet in the United States where transplants occur in some of the finest hospitals in the world operating on a "don't ask, don't tell" policy. The donors come from "seller" countries such as India, Nigeria, the Philippines, or Russia.[65] There are reports of Russians and other Eastern Europeans being trafficked to the United States and forced at gunpoint to sell their kidney.[66]

Europe

A report by the Council of Europe on organ trafficking identifies European's poorest countries as "donor" countries: Bulgaria, Estonia, Georgia, Moldova, Romania, Russia, and Ukraine. The trade has been linked to organized crime. One trafficking network was found to link Israel, Moldova, Turkey, and Ukraine. Buyers and sellers come together in Turkey for transplantation. Turkey serves as a hub for transplant tourism.[67]

Latin America

Brazil, and to a lesser extent Colombia, are the countries most often affected by international trafficking for organ transplant. Brazilian kidney sellers are matched with predominantly Israeli buyers for operations that are performed in South Africa.[68] The World Health Organization reports that Colombia is now becoming a destination for U.S. tourists seeking an organ transplant and other cheap operations. Kidneys and livers can be purchased through several Web sites.[69]

Africa

South Africa is the second transplant tourism hub, which attracts donors from countries as widespread as Brazil, Moldova, Nigeria, and Romania. Recipients come from Botswana, Israel, Mauritius, and Namibia.[70] There have been incidental reports of children being kidnapped and killed for their organs to be used in traditional medical practices in South Africa, and media reports have linked the trafficking of West African children to Europe for use in ritual killings for their body parts. The practice has been documented in Nigeria as well.[71]

Individuals and Organizations Involved in Organ Trafficking

This crime, unlike other forms of trafficking, cannot take place without the complicity of professional medical staff operating in hospitals or private clinics. These doctors knowingly remove healthy organs from individuals not related to the recipients. In addition to the donor and seller, which will be discussed in a later section, a number of brokers and agents are involved. These have been identified as, but are not limited to the following:[72]

- Kidney hunters or brokers (to recruit "donors" locally or internationally from among vulnerable and marginalized populations)
- Medical directors of transplant units
- Hospital and medical staff
- Technicians in blood and tissue laboratories
- Dual surgical teams working in tandem
- Nephrologists
- Postoperative nurses

Others who may knowingly or unknowingly be involved include:

- Travel agents and tour operators to organize travel, passports, and visas
- Medical insurance agents
- Religious organizations and charitable trusts, which sometimes call upon organ brokers
- Patient advocacy organizations, which sometimes call upon organ brokers

The most important link between donor and recipient is the organ broker. These often-unscrupulous individuals have no link to the medical field and are reported to be recruited from bars, flea markets, army barracks, jails and prisons, unemployment offices, and shopping malls.[73] Organ brokers can scour slum areas in poor countries looking for suitable donors, as was the case in the Philippines. Police near Manila raided a house and freed nine men who were being held by a gang that had lured them with the promise of good jobs. Instead, they forced them to agree to "donate" a kidney.[74]

For those looking to purchase a kidney, it is as simple as logging onto the Web sites of such dubious organizations as www.Liver4You.org. For between $85,000 and $115,000, a buyer can purchase a new kidney and pay for the operation in Manila, the Philippines. Liver transplants are more expensive, currently costing $130,000.[75] The organ seller often receives no more than a few thousand dollars of this fee.

In what the Indians called the "mother of all scandals in human organ trafficking in India," police arrested middlemen, donors, and several doctors, including a transplant surgeon, as well as the principal of the Government Medical College. Police estimate that between 1997 and 2002, $31.4 million dollars changed hands between the donors, middlemen, and doctors. The organ sellers, poor migrant laborers from Uttar Pradesh and Bihar states were paid between $525 and $1,050, while the recipients were charged between $104,600 and $209,200.[76]

According to the United Nations, corruption is an integral element in organ trafficking and transplantation.[77] It may be as "benign" as allowing wealthy patients to climb to the top of waiting lists for organ transplants, or may be as insidious as protecting illegal practices. Not more than six years after the first organ trafficking scandal in India, the Indian Government uncovered yet another organ trafficking operation, this time with suspected links to the police. The scale of the operation was "unprecedented" and involved about 500 patients and no less than three private hospitals, 10 pathology clinics, five diagnostic centers, 20 paramedics, five nurses, and four doctors. Additionally, guards were paid to watch and intimidate workers held in safehouses. These unsuspecting individuals thought they were accepting a job. Instead, they were drugged or forced, sometimes at gunpoint, to forfeit a kidney. The police are suspected of tipping off the main suspect before a police raid on at least one occasion, and in spite of an investigative program into the doctor's illegal kidney trafficking, the suspect was allowed to continue operating. One of India's leading newspapers has made accusations of "the nexus between the organ traders and the police."[78]

The Donors and Recipients in the Organ Trafficking Trade

There are about 6,000 international kidney transactions a year.[79] While the procedure remains fairly consistent, the donors and recipients vary from one country to the next and even between regions within particular countries. There are, however, some general trends. Organs are supplied by desperately poor people

Table 7.2 Demographic Data on Organ Sellers in Different Countries

Country (State)	Gender	Age	Income	Education	Occupation
Moldova	Male	18–28	Low	Poor	Laborer
Philippines	Male	29	Annual family income $480	7 years	N.A.
Nigeria	Female	N.A.	Very low annual income	N.A.	N.A.
India (Punjab)	Male	18–30	N.A.	N.A.	Laborer
India (Tamil Nadu)	Female 71% Male 29%	35	Annual family income $420; 71% below poverty line	2.7 years	N.A.

Note: N.A. = not available.
Sources: Data for this table were compiled from Scheper-Hughes (2003, 2005b), Goyal et al. (2002), GTZ (2004), and the Council of Europe (2003).

in poor countries to donors in more affluent ones. Donors are generally minorities and recipients of the organs are white or Middle Eastern. Donors may be males or females, but most recipients are male; rarely are women the recipients of purchased organs.[80] Donors are young; recipients generally older.

In the state of Tamil Nadu, India, almost three-quarters (71 percent) of the 305 respondents in a study of kidney sellers were women. Sixty percent of the women and almost all of the men were street vendors or laborers. Two of the participants reported that they were forced to sell a kidney by their husband.[81] Other studies have found that many organ sellers in India are women, and in some cases the kidney may be sold to pay for the dowry for a daughter's wedding. In the State of Punjab, India, it is generally poor young men (laborers) between the age of 18 and 30 who agree to sell a kidney.[82]

In Nigeria, kidney sellers are usually poor, single women,[83] while in Moldova, kidney sellers are poor, young men from rural areas between the ages of 18 and 28. Most of these men were deceived or coerced in selling their kidney. While they were paid between $2,500 and $3,000 to sell their kidney, recipients were required to pay between $100,000 and $200,000 for the operation.[84]

Consent, Deception, Coercion, and Exploitation in the Procurement of Body Parts

Not all donors consent to sell their organs. Persons can be kidnapped, killed, or sold for their organs. The United Nations reported that "[a]s regards trafficking in children for the purpose of organ removal, although there is no conclusive evidence, a number of reports indicate that many abducted or missing children have subsequently been found dead, their bodies mutilated and certain organs removed."[85] This is often associated with the African traditional practice of magical medicine in which certain body parts are sold and used by deviant practitioners to increase health, fertility, wealth, or influence of a paying client.[86]

Another method of obtaining an organ is through deception or coercion. A person is told that he will be donating blood and is then coerced into selling a kidney. Cases of persons admitted into the hospital in Argentina, Brazil, and India for an accident or unrelated illness have reportedly had a kidney removed without their consent[87] Laudiceia da Silva entered a São Paulo, Brazil, hospital in June 1997 to have an ovarian cyst removed. The woman's family doctor discovered during a routine follow-up examination, that she was missing a kidney. The hospital later told da Silva that her "missing kidney was embedded in the large 'mass' that had accumulated around her ovarian cyst" and that the diseased ovary and the kidney had been discarded. No medical records were produced.[88] A leading expert on organ trafficking documented an asylum for mentally ill persons in Argentina in which the director exploited his patients by providing "blood, corneas and kidneys" to area hospitals.[89]

In other cases, people are promised jobs in a foreign country. Once there, the job fails to materialize, and the victim, who has been kept in a safe-house, is now psychologically or physically threatened into offering up a kidney. In one case, Vladimir, a 19-year-old boy from Mingir, a small village in central Moldova, was lured from his home by a former prostitute-turned-kidney broker who promised him a good job in a dry cleaning store in Istanbul. Nina, the kidney broker, arranged the papers and after a 17-hour bus ride to Istanbul, Vladimir was locked in a hotel room for a week. When Nina appeared again, it was to tell Vladimir that he would have to start selling blood and "after a 'match' was made, he would sell his 'best' and 'strongest' kidney for $2,700 minus his rent and food."[90] The young victim was frightened and felt he had no choice but to cooperate, which was the only way he could get home.

The most common form of trafficking in organs involves cases in which the donor and recipient agree to the sale.[91] While donors may initially consent to selling a kidney, buyers exploit their desperation, poverty, and ignorance. The organ trafficking expert, Scheper-Hughes, identified a case in Tel Aviv where a mentally deficient criminal sold a kidney to his lawyer who then paid the man half of what was promised. In another case in Canada, a man received a kidney from his Filipino domestic worker. He justified this "donation" using the argument that "Filipinos are a people who are anxious to please their bosses."[92]

Kidneys vary according to their abundance and bring their donors different amounts, depending on where the donor is living. According to one expert, an African or an Indian kidney may bring the donor as little as $1,000. A Filipino kidney is worth slightly more and could bring the donor $1,300; a Moldovan or Romanian kidney is worth $2,700; and an urban Peruvian or a Turkish kidney can command up to $10,000 or more. Sellers in the United States can receive up to $30,000.[93] This is just the offering price and the actual price paid to a donor can decrease dramatically depending upon supply of the organ. Alberty da Silva, an over-30 semiliterate Brazilian laborer and slum dweller in Recife, Brazil, was approached by an organ broker. He was initially offered $10,000 for a kidney—$200 upfront and the remainder payable after the surgery. Alberty was told he would be flown to South Africa, given a good hotel, and receive the best medical care at a private luxury hospital. A little sightseeing tour would round out his trip. This unsuspecting victim was told that only one kidney works, while the other one sleeps, and that the doctor would remove his "sleepy" kidney and leave him with the good one. By the time the preoperative medical testing had been completed and a passport and visa had been obtained for Alberty, the offer to purchase his kidney had dropped to $6,000. So many people had signed up to donate a kidney that, within a six-month period, the price being offered for a kidney had dropped to $1,000 and the list of those waiting to sell a kidney was still long.[94]

It is not clear how much money is being earned by the illegal organ brokers. In one case, an American was told that the operation would cost her $65,000, which would include her and her donor's travel to Durban, South Africa. The operation would be carried out in a "private transplant clinic in a five star hospital" and a $6,000 payment would be made to her donor, Alberty da Silva. In the world of transplant tourism, this is considered a bargain.[95]

Case 7.2. A Kidney Ring in Israel

John Allan (formerly Mohammad Gheit), 59, and Hassan Zakhalka, 32, persuaded developmentally challenged or mentally ill Arabs from the Galilee and central Israel to sell a kidney. By placing ads in the newspaper offering money for organ donation, the pair was able to identify potential donors. They gave false information and pressured and threatened the donors to give up their kidney. Following the surgery, the organ brokers refused to pay the donors as promised.

A 32-year-old single mother from an Arab village in Israel initially agreed to undergo the operation that, she was told, was a simple procedure allowing her to be fully functional after two days. When the woman changed her mind, the brokers threatened to report her to the police for her agreement to participate in the illegal activity of organ selling. As was the case with the other victims, the woman was flown to Ukraine where the surgery was performed. Upon her return to Israel, the brokers refused to pay the promised $7,000.

The two brokers were part of a criminal ring that included an Israeli surgeon. The surgeon sold the illegally obtained kidneys for between $125,000 and $135,000, paying the brokers $10,000 dollars.

The two brokers were convicted in a Haifa court of organ trafficking. The surgeon is awaiting extradition from Ukraine.[96]

Exploitation extends beyond the mere fact that donors are not adequately advised of the risks or compensated for the loss of a kidney. Victims of organ trafficking may be promised complete postoperative medical care, but this rarely happens. Organs Watch,[97] which carried out research on organ trafficking in countries around the world, found that none of the donors interviewed in Brazil, Manila, Moldova, and Turkey had been treated by a doctor a year after the operation, despite frequent complaints of weakness and pain. Some had even been turned away from the same hospitals that had performed the surgery. In one case, a kidney seller was given a prescription medicine for the pain, but was unable to pay for the prescription of painkillers and antibiotics. Others interviewed also reported being fearful of not being able to pay for medication if they needed it.[98]

Economic, Physical, and Psychological Consequences to Organ Donors

Studies on those who have been trafficked for their organs, including those who willingly sold their organs, show that the quality of the life of these patients is not better off than before the operation. The consequences can be dire and individuals suffer economically, physically, and psychologically.

In a study of 305 Indians who sold a kidney in Chennai, India, an average of six years before the survey, doctors found that 96 percent of the sellers sold their kidney to escape debt. The sellers received, on average, $1,070, which was spent repaying debts, on food, and on clothing. The average family income declined after the operation, families were still in debt, and the number who now lived below the poverty line had increased.[99] Further studies on kidney sellers in Iran, India, Moldova, and the Philippines indicate that donors experience unemployment, reduced income, and economic hardship. Due to the fact that they are unable to sustain the heavy demands placed on them after the operation, those previously involved in agriculture or construction work find themselves unemployed. In Moldova, kidney sellers reported having to spend their earnings to hire laborers to compensate for the heavy agricultural work they could not do.[100]

Victims are exposed to serious consequences to their health either during or after the operation. One criminal gang in the Philippines was dismantled when the police raided apartments where, under poor hygienic conditions, surgical operations were being carried out to remove kidneys. The local media reported that persons have died under such circumstances.[101] If patients survive the operation, they often face dire health problems. The physical health of kidney sellers often deteriorates after the operation, with patients complaining of chronic pain, weakness, and ill health. This was reported in 86 percent of the patients interviewed in India.[102] Health problems plagued patients in the Philippines and Eastern Europe, where donors suffered from hypertension and kidney insufficiency. In many of the cases investigated, few of the donors in Brazil, Manila, Moldova, or Turkey had seen a doctor or received

Case 7.3. A Kidney Donor Falls Ill

Seeing how another villager bought a car with the money he had been paid for selling his kidney, Niculae Bardan agreed to the same. He was trafficked from Mingir, Moldova, to Instanbul in 2000 at the age of 22. Niculae was paid $3,000 for his kidney from which he had to pay $100 in travel expenses and a $100 to each of the female brokers—one on Mingir and the other in Istanbul, leaving him with $2,700. Four years later, Niculae was suffering from high blood pressure and was in constant pain and unable to work. His doctor diagnosed him with the early stages of kidney failure stating, "If he does not get immediate treatment, he will lose his only kidney and he won't live to see his children leave primary school."[103]

postoperative health care—a year after the operation. Patients were either refused medical care or were unable to pay for the services.[104] Police in Pujab, India, reported that donors were not provided proper postoperative care, were thrown out of the hospital one week after the surgery, and were threatened with imprisonment for participating in illegal organ transplants. Six persons died as a result of the transplants.[105] Health authorities in the Philippines report that because of the lack of postoperative treatment for poor patients, many donors develop health problems such as high blood pressure and urinary tract infections.[106]

Donors also suffer psychologically as a consequence of the transplant. Reports of a sense of worthlessness, serious depression, social isolation, and family problems are not uncommon. In Moldova, sellers are excommunicated from the local Orthodox church, their chances of marriage are nonexistent, and many are alienated from their families. There are reports of kidney sellers disappearing from their families and one committed suicide. Fear of being labeled disabled or weak results in male kidney donors from seeking follow-up medical care.[107]

Finding Solutions

The problem is a complex one that needs to address medical, ethical, and legal issues. A number of governments have experimented with legislation prohibiting the sale of organs. In Great Britain, for instance, the Human Organ Transplants Act 1989 prohibits commercial transactions in human organs and establishes general guidelines, such as placing restriction on the transplantation of organs between persons who are not genetically related.[108] India, too, has legislation. The 1994 Transplantation of Human Organs Act prohibits commercial dealings in human organs and restricts live donations to relatives. A loophole in the law, however, allows for live donors to provide organs to unrelated persons on the basis of "affection or attachment toward the recipient" when approved by an authorization committee.[109] In the Philippines, the government has introduced a permanent ban on organ transplants for foreigners in the country (unless the donor is a blood relative) and restricts the number of transplants to be carried out on foreigners to 10 percent.[110] Iran is the only country that regulates the sale of organs from live donors, but due to its lack of transparency and regulation ("no medical registry of paid donors and no medical accountability, mandatory reporting of mishaps, or seller follow up"), it has been argued that illegal trafficking of organs in the country has not been eradicated but simply become official policy.[111]

While these laws may prohibit their citizens from purchasing or selling an organ on the black market, it does nothing to address the displacement effect that occurs or the problems of organ shortages. When India's Transplantation of Human Organs Act went into effect in 1994, Malaysian transplant patients immediately found a new destination in China.[112] According to the Council of Europe, there are 120,000 patients on chronic dialysis treatment and nearly 40,000 patients waiting for kidney transplants. Fifteen to 30 percent of these people will die due to a shortage of organs.[113] In the Netherlands in 2007, 152 patients died while waiting for a suitable organ for transplant.[114]

Two approaches to meet the demand can be taken. One would be to increase the number of cadaver donors. This could be done by implementing a "presumed consent" or "opt-in" system (the Dutch refer to it as donor-unless-you-say-no approach) meaning that a person is automatically presumed to be an organ donor upon death unless the person specifies that he or she refuses to be a donor (this or similar systems are in place in Belgium, Spain, South Africa, and Singapore). The presumed consent system in Spain has resulted in 31.5 donors per million population compared with 21.2 in the United States, 16.9 in France, and 16.7 in Portugal.[115] Organizations (such as the Multi Organ Harvesting Aid Network Foundation [MOHAN]) can provide predeath counseling to family members that could increase the donation of cadaver organs.[116] The second approach involves transparency and regulating the system using live donors so that impoverished donors can provide their organs in exchange for money, but at the same time be aware of their rights and receive excellent postoperative care.[117] It is essential, in addition to punishing those criminals that ply the trade, to protect the vulnerable victims.

FORCED MARRIAGE AND MAIL-ORDER BRIDES

A number of factors combine to result in the selling of women as brides. Demographic inequality in certain parts of the world creates a gender imbalance with men seeking wives outside of their community. This situation can be found in China where the situation may have been caused or exacerbated by the one-child-per-family policy. Chinese families, preferring a male child to carry on the family name and inheritance, may abandon or abort female fetuses or put the child up for adoption to foreigners.[118] By 2020, predictions are that there will be a surplus of 40 million men in China looking for wives. With lower social and economic status males unable to compete for suitable mates, they must find alternative means of finding a bride.[119] They may resort to purchasing their partner, which fuels the bride-selling market.

Other men in destination countries may seek something "new and different." They may be looking to meet a bride who is exotic, traditional, or submissive. Research on men in the United States who use mail-order companies to meet their brides indicates that they want women who are traditional. Others report that they want women who they can mold or control.[120]

At the same time, women often see foreign marriage as a way out of poverty. In Vietnam, overseas marriage is seen by some women as a way to end poverty and in some rural areas the practice is widespread.[121] According to the U.N. Special Rapporteur on Violence against Women, trafficking accounts for 30 to 90 percent of marriages in some Chinese villages.[122]

From the slums of South American cities to rural villages in Asia, traffickers have used offers of marriage to recruit women for forced labor and the sex trade. Vulnerable and impoverished women have been recruited through direct offers of marriage and, after having married, have been delivered to a sweatshop or brothel by the trafficker "husband." He is then rewarded for having delivered the victim.

The mail-order bride industry is a business and, as a business, the central concern is the customer's (male client) satisfaction. The bride represents nothing more than a commodity. While protective mechanisms are in place in many businesses to safeguard the potential husband, the potential bride is at risk and is often in a vulnerable condition before and after the marriage takes place. These vulnerabilities are in the economic, informational, cultural, and legal spheres. Women are often not provided with as much information about their future husbands as the husbands are able to obtain about their future wives. Not all organizations provide background checks on potential husbands. Women often come from economically deprived areas and may be willing to take more risks for the promise of a more secure future. Once the wife immigrates, she is often isolated socially and may not speak the language of her new husband and host country. Lastly, the new wife is subject to the immigration laws of the new country.[123]

The Source and Destination Country of Brides and Their "Husbands"

The pattern may differ per country. In the United States, the international mail-order bride trade follows traditional trafficking patterns. Brides traditionally come from Asia (specifically China, the Philippines, Thailand, and Vietnam), Latin America (in particular Brazil, Colombia, and Costa Rica), Eastern Europe, and the former Commonwealth of Independent States (CIS) (Russia and Ukraine); the clients generally come from the Western Hemisphere (including Europe and North America). Male clients are generally from Canada, Europe (often Germany, Norway, and Sweden), Japan, and the United States. In 2002, 18,621 fiancées were given permanent residence status in the United States. The majority (9,358) came from Asia (2,418 from Vietnam, 2,392 from the Philippines, and 1,361 from China) followed by 4,739 from Europe (1,476 from Russia and 861 from Ukraine); 966 came from South America (346 from Brazil, 301 from Colombia).[124]

The practice of selling women from Mongolia, Vietnam, and other poor countries in Southeast Asia as commodities to single men in Japan, Malaysia, the Republic of Korea, and Taiwan, China, is not uncommon. International marriage specialists advertise on billboards in the Republic of Korea: "Vietnamese—They Don't Run Away!"[125] Tours are organized for men to visit source countries, or in some cases, prospective brides are exhibited like goods at trade shows. The U.S. Department of State reports that NGOs and governments in the region are reporting an increased number of brokered international marriages. International marriages rose threefold to 43,121 between 2002 and 2007, 72 percent of which involved men from the Republic of Korean marrying women from Mongolia, Vietnam, and other Southeast Asian countries. More than 20,000 women between 2004 and 2007 married men in Taiwan, many of whom were introduced through marriage brokers based in Taiwan and who worked together with recruiters in southern Vietnam.[126]

Forced Marriage as a Form of Trafficking

Not all women willingly enter into brokered marriages. In Afghanistan, it has been reported that men whose opium crops have failed or been destroyed, and who are unable to repay loans to drug warlords, give their young daughters away in marriage as payment for debt. Research carried out by an Afghani schoolteacher and local television reporter found that "opium weddings" are not uncommon in parts of Afghanistan. In two of Nangarhar's districts, she interviewed more than 100 families and found approximately half the

---

Case 7.4. A Daughter Is Used to Pay Off a Debt

Sayed Shah borrowed $2,000 from a local drug trafficker, promising to repay him with 24 kilos of opium after the harvest. The government of Afghanistan eradicated the opium crops in Laghman destroying Shah's entire two and a half acres of poppies. Unable to repay the loan, Sayed Shah fled with his wife and 10 children to Jalalabad, in the neighboring Nangarhar province. The drug trafficker found Shah and demanded payment. Shah took his case before the tribal council begging for leniency. Instead, the elders informed him he would have to give his 9- or 10-year-old daughter, Khalida, in marriage, as payment for the debt to the 45-year-old trafficker.[127]

weddings were arranged as repayment for opium debt. Girls tend to be young teenagers, often promised to older men. Among the new brides were children as young as five who are used as domestic servants in their in-laws' home until they are old enough to consummate the marriage. The researcher documented cases of suicide.[128]

The mail-order bride or "bride for purchase" industry spans the globe. While not new, its growth can be attributed, in part, to the use of the Internet, a topic covered in more depth in the following chapter.

Exploitation of Purchased Wives

The woman is not necessarily and, in most cases, probably not a trafficked victim in an arranged marriage. Women may be marrying for love or money or a spouse visa, which in many countries is easier to obtain than other types of visas. In a study carried out for the United Nations on the trafficking of Filipinos, 5 of 20 trafficked women who went to Japan did so on a spouse visa. These visas provide more long-term protection to women seeking to enter a country and work. Four of the five women knew their marriage was a sham.[129]

Brokered marriages are not per se trafficking in human beings. Even if the wife is abused by a husband who has purchased her, this does not necessarily constitute human trafficking. If, however, the husband marries a partner *for the purpose of exploiting her*, this is human trafficking.

Exploitation of trafficked women takes on many forms. Traffickers pretend to be husbands, and then import and marry their wives only to force them into commercial prostitution. Others force their wives into exploitative domestic or farm work. "Husbands" can work as members of trafficking rings or as individuals who feel that they are entitled to exploit their wife. In the United States, a man pled guilty to having forced his Ukrainian mail-order wife to hold several jobs and to having sexually abused her young daughter.[130] Police in Taiwan, China, broke up a trafficking ring that had brought Indonesian women into the country with legal but fraudulent marriages arranged through brokers, only to exploit them in factory work.[131]

Case 7.5. Women Promised Husbands are Sold to Brokers

Between April 2005 and June 2006, a gang of six people trafficked 126 women from Vietnam to Malaysia. The women were promised husbands, but instead, they were sold to a broker in Malaysia for between US$1,500 and $2,000. The price varied depending upon their looks and age. Once in Malaysia, the women were sold in bars to mostly disabled or elderly men for as much as $6,300. The judge handed down a 12-year sentence to the female ringleader for human trafficking. Her Taiwanese husband and the other four suspects were sentenced to up to 10 years.[132]

Addressing the Problem

A number of countries, including the United States, have passed legislation in an attempt to protect women and regulate the international dating-service/mail-order bride market. In 2006, the highly controversial International Marriage Broker Regulation Act (IMBRA), attached to the Violence Against Women Act, was passed into law and upheld by a federal judge in 2007. IMBRA requires men using international marriage agencies to submit to a background check by the U.S. Citizenship and Immigration Services, which ensures that there is no history of (family) violence and that applicants have not submitted multiple applications.[133] Information on the applicant's background must be submitted to the woman in her local language. Larger, well-established legitimate Internet dating sites in the United States must comply. Others may operate illicitly.

In 2004, the government of Taiwan enhanced interview requirements. This and other eligibility restrictions resulted in a sharp decline of the total number of visas issued to potential spouses from Vietnam. The country began to more closely monitor existing international marriage broker companies and barred the registration of new ones.[134] Republic Act No. 6955 (Mail Order Brides) came into law in 1990 in the Philippines to prohibit "the practice of matching Filipino women for marriage to foreign nationals on a mail order basis and other similar practices including the advertisement, publication, printing or distribution of brochures, fliers and other propaganda materials."[135] Personally introducing Filipino women for a fee is also outlawed. The U.S. government reports that the Republic of Korea has established a program of action to assist foreign brides in the country, but little has thus far been done to regulate the activities of marriage brokers.[136]

It is impossible to diminish the demand for such broker services, but safeguards can be put into place to ensure that international marriages are legitimate and that vulnerable women are protected.

TRAFFICKING FOR ILLEGAL ADOPTIONS

International adoptions, like international marriages, do not necessarily involve human trafficking practices. Unless the child is adopted for the purpose of exploitation, the practice is not a form of human trafficking. What is disconcerting, however, is that organized criminal groups and corruption are often involved in the process of providing babies from developing countries for international adoption to Western couples. Furthermore, there are indications that not all of these children were voluntarily put up for adoption by their biological parent(s).[137]

According to Europol, there are "indicators of a global child trafficking market which agencies estimate involved more than 1 million children and is worth 1 billion Euro a year."[138] Bulgarian gangs were involved in the illegal adoption market; investigations into illegal adoptions were carried out in France, Italy, and Portugal. In 2005, Europol reported that Russian officials had also begun looking into combating the illegal adoption of Russian children.

The U.N. Inter-Agency Project on Human Trafficking in the Mekong subregion reports that Cambodian babies are abducted and sold to unsuspecting couples in the United States who pay a $20,000 adoption fee. This fee has in part fueled the demand for nonorphaned babies and is used to pay bribes in the country.[139]

Dutch journalists traveled to the Chinese province of Hunan in 2008 to investigate allegations that children had been forcibly removed from their families and illegally adopted out to Chinese and foreign couples, among them, Dutch. In Hunan, one of the poorest provinces in China, journalists uncovered a number of unethical and illegal practices. In two families, the child was removed because the parents were not married and were too poor to pay the fine. In another case, one twin was taken from the family because the twins violated the strictly enforced "one child per family" policy. The parents were told that the children were placed in the Shaoyang orphanage and that the children had been put up for adoption—without the parents' knowledge or permission. Government officials offered illegally seized children to the orphanage that made the highest bid. Children generally "sold" for between $400 and $600. A number of directors of orphanages were convicted in 2005, and the government acknowledged the illicit practice of seizing and selling babies, but it still denies the extent of the practice.[140]

Guatemala, too, has been touched by allegations of illegal adoptions. In May 2008, police raided a home searching for a kidnapped child, but instead found nine other children ranging in age from 7 to 12 months. The suspect, who was unable to identify the childrens' biological mothers, is the sister of a congressman who also serves as president of a congressional committee on minors and family affairs. The attorney general pledged a full review of all of the country's 2,286 international adoptions while the country's adoption system, plagued by corruption and fraud, will be overhauled.[141]

Allegations of baby-selling, fraud, and corruption have surfaced in Vietnam. With 42 U.S. adoption agencies working in Vietnam, competition is intense and parents pay up to $25,000 for a child. According to a report released by the U.S. Embassy in Hanoi, illicit practices involved a mother who was pressured to give up her baby when she could not pay the inflated hospital bills and other mothers who were pressured by orphanages to sell their children for about $450 (a year's salary). At the same time, agencies were paying orphanage directors $10,000 per referral or taking them to the United States on shopping sprees or junkets to guarantee "a steady flow of babies."[142]

In 2007, U.S. adoption visas were issued for 5,453 Chinese, 4,728 Guatemalan, and 2,310 Russian children.[143] In the case of illegal adoptions, the demand creates the supply. The danger of a market demanding more and more children for international adoption creates the possibility of illicit practices, corruption, and the involvement of organized criminal groups in providing these babies. In areas of countries in which births are not registered, parents are poor and unaware of their rights, and government officials are corrupt, the practice of putting children up for adoption is particularly susceptible to abuse.

CONCLUDING REMARKS

This chapter has examined a number of different practices, which may or may not qualify as human trafficking. If we return to the definition put forth in the U.N. Trafficking Protocol, only the recruitment and use of child soldiers—under any and all conditions—would qualify as human trafficking.

In the case of organ trafficking, when the organ is obtained through fraud, deceit, threat, or use of force, the practice constitutes human trafficking. This is not always a straightforward situation, when, in poverty stricken areas, persons agree to voluntarily sell a kidney for a mere $2,000. The deception is related to a lack of information concerning the consequences of kidney donation, but not the sale itself. The situation becomes even more complex when the kidney broker and doctor argue that the kidney was purchased "not for the exploitation of the donor" but for improvement in the health of the recipient. After all, the donation of an organ is per se not illegal. The donation of an organ to a stranger for money is a crime in many countries, however, and obtaining a donation through deceit, coercion, or violence is at best unethical and immoral, and at worst illegal. This chapter has clearly identified cases and countries in which this practice has been documented and in some areas the practice is widespread.

More likely than not, international marriages and adoptions arranged through brokers and agencies are for legitimate purposes. The argument that Chinese officials gave one family in Hunan—that their child had been put up for international adoption and was much better off with the new, wealthy family—may be true for the child, but not for the biological parents who wanted to raise that child. As such, this is not human trafficking, but qualifies as perhaps one of the most egregious human rights violations imaginable. The inclusion of illegal adoptions in this chapter highlighted the involvement of international markets dealing in the buying and selling of human beings facilitated by organized criminals and government corruption.

With respect to mail-order brides, adult women should have the right to seek a better future in another country and adult men wishing to acquire such a spouse should have the right to meet one through whatever means available. With an industry wide open to abuse, some regulation is necessary; at a minimum, those spouses who find themselves trafficked and exploited by their husband must be aware of their rights and must be offered legal protection in the destination country.

The next chapter looks at new opportunities for trafficking in human beings. In particular, the use of the Internet is closely related to the practice of mail-order brides. Other opportunities arise out of natural disasters, war, and sporting events.

New Opportunities for Trafficking

THIS CHAPTER EXAMINES situations or developments that provide new opportunities for human trafficking. The information provided in this chapter is topically related to some of the themes addressed in the previous chapter. The rise of Internet accessibility has resulted in the rapid growth of the mail-order bride market and the spread of child pornography. Natural disasters and wars can facilitate the illegal trade in or adoption of children, or their abduction or recruitment into armed militias. Globalization and increased travel have given rise to child sex tourism. We begin with a discussion of the Internet's role in trafficking, followed by an examination of child sex tourism and the link between trafficking and peacekeeping forces, natural disasters, and international sporting events. The discussion will focus on concrete cases in which either trafficking has been suspected or discovered.

USE OF THE INTERNET

Online advertising for dating, escort services, and mail-order brides provides access to an audience larger than most newspapers reach. In Israel, a 2004 court ruling convicted the publishing corporations and directors of three major newspapers for "publishing advertisements in their newspapers relating to the provision of prostitution services." From that point on, Israeli newspapers refused to print advertisements offering sexual services,[1] pushing the entire market onto the Internet. Internet advertising is not only cheap, but it reaches a broader audience, making sex for hire more "accessible and discrete."[2]

As of March 2008, there were more than 1.4 billion (1,407,724,920) Internet users worldwide. The majority are in Asia (37.6 percent), followed by Europe (27.1 percent), North America (17.5 percent), Latin/America and the Caribbean (9.8 percent), Africa (3.6 percent), the Middle East (3.0 percent), and Oceania and Australia (1.4 percent).[3] New technologies have expanded opportunities for traditional crime to evolve. The Internet offers both sellers and consumers of sex and pornography new opportunities to find customers and market and deliver women and children into situations of trafficking.

Because of its anonymity and the huge number of persons that can be reached through the Internet, it has become a perfect tool to acquire girlfriends and wives, to establish contact with children for the purpose of sex, and to buy, sell, or trade child pornography.

Recruitment and Advertising Sexual Services via the Internet

The recruitment of trafficked victims via the Internet has created a new means to obtain victims. Rather than using dating, marriage, or employment agencies, traffickers can now post free advertisements on the Internet. The two most common means of Internet recruitment for trafficking are through advertisements for dating, escort, marriage, or employment agencies, and in chatrooms.[4]

In a report on Internet recruitment carried out for the Council of Europe in 2007, a simple Google search turned up 128,000 "suspect" Internet sites advertising modeling, dating, escort, and marriage services. What made the sites suspect is the fact that women came from poor and often rural areas in countries known as sources for human trafficking, or marriage sites used "subtle, but often blatant sexualized photographs of the women … to appeal to men."[5] This is not clear proof of trafficking, but trafficked victims may be hidden among the more legitimate offers on such sites. In 2006 in Greece, police officers from the Computer Crime Unit found a Web site offering the sexual services of "famous models." The officers ordered the services of a "model" for €450 and encountered a woman from an Eastern European country who claimed to have been trafficked. She and another trafficked victim had spent three weeks traveling around European capitals for the Internet "modeling service" and had earned €60,000. Interpol was notified, the head of the network was finally caught and charged with trafficking, and the Internet site was taken offline.[6]

Case 8.1. A Finnish Prostitution Ring

In 2006, Finnish police broke up a prostitution ring running between Estonia and Finland. The two leaders of the trafficking network, already in prison in Estonia, were placing ads on Estonia's most popular Internet site and using mobile phones to recruit women. Advertising for sexual services is prohibited in Finland so the site was established in the Netherlands where such activity was not banned. Between October 2005 and March 2006, 15 Estonian women, one of them mentally handicapped, were brought into Finland and forced into prostitution. The women were forced to hand over most of their earnings—the handicapped woman was given nothing for her work—and threatened with violence.[7]

Mail-Order Brides and Dating Services

A Google search of "mail-order brides" yields 921,000 hits.[8] Among some of these sites are advertisements for combined services such as dating. The majority of women profiled on these sites are Eastern European—predominantly Russian and Ukrainian—Asian, and Latina women. Some Internet sites offer tours to meet the prospective bride. A Council of Europe report draws a distinction between mail-order bride sites, referring to them as "slaves who can be purchased online by credit card," and online marriage agencies that are offering sexual services.[9]

A Foreign Affair (at www.loveme.com) boasts on its Internet site that it is not a "Mail Order Bride" company, but the "largest and most respected International Introduction and Singles Tour Company in the industry." The company offers an 11-day tour to a single Russian city for a mere $4,100 and a three-city eight-day tour for about $7,400.[10] Trips generally include airfare and accommodation, as well as social events designed to allow the customer contact with as many women as possible. The site boasts "Meet 500 to 2,000 Beautiful Foreign Women During Our Romance Tours!" There are as many as 2,000 foreign women for 12 Western male clients. These trips may serve as an opportunity to meet a bride or as a front for a high-scale prostitution ring.[11] Internet sites specialize in everything from disabled Russian women[12] to vulnerable women and underage children.[13]

The Internet dating and mail-order bride Web sites are largely unregulated—although regulations are in place for bringing such a bride into the United States and other countries. Low overhead and startup costs combined with the increased use of the Internet and an endless source of foreign women seeking a more stable economic future has created a massive growth in Internet dating and marriage broker services. As if selling a product, many online mail-order bride Web sites have taken a Web-based merchandising approach to their matchmaking, one in which the male clients are taken through a process of "Browse, Select, Proceed to Checkout." One researcher found that "[t]oday, any man with Internet access, an electronic photo (even ten years old) and a credit card number can shop."[14]

That many of these online agencies are selling sexual contacts with the women they advertise in sexually provocative poses and scantily clad clothing is undeniable. But to what degree are these agencies linked to human trafficking? In her testimony before the U.S. Senate, one expert reported that workers in the St. Petersburg (the Russian Federation) Psychological Crisis Center for Women had heard of Russian women being recruited by marriage agencies and then trafficked into prostitution. This same pattern was confirmed by nongovernmental organizations (NGOs) operating in countries of the former Soviet Union. With agencies maintaining a database with extensive information on single women—and their families—who have expressed a desire to go abroad, it is easy to imagine how these agencies could use that information to coerce women into prostitution and thus be involved in trafficking.[15]

Case 8.2. An Israeli Escort Service

Tal Zohar, set up the "Escort Plus" Web site in Israel featuring details of women offering sex for money. Zohar earned a commission on each so-called sale. In 2001, he began traveling to European countries to hire young women to work in Israel via his Web site. He purchased two Ukrainian and two Moldavian women. In addition to purchasing women to work for his virtual brothel, Zohar did not pay the victims the wages that they should have earned. Zohar, convicted of human trafficking, pimping, and exploitation, was sentenced to five years in prison plus a suspended sentence.[16]

Escort Services

While many of the services may be legitimate, other popular websites are used to promote the sale of trafficked victims. The Polaris Project reports that a popular online marketing and sales Web site in the United States is being used to sell trafficked victims under the guise of "legal escort services." Law enforcement in Boston, Massachusetts, arrested a man and his niece and charged them with plotting to sell teenagers as young as 13 to predators from Massachusetts to New York. In Chicago, two women were charged with forcing girls as young as 14 to prostitute themselves to as many as 12 clients a day. Both of these cases involved advertising on the Web site Craigslist. Law enforcement in the United States report that "a spike in online Craigslist ads, and how sex trafficking has 'moved online' lately."[17]

Trafficking and Child Pornography

The demand for child pornography is enormous. According to the international police agency, Interpol, one company in the United States which operated for five months selling access to child pornography sites at $29.95 each, grossed $5.5 million in five months of operation.[18] Law enforcement and researchers believe the production and trade in child pornography is increasing and the increase is related to growing use of the Internet.[19] An international investigation exposed a highly sophisticated operation that was digitally trading more than 400,000 photos of children to members worldwide. Twenty-two men were arrested in Australia, Germany, the United Kingdom, and the United States and about 20 victims were identified and rescued.[20]

The Internet can be used either to recruit victims or to distribute child pornographic materials. Traffickers who recruit and use victims for pornography via Web sites may differ from traffickers who use the Internet to recruit women via escort services, dating or marriage sites, or employment sites. In these later cases, there must be a personal contact between the trafficker, and the victim and the victim is often moved within the country or to a foreign country for the purpose of sexual exploitation. In the case of trafficking for pornography via the Internet, the victim does not even have to leave his or her home, and in fact, may be unaware of the sexual exploitation.[21]

The U.S. government defines child pornography as imagery depicting a minor engaging in sexually explicit conduct, including various forms of sexual activity such as masturbation, intercourse, or lascivious exhibition of the genitals. The possession, distribution, and manufacture of these images is illegal. Pornographic pictures of children can be made easily through the Internet without the child's knowledge. "Grooming" is the term given to those who seek contact with children—usually in chatrooms—with the intent to sexually abuse them online—by having them perform sexual acts while the predator watches or records the acts via webcam—or offline—in which case the predator seeks personal contact with the child for the purpose of a sexual encounter.

The television reality show *NBC Dateline* ran a series of undercover sting operations in various cities portraying adult men who had been chatting online with an individual who they thought was a minor. These men showed up at the home of the minor—who was, in fact, an adult volunteer working for the Internet watchdog agency Perverted Justice—anticipating a sexual liaison, only to be taped by hidden cameras. Some of the men had sent suggestive or explicitly sexual material to the "child," prepping him or her for the encounter. A number of persons were arrested and prosecuted.[22]

The buying and selling of child pornography, while illegal, does not constitute human trafficking; however, the production of child pornography may constitute trafficking in situations in which a child or young person is purchased or recruited for the purpose of exploitation. Many of the children used in pornographic pictures have been subjected to rape or other forms of sexual violence. The production of child pornography has been directly linked to the sexual exploitation of children. In a study of U.S. offenders arrested for having sex or intending to have sex with minors in foreign countries, 21 of the 50 offenders were found to be in possession of child pornography. Some of the pictures were produced by the perpetrator during the molestation of the child.[23]

Child Sex Tourism

International tourism has grown sevenfold since the 1960s providing economic support to developing countries. With the growth in tourism, comes the potential for a growth in child sex tourism. The International Labour Organization (ILO) reports that 2 to 14 percent of the gross domestic product of Thailand, the Philippines, Malaysia, and India is generated from sex tourism.[24] The crime typically is fueled by the ease of travel, poverty in the destination country, the Internet, weak laws, and government corruption.[25]

Child sex tourism is tourism with the primary purpose of consummating a commercial sexual relationship with a person under the age of 18. It is an act involving mostly men from Western countries exploiting the poverty and vulnerability of children—usually in developing nations. Although the child is abused in his home country or city and thus does not fit the pattern of trafficking to which we have become so accustomed—that is, foreign women or children being imported *into* a country for the purpose of forced prostitution—child sex tourism does represent a form of sexual exploitation that falls under the U.N. definition of trafficking. It is the recruitment or purchase of a child for the purpose of exploitation. A report examining child sex tourism in the United States found that it occurs in tourist cities as well, such as Las Vegas.[26]

Patterns of Child Sex Tourism

The U.S. Department of Justice reports that Asian countries, in particular India, the Philippines, and Thailand, have long been the preferred destinations for child sex tourists. These predators, however, are spreading out to destinations in Central America and Mexico as well.[27] Tourist destinations in Africa are hotbeds for child sex tourism—for example, in Kenya, where it is reported that along the Kenyan coast, child sex tourism has become rampant with between 10,000 and 15,000 girls being prostituted.[28]

Sex tourists generally do not travel far to exploit children. U.S. and Canadian child sex tourists are traveling closer to home and countries in Central and Latin America are becoming preferred destinations. Among countries in this region, Costa Rica and Mexico are popular destinations and to a lesser extent Brazil and the Dominican Republic. Europeans prefer African countries such as Cameroon, The Gambia, Ghana, Kenya, Morocco, Nigeria, and South Africa. Child sex tourists from Asian countries tend to remain in the region, but they have been arrested in other countries as well.[29]

According to Australian National Police, Australian child sex tourists typically visit Southeast Asia, in particular Indonesia, the Philippines, and Thailand. Their victims are generally between the ages of 5 and 18 years and both boys and girls are targeted. Australian police report that the Internet is increasingly being used as a source of information to assist predators in their travel plans. The use of pedophile-friendly travel agencies also assists child sex tourists in organizing their trips.[30]

The nonprofit organization End Child Prostitution, Child Pornography, and the Trafficking of Children (ECPAT), reports that child sex tourism is particularly prevalent in Central and South America and Asia, with Costa Rica, Cambodia, and Thailand being some of the most popular sex tourist destinations for child sex tourism.[31] Table 8.1 portrays established or emerging major child sex tourist destinations identified by the organization and in research carried out by the Protection Project.[32]

ECPAT estimates that more than 1 million children worldwide are drawn annually into the sex trade.[33] In Thailand, an estimated 22,500 – 40,000 children are exploited in the commercial sex industry, between 60,000 – 75,000

Table 8.1 Major Known and Emerging Destinations of Child Sex Tourism by Region and Country

Region	Country
Africa	Cameroon, The Gambia, Kenya, Senegal, South Africa
Southeast Asia	Bali (Indonesia), Cambodia, Laos, Philippines, Thailand, Vietnam
Central and South America	Brazil, Colombia, Costa Rica, Dominican Republic, Guatemala, Honduras, Mexico
Northern Russia, Eastern and Southeastern Europe	Romania, Moldova

Source: Information from Protection Project (2007).

children are victims in the Philippines, and as many as 30,000 children are exploited in the child sex tourism industry in Mexico.[34]

Situational child sex tourists generally travel to another country for a short period of time and return home. If the opportunity arises, they will have sex with a child. Preferential child sex tourists travel to a country with the sole purpose of abusing children and may even take up residence in the country.[35] This trend was noted in Southeast Asia[36] where child sex offenders, rather than short-term visitors, tend to be more long-term residents of the region and may be working there as well. Exploiters are infiltrating more isolated communities and are taking on jobs that bring them into contact with children—as teachers, aid workers, or tutors, occupations which give them unrestricted access to children.[37] The same pattern is being reported in Central America and Africa. In Kenya, reports have surfaced of children being abused by expatriates who are setting up charitable organizations to help them.[38]

Case 8.3. A School Teacher's Young Victims

In June 2006, a U.S. citizen was arrested in Phnom Penh, Cambodia, for allegedly torturing and raping a 20-year-old woman and at least three young girls between the ages of 9 and 11. The 53-year-old offender, Michael Joseph Pepe, was a school teacher.

The offender bought one of the children from her mother for $300; the other two girls he rented from their mother for $30 a month.[39] The children were brought from the countryside to Pepe's house so he could torture them while raping them. While he did this, he filmed the acts. Police confiscated items, including the rope used to bind the victims, and hundreds of pornographic pictures of young girls. They suspect that there were other victims of Pepe.[40]

The Perpetrators and Victims

"On this trip, I've had sex with a 14 year-old girl in Mexico and a 15 year-old in Colombia. I'm helping them financially. If they don't have sex with me, they may not have enough food. If someone has a problem with me doing this, let UNICEF feed them." These are the words of a retired U.S. school teacher.[41]

Although most perpetrators of this crime are males, the U.S. Department of State reports that wealthier women are also becoming perpetrators by traveling to countries in Africa such as The Gambia and Kenya and paying for sex with young males.[42] The difference, however, is that while women may be feeding prostitution by purchasing the sexual services and companionship of young males, and while these boys may be under the age of 18, they are not extremely young children.

Because of the clandestine nature of child sex tourism and the fact that most perpetrators escape criminal liability in the countries in which they perpetrate their crimes,[43] limited data are available on the offenders and victims. Data provided by arresting agencies on 50 U.S. child sex tourists shows that 49 of the 50 perpetrators were male, and two-thirds of the offenders were between the ages of 40 and 59. Where data were available regarding the gender of the victims, 61 percent of the offenders intended to or actually engaged in sex with young boys. The researchers argue that men seeking sexual contact with boys may be easier to detect and therefore more likely to be arrested. Whereas sexual contact with girls can be arranged through prostitution channels, men seeking contact with boys must approach them directly, and often in public places.[44]

Data provided on child sex tourism in a limited number of countries in the Association of Southeast Asian Nations (ASEAN) region on the nationality of offenders and the age and gender of victims paint the following picture: Of the 30 offenders arrested in Cambodia, the Philippines, Thailand, and Vietnam, all were male and eight offenders were from the United States, seven from Germany, four from Australia and England, three from Italy, two from China, and one each from Austria, Belgium, Switzerland, Korea, and India. Where age of the offender was available, the majority of offenders were between the ages of 40 and 49 years.[45]

With respect to the age and gender of the child victims, table 8.2 provides a distribution, based on information provided by Cambodia, Myanmar, the Philippines, and Thailand. Female children were the victims more often than male children, and very young children, between the ages of 6 and 11, are the largest single group of those exploited.

What's Being Done about Child Sex Tourism?

In addition to such international instruments as the U.N. Convention on the Rights of the Child and its optional protocols, which specifically require member states to combat child sex tourism, a number of countries have passed

Table 8.2 Age and Gender of Victims of Alleged Traveling Child Sex Offenders Arrested in 2006

Age-Group	Number of Males	Number of Females	Total	Percentage
6–11 years	17	15	32	39%
12–15 years	8	17	25	30.5%
16–17 years	11	14	25	30.5%
Total	36	46	82	100%
Percentage	44%	56%	100%	

Source: The table is a composite of information gleaned from the tables in Child Wise (2007) in the sections on Cambodia, Myanmar, the Philippines, and Thailand.

legislation allowing for the prosecution of their citizens who travel abroad and engage in illicit sexual relations with children. The U.S. PROTECT (Prosecutorial Remedies and Other Tools to End the Exploitation of Children Today) Act of 2003, punishes anyone who "travels with intent to engage in illicit sexual conduct" or those who "engage in illicit sexual conduct in foreign places." This covers interstate travel within the United States.[46] Similarly, Australia has passed the Crimes (Child Sex Tourism) Amendment Act 1994 No. 105, punishing its citizens for having sexual relations with a child under the age of 16 outside of the territory[47] and under the U.K. Sexual Offences Act, 2003, Article 72, persons can be prosecuted for a crime that is viewed as a criminal offence in both countries.[48] More than 30 countries have passed some type of extraterritorial legislation allowing the country to prosecute its own nationals for sexual offenses that have been committed against children in another country.[49]

On April 21, 2004, a campaign called the Code of Conduct for the Protection of Children from Sexual Commercial Exploitation in Travel and Tourism was launched. The Code is a joint effort by international organizations, NGOs, and the travel industry to create more awareness and to identify and report suspected abusers.[50] Other international initiatives to end child sex tourism include national awareness campaigns (Brazil); a film on the dangers of child sex tourism, which is shown to children in schools (Madagascar); and the in-flight videos highlighting the crime and penalties for child prostitution, shown on Air France flights.[51]

TRAFFICKING, THE MILITARY, AND PEACE SUPPORT OPERATIONS

Trafficking During Times of War and Civil Unrest

It is impossible to document the degree to which trafficking increases during times of war or armed conflict, but anecdotal evidence supports the allegation.

This is due, in part, to the collapse of state institutions and border controls, and an increase in lawlessness—all factors that increase the risk of trafficking in persons, in particular, women and children.

According to the United Nations, the breakdown of law and order combined with the increased demand for sexual services by members of the military or fighting factions can lead to a situation in which a conflict area becomes a destination for human trafficking. Organized criminal groups take advantage of the chaotic conditions to run trafficking operations knowing that the chances of detection are minimized.[52] Forms of trafficking vary according to the nature of the armed conflict and "the specific political and economic factors on the ground." A common thread, however, is that women and children, who constitute the majority of internally displaced persons, are the most vulnerable to traffickers.[53]

The link between prostitution and the military is well documented. Military servicemen deployed far from home have been a "long-standing source of demand for sexual services from local populations." American soldiers, during the Vietnam War, used military-inspected and certified prostitutes during "rest and recreation" breaks in Thailand, Vietnam, and the Philippines.[54] U.S. military stationed in South Korea drew "entertainers" from Southeast Asia.[55] According to one expert, the U.S. military deployed abroad in combat and peacekeeping operations may be "one of the largest sources of demand for sexual services around the world, some of which would likely be provided by trafficked women."[56]

Postwar Trafficking

To support countries trying to stabilize and rebuild after war, international assistance initiatives provide monitoring, maintenance, establishment of peace, and prevention of resurgent violent conflict. Peacekeeping operations support and monitor the building of peace, whereas peace enforcement operations create conditions of peace but are allowed to use force. Both of these are forms of Peace Support Operations (PSOs).[57] United Nations staff make up a small minority of peacekeeping missions. The majority of soldiers serving in these missions are "on loan" from troop-contributing countries. These troops are members of their own military and the United Nations has no disciplinary authority over them.[58]

According to the United Nations Interregional Crime and Justice Research Institute (UNICRI), the links between human trafficking and peace support operations are threefold. First, the international community is the only or primary source of law enforcement, therefore the primary authority for combating human trafficking. Second, in most PSO situations, staff are paid a wage much higher than that earned by the communities they serve. This advantage may make them the primary source of demand for domestic labor and trafficked persons in brothels. Last, members of PSOs have been directly implicated in human trafficking.[59]

The United Nations Department of Peacekeeping Operations (DPKO) has recognized that these operations "trigger human trafficking rings in the regions in which they operate because of the mass influx of a relatively wealthy, predominantly male peacekeeper population potentially interested in purchasing sexual and other services from trafficked women and girls."[60]

U.N. observer, peacekeeping, stabilization, or disengagement forces are currently serving in the following countries:

- *Africa*: Chad and the Central African Republic, Côte d'Ivoire, Darfur, the Democratic Republic of Congo, Ethiopia and Eritrea, Liberia, Sudan, and Western Sahara
- *Europe*: Cyprus, Georgia, and Kosovo
- *Americas*: Haiti
- *Asia-Pacific*: East Timor, India, and Pakistan
- *Middle East*: Lebanon, the Golan Heights, and the "Middle East"[61]

Although most of the deployed soldiers serve without incident, there have been documented cases or allegations of peacekeeping troops from Cambodia, East Timor, Morocco, Nepal, Pakistan, South Africa, Tunisia, Uruguay, and countries in West Africa involved in allegations of pedophilia, prostitution, and rape, while commanders failed to investigate or protect whistleblowers.[62] The arrival of peacekeepers in postconflict countries was found to be responsible for the rise in child prostitution,[63] and the reestablishment of international peacekeeping operations in East Timor in 2006 is thought to be the impetus for the reopening of businesses suspected of involvement in sex trafficking.[64]

The 50,000 peacekeepers that were deployed to Bosnia and Herzegovina in the early 1990s were directly responsible for the trafficking in women for prostitution, which "sprang up overnight outside the gates of the U.N. compounds." According to a regional human rights officer in Bosnia after the war, "[t]he sex slave trade in Bosnia largely exists because of the U.N. peacekeeping operation. Without the peacekeeping presence, there would have been little or no forced prostitution in Bosnia."[65] Investigations were carried out to determine the involvement of U.N. policing officials' involvement in the sex slave trade in Bosnia and enough evidence was found to justify a full-scale criminal investigation into the matter. In addition to visiting brothels where trafficked women were kept, cases were reported of members of the Stabilization Force (SFOR) and International Police Task Force members involved in the actual trafficking of women. In three cases, International Police Task Force monitors purchased women and their passports from traffickers and brothel owners.[66]

By patronizing brothels in which trafficked victims were held or purchasing them directly from brothel owners, military and civilian contractors operating under U.N. impunity abused the human rights of their trafficked victims and further supported organized crime, which ran the brothels and trafficked the women. Revenues generated through trafficking are used to corrupt law enforcement and to invest in the further growth of the trade.[67]

The Washington-based Center for Strategic and International Studies, in its report "Barracks and Brothels," wrote,

> The United Nations has an especially troubling track record of peacekeeper involvement in trafficking as well as in other forms of sexual exploitation in conflict and post-conflict regions. Yet decision makers at the UN seem to fear that creating a taboo against trafficking for peacekeepers will negatively affect the UN's ability to attract peacekeepers.[68]

Finding Solutions

After a 2004 U.N. Department of Peacekeeping Operations (DPKO) investigation into the misconduct of U.N. peacekeepers in the Congo, the seriousness of the situation was finally recognized. Since mid-2005, the United Nations has provided training on prevention of sexual abuse for all peacekeeping personnel on arrival in a mission. The DPKO has developed a wide range of training materials. Strategies have been developed and expanded to prevent trafficking and provide protection to victims of sexual abuse by U.N. peacekeeping personnel.[69] An Anti-Trafficking Focal Point or special investigative unit has been established in some missions. In Kosovo in 2000, a Trafficking and Prostitution Investigation Unit was established with UNMIK (United Nations Mission in Kosovo) police, and a female trafficking officer was appointed to the U.N. Civilian Police in the Liberian PSO. This trafficking officer, along with her team, raided nightclubs in the area and rescued girls and women who had been trafficked.[70] The DPKO has encouraged personnel to report violations and now systematically monitors and records complaints.[71]

In 2007, additional measures were adopted by the United Nations to prevent military and civilian personnel in peacekeeping and humanitarian missions from engaging in abuse and sexual exploitation. Measures are aimed at prevention, victim assistance, and investigation. In 2007, allegations of sexual conduct and abuse were levied against Moroccan peacekeepers at the U.N. mission in Côte d'Ivoire and against peacekeepers in missions in Haiti and the Democratic Republic of Congo. The United Nations. registered 127 allegations of sexual misconduct, a decrease from the 357 allegations in 2006. By the end of 2007, the United Nations had investigated 123 cases and had repatriated 114 personnel.[72]

UNICRI has developed a predeployment, in-service training program for international law enforcement personnel deployed, or to be deployed, in PSOs in the Balkan area.[73] The purpose of the training is to raise awareness of all aspects of human trafficking. Participants are taught how to identify and protect trafficked victims, while learning how to counter the activities of organized criminal networks through reactive and proactive investigations and disruptive police actions.

Other international entities such as NATO (North Atlantic Treaty Organization) and the Organization for Security and Co-operation in Europe (OSCE), have adopted policies condemning trafficking and have implemented measures to ensure that members participating in missions are not involved in the abuse. NATO requires member states to take a variety of actions to reduce human trafficking, including the following: provisions that prohibit contractors from engaging or facilitating human trafficking; training of all personnel taking part in NATO-led operations; committing to evaluate implementation of their efforts; and ratification of the U.N. Trafficking Convention.[74]

In 2004, the U.S. Department of Defense implemented a zero-tolerance policy regarding sex trafficking and activities—such as prostitution—that may contribute to trafficking. Since the end of 2006, patronizing a prostitute is a criminal charge under the Uniform Code of Military Justice. An antitrafficking program was developed by U.S. Forces in Korea focusing on awareness, victim identification, demand reduction, and cooperation with local authorities. Considered a model approach, it now serves as the basis for NATO's training modules.[75] Antitrafficking training (available online[76]) is now mandatory for all U.S. service members and military police are receiving specialized training to assist them in recognizing and identifying possible trafficking situations and victims, especially overseas.[77]

Forty-five other countries provide antitrafficking, sexual exploitation, or human rights training to personnel being sent to PSOs.[78] Training is provided either by the government or in conjunction with international organizations, such as the International Organization for Migration (IOM).

OTHER OPPORTUNITIES

Sporting Events

Fears of an increase in forced prostitution during the World Soccer Cup in Germany in 2006 were raised in international media before the games. Estimates of 40,000 foreign prostitutes, among them trafficked victims being forced into prostitution directly before and during the World Cup, led the IOM to conduct research into the possible link between human trafficking and the World Cup and other major sporting events. Their results with respect to the Germany World Cup were inconclusive, but what was evident is that the figure of 40,000 prostitutes to provide sexual services to the fans of the games was "unrealistic and unfounded hype."[79] The fact that this figure of 40,000 was only hype may be attributable to a large-scale awareness-raising campaign, NGO hotlines, and extra police operations and patrols at the borders.[80]

To prevent this occurrence at the European Football Championships in June 2008, media campaigns were launched in Switzerland. The threat of trafficking at such major sporting events is being taken seriously by host countries preparing for the 2010 Olympics in Vancouver and the 2012 Olympics in London.[81]

Natural Disasters

Natural disasters, along with wars and HIV/AIDS, make orphans of children, which increases their dependency on others and the risk that they will fall prey to traffickers. Following the tsunami on December 26, 2004, that destroyed much of the coastal areas of Indonesia, Sri Lanka, Thailand, and India, the United Nations Children's Fund (UNICEF) reported cases of child trafficking out of Aceh province in Indonesia. The pattern was similar in Myanmar when cyclone Nargis hit the country on May 2, 2008, and left hundreds if not thousands of children orphans. A child protection officer from UNICEF reported evidence of child traffickers attempting to lure orphaned children from a shelter in Rangoon.[82]

Countries were quick to respond. In the case of the 2004 tsunami, fearing that the chaos and breakdown in social control would facilitate child trafficking, Indonesia (followed by Thailand) increased monitoring of children, prohibiting the removal of children from the region unless accompanied by a verifiable family member. Furthermore, countries banned the foreign adoption of such children in the immediate wake of the disaster.[83] In Myanmar, police intervened and arrested suspected child traffickers. Aid organizations are alert to the dangers and are pressing governments in such situations to respond rapidly.

Concluding Remarks

This chapter examined new opportunities for human trafficking. Unlike material addressed in previous chapters, this one examined a number of gray areas—Internet dating services, escort services, and marriage bureaus—which may be legitimate but also are areas in which trafficking can thrive. The issue of child sex tourism and the production of child pornography is more straightforward. Clearly, most countries have laws that would allow for the prosecution of offenders who sexually abuse children. By classifying such acts as trafficking, governments in the destination countries are able to prosecute the parent for selling the child, a facilitator for procuring the child, or the taxi driver for transporting the child to the abuser, if such acts were knowingly done to exploit the child.

Peace support operations have, in the past, supported the local prostitution market, and in the case of the war in Bosnia and Herzegovina, PSOs were believed to be directly responsible for women being trafficked into prostitution. The military and international organizations are sensitized to the issue and have taken measures to ensure that human trafficking is no longer tied to military and peacekeeping deployments. The predicted increase in trafficked victims and prostitution during the 2006 World Soccer Cup never materialized. Whether the international media acted irresponsibly or whether measures taken by the German government, law enforcement agencies, and NGOs accounted for the absence of trafficking during this major sporting event is difficult to determine. It appears that preparatory actions both before and during this sporting event, as well as immediately after the natural disasters in the Indonesia, Thailand, and Burma, may have prevented the trafficking of victims.

The following chapter will explore measures that have been taken by various actors in the field to win the battle against this modern-day form of slavery.

Ending Human Trafficking

Every man is guilty of the good he did not do.
—Voltaire (November 21, 1694—May 30, 1778)

ENDING HUMAN TRAFFICKING, forced labor, and slavery are high on the agendas of many governments and their enforcement branches as well as local and international human rights organizations. The battle is a long, difficult one, in part, because the success stories in terms of the number of victims rescued and the number of offenders prosecuted remains small, compared with the estimates of the number of people trafficked.

A $15 million dollar grant on behalf of the United Arab Emirates' General Shaikh Mohammed bin Zaycd Al Nahyan, Crown Prince of Abu Dhabi, helped launch a united global initiative against human trafficking in March 2007. Launched as UN.GIFT (United Nations Global Initiative to Fight Human Trafficking), the program is managed by the United Nations Office on Drugs and Crime (UNODC) in collaboration with the International Labour Organization (ILO), the International Organization for Migration (IOM), the United Nations Children's Fund (UNICEF), the Office of the High Commissioner for Human Rights (OHCHR), and the Organization for Security and Co-operation in Europe (OSCE). Operating under the principle that "human trafficking is a crime of such magnitude and atrocity that it cannot be dealt with successfully by any government alone," the program calls for stakeholders— governments, business, academia, civil society, and the media—to work together to creative effective tools to fight human trafficking.[1] The Vienna Forum to Fight Human Trafficking, held in Vienna, Austria, from February 13–15, 2008, brought together representatives from government bodies, international and local nongovernmental organizations (NGOs), researchers, the private sector, and religious organizations from 116 countries. Its mission was to "raise awareness on all forms and dimensions of trafficking, facilitate cooperation, and forge new partnerships among participants" and to provide suggestions on innovative measures and directions for future actions.[2]

At the international level, a number of organizations are active, often in collaboration with local NGOs or government authorities in conducting research; organizing prevention campaigns; offering training to NGOs, police, prosecutors, and judges; assisting in the development of legislation or national action plans; or providing protection and assistance to trafficked victims. Among these organizations are the Free the Slaves, ILO, IOM, the International Centre for Migration Policy Development (ICMPD), La Strada, the Office of the High Commissioner for Human Rights (OHCHR), OSCE, the United Nations Educational, Scientific and Cultural Organization (UNESCO), UNICEF, the United Nations Development Fund for Women (UNIFEM), the United Nations High Commissioner for Refugees (UNHCR), UNODC, Terre des Hommes, and Save the Children.[3] Some organizations such as the OSCE and the United Nations Office for the Commission on Human Rights (UNOHCHR), have appointed a special representative or rapporteur to combat trafficking in human beings.

At the national level, a variety of specialized institutions have been established within countries to address the problem of trafficking. These institutions can take the form of national rapporteurs (as in the Netherlands) or offices such as the Office to Monitor and Combat Trafficking in Persons (in the United States), interministerial or interagency coordination (such as Nigeria's National Agency for the Prohibition of Traffic in Persons and Other Related Matters—NAPTIP), or bodies that coordinate the provision of services to trafficked victims (as the Trafficking Watch Group in the Philippines). In some countries, special law enforcement and prosecutorial units have been established. For those countries that have not yet developed the much-needed expertise to deal with the problem, a number of training manuals and projects have been developed to provide practical help to governments, policymakers, police, prosecutors and judges, NGOs, and others.

The antitrafficking literature has generally discussed the three Ps: prevention, prosecution, and protection. A suggestion was made at the Vienna Forum to include a fourth P—partnership. It is impossible to discuss the myriad of antitrafficking projects implemented worldwide. This chapter instead looks at some of the broader measures taken to address the problem within the areas of prevention, law enforcement and prosecution, victim protection, and assistance and goes beyond those topics to also examine data collection efforts, regional and international instruments, and legislation and national action plans aimed at eradicating trafficking. A number of specific projects will provide examples of the measures being implemented. The chapter closes with comments on more permanent solutions.

PREVENTION

Governments, international, and grassroots organizations alike are actively involved in raising awareness among vulnerable populations and citizens at large to prevent initial victimization of those at risk or to increase the reporting of suspected cases of trafficking. One example of this international initiative is Stop the Traffik, a global nongovernmental movement against human trafficking. The movement has more than 1,000 member organizations in 50 countries, most of them at the grassroots level. Member organizations engage in raising awareness and educating communities about human trafficking. Prevention campaigns are often initiated in countries from which people are trafficked, but should also be aimed at raising awareness in destination countries.

Awareness Raising

Awareness raising campaigns include everything from radio and television ads to education programs at schools, to posters at airports providing telephone hotline numbers for incoming passengers to call should they become victims of trafficking. It is essential that awareness-raising campaigns target the groups at risk (as well as their family members) and accurately portray the recruitment methods of the traffickers and the markets into which victims from that country or region are trafficked. Because so many young Albanian women were "seduced" with marriage proposals and trafficked into prostitution in Italy, the Albania IOM's television antitrafficking announcement showed a young girl in a wedding dress, smiling, holding money in her hands. She was repeatedly slapped across the face by a male wearing a suit, who, each time he hit her, took some of her money until she was left empty handed, make-up smeared, the smile gone and a tear running down her face.[4]

Among some of the more far-reaching media campaigns was a trafficking documentary MTV EXIT (Music Television's End Exploitation and Trafficking) aired by MTV. In 2006, MTV launched its Pan-European Campaign "No Exploitation and Trafficking"[5] and later the program was introduced across the South Asia and the Asia-Pacific regions. The campaign is a "youth-focused pan-regional initiative created to raise awareness and increase prevention of human trafficking"[6] and portrays stories of victims trafficked into prostitution, domestic servitude, and forced labor. The documentaries in Asia premiered in September 2007, followed by a series of public service announcements and fictional short films in 2007 and 2008. A multilanguage Web site was launched (www.mtvexit.org) and the campaign included live awareness and prevention events.[7] Numerous films and documentaries have been produced and distributed worldwide in different languages.[8]

National hotlines have been introduced in numerous countries. The launch of such hotlines is generally combined with awareness-raising campaigns. In the United States, a toll-free number is run by the Covenant House, sponsored by the Department of Health and Human Services in collaboration with the Department of Justice. Victims of trafficking can be instantly referred to a prescreened aid organization in the victim's area.[9] In January 2006, the Dutch Crime Stoppers organization, *Meld Misdaad Anoniem*, launched a campaign to raise awareness of trafficking among clients of prostitutes, taxi drivers, store owners, and local residents to help them recognize the signs of sexual exploitation. People are encouraged to report suspected cases or victims to the police or anonymously to the Crime Stoppers number. In the year of the campaign, 120 tips came in to the organization concerning forced prostitution.[10] An antitrafficking hotline launched by the Interior Ministry in Azerbaijan in 2006 services both trafficked victims who may be seeking counseling or legal advice, as well as the public, which may want to report human trafficking and other crimes.[11] Some hotlines inform individuals of the danger of illegal or unregulated migration. The Serbian NGO ASTRA runs a hotline that people can call to request assistance, report incidents, or receive information on the authenticity of travel, job, or study offers. The hotline has received more than 7,500 calls over the last six years—more than half of them over the past two years, the majority of which were from victims of human trafficking.[12]

Some prevention campaigns do not have the luxury of in-depth, prelaunch preparation. During the emergency evacuation of foreigners when armed conflict escalated in Lebanon in mid-2006, some 300,000 domestic workers from Ethiopia, Sri Lanka, and the Philippines were left behind. Knowing that this group was particularly vulnerable, and becoming aware that traffickers were targeting this group, UNODC put together an emergency information campaign within days. The 12,000 pages of information in various languages were distributed in shelters, churches, embassies, shops, and markets and included the number of a telephone hotline run by the NGO Caritas Migrant, which could provide assistance and support.[13]

More Permanent Prevention Measures

It is essential that prevention campaigns are aimed at the target group. Not all persons, even from poor communities, are equally susceptible to being trafficked. Risk assessment of the most vulnerable persons within a community or society is essential to prevent trafficking. Research needs to identify what factors promote trafficking—whether it is an ethnic minority identity (Roma children are at high risk of trafficking and being forced into begging and stealing), life experience (runaway child victims of domestic violence and domestic sexual violence are at high risk of being trafficked into prostitution), or a simple general lack of education and job skills. Migrants or those planning to migrate must be aware of their rights and how to verify the veracity of job or marriage offers.

Because many of those trafficked are from poorer countries or are the most disadvantaged and marginalized in a society, it is important to promote income-generating activities and opportunities. Education opportunities and job training skills are important, but in addition to skills, individuals must be provided with the tools to ply their trade. Microcredit loans may assist trafficked victims or those at risk to start a small business and generate enough income to allow them to remain in their village or city. Strengthening social protection systems for high-risk children can prevent their victimization. In parts of Southeastern Europe, multidisciplinary teams of professionals (such as social and health workers and law enforcement officials) help identify high-risk children and implement measures to protect them.[14]

It is essential that governments, in countries to which victims are likely to be trafficked, regulate the labor market and areas into which victims may be trafficked. This regulation demands looking beyond the traditional brothels, nightclubs, karaoke bars, and massage parlors into more nontraditional markets such as the construction, agricultural, fishing, hotel, and restaurant industries. It also demands that publicity campaigns draw the attention of citizens who may see signs of trafficking in their surroundings and ensure that they know which agencies or organizations to contact in such cases.

Unlikely Allies: The Private Sector

According to the U.S. Department of State, in 2007, forced labor was involved in the production of pig iron made in Brazil; bricks made in India, China, and Pakistan; shrimp processed in Thailand and Bangladesh; parboiled rice made in India; sugar cane harvested for ethanol production in Brazil; cotton harvested in Uzbekistan; clothing made in Bangladesh, India, Jordan, and Malaysia; and cocoa harvested in Ghana and Côte d'Ivoire.[15]

The private sector cannot escape its responsibility in preventing human trafficking and has either conformed to the pressure of NGOs or has, in some cases, taken the lead itself to find solutions. Better supply chain management of goods, to ensure that they are not produced with slave labor, could eradicate trafficking in all industries. A number of public-private initiatives have been launched around the world aimed at sharing experiences and raising awareness of the private sector's ability to prevent and fight human trafficking. Among others, was the Global 1000 Initiative launched in Geneva on December 6, 2006. The senior vice president of corporate affairs of Manpower, Inc. sent an invitation to the chief executive officers of the 1,000 biggest corporations worldwide to join in the End Human Trafficking Now! campaign. The idea was to get the companies to encourage other companies with which they work to monitor the supply chain and ensure that nowhere in this chain are humans trafficked and exploited.[16]

Thousands of children have been working as slaves on cocoa farms in Côte d'Ivoire, which is the world's largest cocoa producer.[17] To ensure that chocolate is "child-slave-free," major players in the food industry in October 2007 initiated a program for a more sustainable "cocoa supply chain" in Côte d'Ivoire aimed at improving environmental and social practices. A draft farm-level certification code, developed by local stakeholders (government departments, NGOs, and farmers) is being tested in pilot projects in the country.

Independent certifiers are being trained and the program, which has also been launched in Ghana, is expected to expand to other West African nations.[18] The British Biscuit, Cake, Chocolate, and Confectionery Association, which opposes the use of trafficked persons in the production of cacao, reports that U.K. manufacturers were spending about $12 million dollars annually to develop monitoring and certification schemes.[19] The United Kingdom's Bettys & Taylors of Harrogate, a traditional family business specializing in coffees and teas, has trained their buyers as social auditors, visiting farms that grow tea and coffee purchased by the company, to ensure that workers throughout their supply chain are fairly treated.

Microsoft, together with the Canadian police and international law enforcement has developed the Child Exploitation Tracking System (CETS) to help fight child exploitation online and has provided training for law enforcement.[20] Through Microsoft's Unlimited Potential Program in Asia, the organization awarded grants to projects in communities where trafficking is concentrated. Local NGOs, through the program, established 135 community technology centers where the ICT (information and communication technology) curriculum has been adapted to the local enterprise. The program has been used as a rehabilitative tool for trafficked victims as well as for others in the community who may have turned to illegal migration had they been denied opportunities at home.[21]

The financial sector can be instrumental in the fight against trafficking and exploitation. Investigators at the International Centre for Missing and Exploited Children (ICMEC) identified 70,000 customers using their credit cards and paying $29.95 per month to access graphic images of small children being sexually assaulted. Determined to eradicate the problem, the ICMEC teamed up with the U.S. National Center for Missing and Exploited Children and 30 major online companies[22] and financial institutions to form the Financial Coalition against Child Pornography. The Coalition was launched on March 15, 2006. Members of the Coalition cover 90 percent of the credit card industry. The aim of the group is to shut down the payment accounts being used by traders and purchasers of child pornography and thus shut down the operations.[23]

Unlikely Allies: Religious Institutions

Faith-based groups and institutions can be instrumental in addressing the issue and raising awareness of human trafficking, pressuring governments to pass and enforce laws against human trafficking, and to protect and assist trafficked victims. In some communities, religious institutions are one of the most influential social institutions. Recognizing this, IOM has launched a training course for religious leaders across Ukraine. Those who are trained, train other religious leaders to conduct prevention activities in their communities. Trainers from various faiths across the country have participated.[24]

In Moldova, the IOM launched the Inter-Denominational Coalition for the Prevention of Trafficking in Human Beings, involving religious institutions representing the majority of faiths in the country. More than 650 religious leaders, including monks, have participated. Seminars offered to religious leaders teach them how to become active in prevention activities within their communities, alerting them to the risks of trafficking and encouraging "a tolerant attitude toward victims among lay and religious communities"—not always a simple task when many of the child and women victims have been forced to work in prostitution. Once victims have been returned to Moldova, priests have been instrumental in granting protection and support and assisting in victims' reintegration back into society.[25]

The Church of Bangladesh, through its social development program and commitment by its parishioners, is actively involved in raising awareness among vulnerable people and in the community at large on the dangers of trafficking. At the same time, it provides support to former trafficked women.[26] The Catholic Diocesan Development and Welfare Society in India established a Catholic rehabilitation center, the *Bal Vikas Ashram,* for child slave victims in Uttar Pradesh, India. In Rome, Sister Eugenia Bonetti, coordinates the work of 250 religious nuns from 70 different world congregations. Her full-time work involves helping young trafficked women forced into prostitution regain their independence. Across countries in South America and the Caribbean (including Bolivia, Colombia, Peru, and the Dominican Republic), India, and Japan, the Sisters of Adoration, Slaves of the Blessed Sacrament and of Charity operate missions to provide support to victims of sex trafficking.[27]

LAW ENFORCEMENT AND PROSECUTION

Law Enforcement Investigations and Arrests

The job of law enforcement is made particularly difficult due to the fact that victims seldom cooperate with investigations. This forces the police to rely on other means to secure evidence against the traffickers. Telephone taps are becoming more difficult as criminals dispose of or rotate telephones and numbers and interpreters often are needed to translate telephone taps. A successful investigation demands a coordinated approach among local, regional, or international partners and often involves months of investigative work. In the Netherlands, it took 35 detectives from the national police, three from the Social Intelligence and Investigative Service, four detectives involved in the investigation of the network's financial structure, the military police, assistance from the regional police departments, cooperation with the German police, and 26,000 telephone taps to arrest the members of the trafficking network in the investigation known as Sneep.[28]

Table 9.1 Investigations and Arrests by U.S. Law Enforcement Agencies and Initiatives, 2005–2007

	2005		2006		2007	
Organization	Investigations	Arrests	Investigations	Arrests	Investigations	Arrests
FBI	146	51	126	142	120	155
Project Innocence Lost	71	382	103	157	125	308
ICE	322	186	299	184	348	164
Operation Predator		2,380		2,381		1,630

Note: FBI = Federal Bureau of Investigation; ICE = Immigration and Customs Enforcement.
Source: U.S. Department of Justice (2008a).

In the United States, in the summer of 2005, the Federal Bureau of Investigation (FBI) began its Human Trafficking Initiative. Field offices participate in antitrafficking task forces and have established and maintained relationships with community organizations and local NGOs. In addition to determining the existence and scope of the trafficking problem in their region, officers conduct victim-centered investigations. Arrests increased dramatically since the creation of the initiative. The FBI's Innocence Lost Project targets sex trafficking within the United States, often involving U.S. citizen or lawful permanent resident children, while the Immigration and Customs Enforcement's Operation Predator is a comprehensive initiative aimed at safeguarding children from human traffickers, Internet child pornographers, foreign national sex offenders, and international sex tourists.[29] Table 9.1 provides information on cases open or investigated and the number of arrests by these agencies and operations.

Law Enforcement Training

To strengthen the law enforcement response to trafficking, a number of (international) organizations have developed training manuals or modules. UNODC has developed a "Toolkit to Combat Trafficking in Persons," providing practical help to governments, policymakers, police, NGOs, and others through "best practices."[30] The United Nations Development Program (UNDP) together with the ICMPD has developed a comprehensive training scheme targeting specific groups, using their "Law Enforcement Manual for Combating Trafficking in Human Beings."[31] The OSCE, spanning 56 countries from North America and Europe to Central Asia, provides law enforcement assessment needs and training. The Government of India, in conjunction with

UNODC, published a "Compendium on Best Practices on Anti-Human Trafficking by Law Enforcement Agencies," outlining best approaches on investigating and prosecuting traffickers, protecting victims, and preventing trafficking.[32]

Additionally, some departments are looking beyond training police. In Forth Worth, Texas, code officers who inspect property for violations of city codes have been trained to also look for signs of human trafficking.[33]

U.S. Prosecutions

Between 2001 and 2005, a total of 555 suspects were referred to U.S. attorneys with human trafficking as the lead charge. The largest group comprised suspects charged with sale into involuntary servitude (155 or 28 percent), followed by forced labor (134 or 24 percent) and sex trafficking of children (129 or 23 percent). Of the 75 defendants convicted, 57 pleaded guilty and 18 were convicted at trial. The majority (85 percent) were sentenced to prison and the median sentenced imposed was 70 months.[34] In 2006, federal prosecutors charged 222 defendants and got 98 convictions.[35]

In 2007, 42 antitrafficking task forces were operating throughout the United States. The Department of Justice introduced a human trafficking prosecution unit within the Civil Rights Division focused solely on prosecuting human trafficking cases.[36]

Global Criminal Justice Data

Currently, reliable data on human trafficking are lacking, in particular, data related to the response of the criminal justice system. A limited number of countries provide data on arrests and prosecutions. In its annual report to the government, the Dutch National Rapporteur provided detailed information on the (suspected) victims of trafficking, the offenders, as well as police investigations and court outcomes and the legal status of victims.

Germany also provided demographic data on suspects arrested for human trafficking and the number and outcome of cases that go to trial.

Limited information on individual countries can be obtained from the U.S. Department of State's annual Trafficking in Persons Report. In table 9.2, information is provided on the number of trafficking prosecutions and convictions worldwide for the years 2003–2007. Prosecutions have declined, but convictions (as a percentage of total prosecutions) are on the rise.

Cooperation between Law Enforcement and Civil Society

In 2006, the United Kingdom's law enforcement community and its partners launched a multiagency operation focused on trafficking for sexual exploitation. This campaign, known as Pentameter, was a coordinated and

Table 9.2 Global Criminal Justice Data and Legislation

Year	Prosecutions	Convictions	New or Amended Legislation
2003	7,992	2,815	24
2004	6,885	3,025	39
2005	6,618	4,766	41
2006	5,808	3,160	21
2007	5,682 (490)*	3,427 (326)	28

Note: * Numbers in parentheses are those of labor trafficking prosecutions and convictions.
Source: U.S. Department of State (2008a, 37).

intelligence-led proactive operation and reactive investigation. Police first gathered information on businesses and premises where trafficking might take place—brothels, massage parlors, and saunas. Where intelligence indicated the presence of possible trafficked victims, reactive teams responded immediately to rescue the victims. This coordinated effort took place in all 55 police forces in the United Kingdom.[37] Operation Pentameter resulted in the rescue of 84 women, including a 14-year-old African child. Twelve minors, ages 14 to 17, were rescued from pimps.[38] The operation led to the arrest of 232 people, and 134 persons were charged.[39] Additionally, police focused on asset recovery. Police seized well over £300,000 cash.

At the heart of the operation was "harm reduction and victim care." NGO partners, serving on an independent advisory group were instrumental in informing police on how victims should be treated during that important initial contact. Police forces inventoried available resources for victim support within their jurisdiction and worked closely with organizations providing victim support and assistance.[40] A media campaign was launched to raise awareness among the general population, and in particular, the users of prostitutes. NGOs provided police with advice on the media campaign. The success of this operation has led to similar operations in Ireland, the Netherlands, and Poland.[41]

A year later, the United Kingdom launched Pentameter 2, a "victim focused operation" aimed at treating victims sensitively and providing a wide range of assistance from voluntary and statutory agencies. A support staff member of the NGO, Poppy Project, was assigned to the U.K. Human Trafficking Centre to help with victim liaison for the duration of the Pentameter 2 Operation.[42] Pentameter 2 proved to be more successful than its predecessor. The operation identified 167 victims, 13 of whom were children (the youngest was 14 years old). The police visited 822 premises (157 massage parlors and saunas and 582 residential properties) and arrested 528 criminals. More than £500,000 worth of cash was recovered and the police are attempting to seize further criminal assets believed to be worth several millions of pounds.[43]

The U.S. Immigration and Customs Enforcement's (ICE's) victim-centered approach to disrupting trafficking places equal value on the identification and rescue of victims and the arrest and prosecution of traffickers. To accomplish this first goal, ICE has more than 300 "collateral duty victim/ witness coordinators" who work with NGOs to assist in providing services to victims.[44]

Other actions are initiated by NGOs. The NGO *Action Pour Les Enfants* (APLE) provided information to police in Cambodia that led to the arrest of 21 child sex offenders. The organization monitors the activities of local police and judicial officials and facilitates the involvement of foreign police.[45] The Ethiopian NGO, Forum for Street Children, has collaborated with international NGOs and local and regional law enforcement to help establish Child Protection Units within police stations in the capitol and nine towns throughout the country. The NGO provides training to the police and has rescued and repatriated more than 1,000 children with their families.[46] The human rights organization International Justice Mission (IJM), has been working to free young women from forced prostitution and assist local authorities in building cases against traffickers in Cambodia, India, the Philippines, and Thailand. IJM lawyers work to secure conviction and sentencing of traffickers and ensure that victims get access to aftercare services. The work of the organization has assisted in the freedom of hundreds of girls and women trafficked into the commercial sex trade. In one operation alone, 95 victims were rescued.[47]

What Will Ensure Law Enforcement's Success?

Law enforcement officers must be taught where to look for and how to identify victims of trafficking—particularly in areas outside of the commercial sex industry. More awareness and sensitivity to the trafficking of their own citizens is needed. Traditionally, in destination countries, law enforcement has identified foreign women working in prostitution who do not speak the local language and are not in possession of legitimate identity documents. Other indicators are necessary to recognize, for instance, American children and women who have been trafficked into the commercial sex industry or forced labor within the United States. Appendix 3 provides a list of general and child trafficking indicators as well as indicators to assist in the identification of victims who have been trafficked into domestic servitude, labor and sexual exploitation, begging, and petty crime. Some of these indicators apply to illegal migrants as well as trafficked victims and whether a person is a victim of trafficking may be apparent only to personnel from an NGO or police following an investigation. Below are a number of signs of trafficking that might be clearly visible to ordinary citizens at their workplace or in other settings.

Case 9.1. Indicators that a Person May be Trafficked

Adults who are trafficked may exhibit the following characteristics:

- Live in groups in the same place where they work and leave those premises infrequently, if at all
- Be unable to leave their work environment or only under the control or supervision of their employer
- Show fear or anxiety of their employer
- Suffer injuries inflicted by their employer
- Are unable to quit their job or change their accommodation
- Live in degraded, unsuitable places, such as in agricultural or industrial buildings
- Not know their home or work address
- Work excessively long hours over long periods without being allowed to take days off
- Have extremely little or no cash of their own
- Be unfamiliar with the local language or, for prostitutes, only know sex-related words in the local language or the language of their clients
- Have limited or no social interaction
- Have limited contact with their families, friends, or with people outside of their immediate work environment
- Be unable to communicate freely with others

Children may also exhibit the following characteristics:

- Be under the control of persons unrelated to them
- Look fearful and behave in a way that does not correspond with behavior typical of children their age
- Have no friends of their own age outside of work
- Have no access to education or time for playing

It is essential that law enforcement take a human rights approach to dealing with trafficked victims. Until victims feel safe, they will not cooperate with law enforcement or government officials. It is important that during the interviewing phase, victims understand that they are victims who will be protected and not criminals who will be deported. When potential victims have been uncovered during trafficking police raids in the United Kingdom, the police can use a digital audio player with prerecorded voice files in the language of the potential victim. This prerecorded message explains to the victim exactly what is happening and what the victims can expect from the police in terms of their rights.[48] Interpreters must be present during interviews so that victims clearly understand what is happening and, throughout the entire process, the safety and rights of victims must be guaranteed. This may mean introducing protective measures so that victims do not have to confront their traffickers in court (screens to separate the victim from the accused or video-audio testimony from an undisclosed location). An NGO victim liaison contact person may be useful in supporting the victim throughout the investigation and trial.[49]

VICTIM ASSISTANCE AND PROTECTION

In the Host Country

Victim assistance must be offered in the host (destination) as well as in the source (home) country of the trafficked person. Victims may suffer severe trauma upon being rescued, and it is important to provide them with a physically secure and safe environment to recover. Experts in the field recommend that victims be provided a "reflection period" of a minimum one month and preferably three months in which to heal, consider their options, and if they so desire, cooperate with law enforcement officers in building a case against their traffickers. During this reflection period, victims (some prefer the word "survivors") should be provided with shelter, medical, psychological, and legal support. Their ability to remain in the country should not be contingent on their cooperation with criminal justice authorities, and victims of severe forms of trafficking should be granted the right to seek residence in the host country.

Risk analysis should be conducted to determine whether it is safe to repatriate the trafficked victim to his or her home country or community. If this is not possible, governments should consider granting asylum or special status to the victim. One of the trafficked Albanian women in an IOM shelter that the author visited had a price placed on her life for testifying against her trafficker. The author was told by an OSCE representative working on her case that the OSCE was in negotiations with a third country to grant the young woman asylum.[50]

More and more countries are providing civil compensation and remuneration to victims of trafficking. This is an important measure to assist victims in reclaiming their lives and building their future. Compensation and remuneration are important measures that should be incorporated in all national legislation.

Upon Returning Home

Most assistance strategies are aimed at safely returning and reintegrating the trafficked victim into his or her home country or community. This is no easy task as victims may not wish to return home. Their decision may be influenced by the shame and social stigma of having worked in prostitution, fear of reprisals from the traffickers, rejection by family members, or lack of adequate medical and psychosocial services or education and employment opportunities in the villages from which they came. With young children, the situation may be complicated by the fact that the child might have initially left to escape a home filled with sexual or physical violence or because it was a parent who sold the child into slavery. Returning a child to its parental home might not be a safe and sustainable option.

Victims of trafficking are highly susceptible to being retrafficked. A study of girls and women trafficked into commercial sexual exploitation in India revealed that 10 percent of the 464 victims and 24.2 percent of the survivors interviewed had been retrafficked.[51] The director of the Vlora Women's shelter in Albania, the Hearth, estimated that 80 percent of the women in the shelter end up retrafficked. According to the Immigration Law Practitioners' Association in the United Kingdom, "the question is not whether retrafficking takes place, but how fast?"[52]

Victims return home after weeks, months, or years of having lived in another city or country and after having been exposed to the most egregious crimes and human rights violations. They lack the most basic needs. Therefore, effective reintegration programs must address issues of housing, education and job training, employment, mental and physical health, trauma, and substance abuse, while ensuring the protection and safety of the victim. Any successful reintegration program must be tailored to the specific needs of the individual, who should also be able to make decisions regarding the program. A program can be considered "successful" when the trafficked victim has safely reintegrated into the community and is no longer at risk of being retrafficked. Experts in the field who provide assistance to victims of trafficking do agree that monitoring of repatriated victims is often short lived and thus it is impossible to determine the long-term efficacy of their efforts.

Data Collection

One of the main obstacles to effective antitrafficking policies is the lack of accurate and reliable statistical data. Comparative data are almost impossible because of a lack of common definitions in national legislation or definitions used by different agencies. Data on trafficking in sectors other than that of sexual exploitation of children and women is lacking and without coordination; government agencies and NGOs may be double counting victims. The Austrian Ministry of the Interior, in collaboration with IOM Vienna, has launched the project "Development of Guidelines for the Collection of Data on Trafficking in Human Beings, Including Comparable Indicators." Partners in this endeavor include EUROPOL (the European Law Enforcement Organization), the Belgian Federal Police, the Ministry of Justice and Law Enforcement of Hungary, the Ministry of the Interior of Italy, the Police of Luxembourg, the Ministry of Justice of Sweden, and the ICMPD. The project aims to set the basis for improved data collection by developing guidelines and assisting Member States of the European Union to enhance their data collection efforts. The project encourages the collection of data in such a way as to make them comparable across the European Union, thus allowing for an improved analysis of trends and well-targeted policy responses.[53]

Research is needed on the factors that contribute to trafficking, the methods used by traffickers to recruit their victims, the relationship between recruiter and victim, trafficking routes, and methods of manipulation and exploitation. To launch media campaigns warning of job offers from companies that advertise in newspapers, when in fact victims are being recruited by family members, relatives, and friends, will have little effect on stemming the tide of trafficking. Additionally, evaluation research is needed to determine the efficacy of projects with particular groups—these include both prevention as well as victim protection and assistance. Future projects should be evidence-based.

At the national level, such systematic research is being carried out in the Netherlands. The office of the Dutch National Rapporteur reports annually on victims, offenders, and government responses to trafficking in the Netherlands, allowing the country to track trends and reveal new patterns in human trafficking and, using evidence-based data and research, to identify policy gaps and make recommendations on how to best approach the problem.

At the international level, IOM's Counter-Trafficking Module (CTM) database—the largest database worldwide—contains information to assist in case management of trafficked victims (both domestic and international). As of June 1, 2008, the database contained primary data on more than 12,750 registered victims of more than 80 different nationalities trafficked to more than 90 destination countries.[54] The database contains information provided by victims themselves on background variables, their experiences, the routes, and causes of trafficking, the kinds of exploitation, and their traffickers. IOM has further assisted governments enhance their interagency migration data collection systems.[55]

International and Regional Instruments

By 2008, 118 States had ratified the U.N. Protocol to Prevent, Suppress, and Punish Trafficking in Persons, making a commitment to incorporate its provisions in their domestic laws and to implement its measures.[56] In addition to the U.N. Trafficking Protocol, there are a number of other international conventions. These include the ILO Convention 182, Concerning the Prohibition and Immediate Action for the Elimination of the Worst Forms of Child Labor; the Optional Protocol to the Convention on the Rights of the Child on the Sale of Children, Child Prostitution and Child Pornography; the Optional Protocol to the Convention on the Rights of the Child in Armed Conflict; the ILO Convention 29, Forced Labor; and the ILO Convention 105, Abolition of Forced Labor.

The OSCE Action Plan to Combat Trafficking in Human Beings was designed to assist the 56 participating states comply with their antitrafficking commitments and obligations. The Plan contains far-reaching, concrete recommendations concerning prevention of human trafficking, investigation, law enforcement and prosecution, and protection and assistance to victims. Drawing upon best practices of various organizations, the plan covers a broad scope of antitrafficking activities involving a wide range of actors.[57]

On February 1, 2008, the Council of Europe Convention on Action against Trafficking in Human Beings entered into force. In June of that year, 39 states had signed the Convention and 17 had ratified it.[58] This is the first European treaty to address human trafficking mandating governments to prevent trafficking, prosecute criminals, and provide comprehensive support and assistance to victims. Important is the emphasis on residence permits for victims not directly based upon their cooperation with law enforcement officials. The provisions in this Convention extend beyond the recommendations of the U.N. Trafficking Protocol and the U.S. Trafficking Victims Protection Act (TVPA) minimum standards.[59]

Legislation and Comprehensive National Action Plans

Most countries have implemented some form of legislation prohibiting human trafficking. Since the ratification of the U.N. Trafficking Protocol, at least 70 countries amended their criminal codes making trafficking in persons a specific offense. At least 38 countries have enacted trafficking legislation that also provides for measures to protect and assist trafficked victims. Fourteen countries have comprehensive acts combating child trafficking. In nine countries, human trafficking is part of the immigration legislation. Twenty-two other countries are in the process of passing antitrafficking legislation.[60] Now that most governments have legislation in place, enforcement is essential.

To further the goal of eradicating trafficking and assisting victims, many countries have launched National Action Plans that encourage collaborative efforts between government agencies and civil society and foster cooperation with the international community. The action plans generally involve those ministries or departments that are most affected—Foreign Affairs, Internal Affairs, Justice, Social or Family Affairs, Immigration, Tourism, Education, and Labor. Many National Action Plans put forth concrete recommendations involving training of immigration, law enforcement and criminal justice officials, media and awareness-raising campaigns, and provisions for shelters and victim support and assistance.[61]

Effecting Permanent Change

Many of the projects put forth in this chapter provide limited protection to persons at risk, potential and trafficked victims. To truly eradicate the problem of trafficking, governments, donors, civil society, faith-based organizations, and private industry must invest in long-term sustainable strategies. This requires changes in economic and social policies and cultural and historical practices to address structural factors that serve as root causes of migration and exploitation. According to La Strada International, "as long as women cannot live their lives free from the threat of violence and discrimination and do not have equal opportunities in the labour market, they will choose to take on unregulated work opportunities to support themselves and their families, abroad and at home."[62] This applies not only to women, but also to the most disadvantaged and marginalized in a society.

Long-term sustainable strategies include the eradication of poverty and corruption and the provision of education, job, and career opportunities for the most vulnerable populations in the society. At the same time, governments and society must ensure gender equality and focus on the reduction of discrimination and violence in the family aimed at women and children.

By reducing the endless supply of exploitable victims, it may also be possible to affect the demand. Failing to focus on demand reduction addresses only half of the problem. A more permanent solution is to legally or administratively regulate sectors that are known to make use of trafficked victims and to ensure that slave labor is not involved in the supply chain of goods purchased. Companies that uphold their corporate social responsibility should be rewarded, while attention should be drawn to others that do not.

International instruments have been ratified and national legislation is in place in many countries. Where this is not the case, comprehensive antitrafficking legislation must be passed. These instruments and laws must then be turned into commitments and enforced. Partnerships must be strengthened between countries that are part of the source-transit-destination regional and international trafficking chain. Just as important, however, is the development and nurturing of partnerships within a country among government agencies, civil society, the private sector, the clergy, and the media.

Long-term prevention measures must be combined with effective law enforcement and justice responses while at the same time taking a human-rights-based approach to the trafficking problem. As important as it is to wipe out criminal networks, it is equally important to ensure that victims are adequately protected and provided legal, medical, and psychosocial support and the skills to rebuild their lives. Only a merging of these various approaches will guarantee a humane and effective campaign to eradicate human trafficking and end human misery.

Appendix 1 ——————————————————————

Risk Factors of Child Trafficking

INDIVIDUAL RISK FACTORS

General
- Age and sex (i.e., young girls)
- Marginalized ethnic minority – little access to services
- No birth registration/lack of citizenship
- Orphans and runaways
- Lack of education and skills
- Low self-esteem
- Innocence/naivety/lack of awareness
- Consumers, negative peer pressure

In-source/Sending Areas
- Difficulties in school – dropouts
- Experience of family abuse or violence
- Feeling bored with village/rural life
- City attraction/perception of a better life

In Transit
- Traveling alone rather than in group
- Traveling without money
- Traveling unprepared and uninformed
- Traveling without destination or job
- Emotionally upset, drugged, threatened, or constrained
- Traveling without identification and registration
- Traveling illegally
- Go through nonregistered agency or smuggler
- Traveling at night

At Destination
- Isolation
- No social network
- Inability to speak the language
- Inability to understand system in which they live and work
- Illegal status
- Drug and alcohol dependency
- No contact with family
- Work in bad conditions – may result in worst forms of child labor
- Inability to recognize exploitation/bondage

FAMILY RISK FACTORS

- Marginalized ethnic group or subservient caste
- Poor single parent families
- Serious illness (HIV/AIDS) and death in poor family
- Power relations with household – often patriarchal – fathers decide (e.g., Latin America, Africa, South Asia)
- Son/male preference
- Domestic violence/sexual abuse
- Alcohol and drugs in family
- Past debt/bondage relations in family
- Traditional attitudes and practices (e.g., send daughter to extended family)
- History of irregular migration and migration network

EXTERNAL AND INSTITUTIONAL RISK FACTORS

- War/armed conflict
- Large youth populations vs. low labor market absorption capacity
- Natural disaster (e.g., drought, flooding, earthquakes)
- Globalization and improved communication systems
- Absence of fast and transparent migration/job placement services for youth (i.e., youth may go illegally)
- Strict migration controls contribute to pushing movement underground, with large profits for traffickers
- Weak legal framework and enforcement
- Corruption
- Weak education not relevant to labor market
- (Gender) discrimination in education and labor market
- Shifting social mores, ambiguity in teens' roles

COMMUNITY RISK FACTORS

- Youth unemployment
- Location (i.e., close to border with more prosperous country)
- Distance to secondary school and training centers
- Road connection, exposure to city
- Quality of village leadership and community network
- Lack of policing, trained railway staff, border guards
- Lack of community entertainment
- History of migration

WORKPLACE RISK FACTORS

- Unsupervised hiring of workers (e.g., in border areas)
- Limited reach of labor law
- Poor labor protection and enforcement
- Unregulated information economy and 3-D (dangerous, dirty, and demanding) jobs with poor working conditions
- Lack of law enforcement, labor inspection, and protection
- Inability to change employer
- Male demand for sex with girls and sex tourism
- Undercover entertainment (hairdresser, massage)
- Public tolerance of prostitution, begging, sweatshops
- Lack of organization and representation of workers

Appendix 2 ─────────────────────

Trafficking Patterns by Region, Subregion, and Country[1]

---

[1]Information provided in these tables was taken from the U.S. Department of State's *Trafficking in Persons Report 2008* (TIP). Absent in this TIP report and consequently in these tables is any reference to organ trafficking despite the fact that this form of trafficking has been documented in numerous countries.

AFRICA

Eastern Africa

Country	Internal Trafficking	Source (Trafficking to)	Destination (Trafficking from)
Burundi	Children: child soldiering, domestic servitude, and commercial sexual exploitation.	Children to Uganda: agricultural labor and commercial sexual exploitation.	
Djibouti	Girls: prostitution.		Women and girls from Ethiopia and Somalia: domestic servitude or commercial sexual exploitation.
Ethiopia	Children and adults: domestic servitude, commercial sexual exploitation, and forced labor (street vending, begging, traditional weaving, or agriculture). Debt bondage.	Women to Lebanon, Saudi Arabia, and the United Arab Emirates, Bahrain, Djibouti, Kuwait, Sudan, Syria, and the Republic of Yemen: domestic servitude and sexual exploitation. Men to Saudi Arabia and the Gulf States: low-skilled forced labor.	
Kenya	Children: domestic servitude, street vending, agricultural labor, herding, work as barmaids, and commercial sexual exploitation. Coastal sex tourism industry.	Men, women, and children to the Middle East, other African nations, Europe, and North America: domestic servitude, enslavement in massage parlors and brothels, and forced manual labor, in construction industry. Nationals to Middle Eastern nations (Saudi, Arabia, the United Arab Emirates, and Lebanon) and Germany.	Foreign women: brothels and massage parlors. Children from Rwanda, the Democratic Republic of Congo, Ethiopia, Uganda, and Somalia. Girls: prostituion or barmaids.

Madagascar	Women and children: forced labor and sexual exploitation. Children: domestic servitude, commercial sexual exploitation, forced labor, traveling vendors, and mining. Young women: domestic servitude and sexual exploitation. Young boys and girls: child sex tourism.	
Malawi	Debt bondage and forced labor. Children: agricultural labor, animal herding, domestic servitude, commercial sexual exploitation, and forced menial tasks in small businesses. Adults and children: labor and commercial sexual exploitation.	Adults and children to Mozambique, South Africa, and Zambia: labor and commercial sexual exploitation. Women and children from Zambia, Mozambique, Tanzania, and Somalia: forced labor and commercial sexual exploitation.
Mauritius	Female children: commercial sexual exploitation.	
Mozambique	Children: forced and bonded labor. Women and girls: domestic servitude and commercial sexual exploitation.	Women and girls to South Africa: domestic servitude and commercial sexual exploitation. Young men and boys to South Africa: farm work and mining. Children and adults to Zambia: agricultural labor. Women and girls from Zimbabwe: sexual exploitation and domestic servitude.
Rwanda	Girls: domestic servitude and commercial sexual exploitation.	Children from Rwanda's Eastern Province to Uganda: work on tea plantations or use in commercial sexual exploitation. Children: forced labor and soldiering in the Democratic Republic of Congo.

167

(Continued)

Eastern Africa (*Continued*)

Country	Internal Trafficking	Source (Trafficking to)	Destination (Trafficking from)
*Somalia**2	Somali Bantus and Midgaan (tribes): servitude as domestics, farm laborers, and herders. Children: child soldiers. Women and children: sexual exploitation and forced labor.	Women to the Middle East (Iraq, Lebanon, and Syria) and South Africa: domestic labor and commercial sexual exploitation. Men to the Gulf States: labor exploitation as herdsmen and menial workers. Children to Djibouti, Malawi, and Tanzania: commercial sexual exploitation and exploitative child labor.	Men from Cambodia: long-range fishing boats operating off coast of Somalia.
Tanzania	Boys: forced labor on farms, mines, and informal business sector. Girls from rural areas to urban centers and the island of Zanzibar: domestic servitude and commercial sexual exploitation.	Men to South Africa: forced labor. Girls to Oman, the United Arab Emirates, and possibly other European or Middle Eastern countries: forced domestic labor and sexual exploitation.	Children from Somalia: labor and sexual exploitation.
Uganda	Children: forced labor and commercial sexual exploitation. Karamojong women and children forced into domestic servitude, sexual exploitation, herding, and begging.	Children to Canada, Egypt, the United Arab Emirates, and Saudi Arabia: forced labor and commercial sexual exploitation.	Pakistani, Indian, and Chinese workers and Indian children: sexual exploitation. Children from the Democratic Republic of Congo, Rwanda, and Burundi: agricultural labor and commercial sexual exploitation.
Zambia	Children: exploitation in prostitution, agriculture, domestic service, and fishing sectors.	Women to South Africa and to Europe: sexual exploitation.	Adults and children from Malawian and Mozambican: forced agricultural labor.

[2]Countries in italics and marked with a * are designated "special cases" in the TIP report. This special status may be due to a failure to adequately document a "significant number" of trafficking victims within the country, however sources indicate that trafficking may be occurring and may point to trends.

Zimbabwe	Rural men, women, and children to farms: agricultural labor and domestic servitude, and to cities, domestic labor and commercial sexual exploitation. Women and children: domestic labor and sexual exploitation.	Women and children to Botswana, Mozambique, South Africa, and Zambia: domestic labor and sexual exploitation. Young men and boys to South Africa: farm work. Young women and girls to South Africa, the People's Republic of China, Egypt, the United Kingdom, the United States, and Canada: involuntary domestic servitude or commercial sexual exploitation.	South African girls: domestic servitude.

Central Africa

Angola	Women and girls: domestic servitude and commercial sexual exploitation. Young men: agricultural or unskilled labor.	Angolans to South Africa, the Democratic Republic of Congo, Namibia, and Portugal. Young men: debt-bonded agricultural work in Namibia.	Children from Congo to Angola.
Cameroon	Girls: domestic servitude and sexual exploitation. Boys and girls: forced labor in sweatshops, bars, restaurants, and on tea and cocoa plantations.	Women to Europe, primarily France, Germany, and Switzerland: forced prostition.	Children from Nigeria, Chad, the Central African Republic, Congo, Benin, and Niger: forced labor in agriculture, fishing, street vending, and spare-parts shops.

(Continued)

Central Africa (*Continued*)

Country	Internal Trafficking	Source (Trafficking to)	Destination (Trafficking from)
Central African Republic (C.A.R.)	Children: sexual exploitation, domestic servitude, vending, and forced agricultural, mine, market and restaurant labor. Children: child soldiers. Men, women, and children abducted by rebel groups: forced labor, soldiers, and sex slaves.	Children to Cameroon, Nigeria, and the Democratic Republic of Congo: sexual exploitation, domestic servitude, vending, and forced agricultural, mine, market and restaurant labor.	Children from Rwanda to the Central African Republic.
Chad	Children: domestic servitude, forced cattle herding, forced begging, forced labor in petty commerce, the fishing industry, or commercial sexual exploitation, and child soldiers. Chadian rebels recruit children into the armed forces. Men: forcefully recruited into Chadian National Army.	Chadian children to Cameroon, the Central African Republic, and Nigeria: cattle herding.	Children from Cameroon and Central African Republic: sexual exploitation. Sudanese children: child soldiers
Congo, the Democratic Republic of the (D.R.C.)	Men, women, and children abducted: forced laborer (including in mines), porters, domestics, combatants, and sex slaves. Congolese miners in debt bondage. Children: forced prostitution.	Women and children forcibly transported to Uganda by Ugandan troops: sex slaves or domestics. Women and children to South Africa: sexual exploitation. Girls to the Republic of Congo: commercial sexual exploitation. Children to Uganda: agricultural labor and sexual exploitation.	Men and boys from Rwanda, Ugandan, and Congolese: fraudulently conscripted into militias. Children from Rwandan: forced labor and soldiering in the Democratic Republic of Congo.

Congo, Republic of the (R.O.C.)	Girls from rural areas within the country: commercial sexual exploitation. Boys and girls from rural areas to larger cities: forced street vending and domestic servitude.	Children from other African countries (Benin, Mali, Senegal, Guinea, Togo, and Cameroon): domestic servitude, forced market vending, and forced labor in the fishing industry. Girls from the Democratic Republic of Congo: organized prostitution. Children from the Democratic Republic of Congo: forced commercial activities, such as street vending, domestic servitude, tailoring, hairdressing, and food service.
Equatorial Guinea		Children from Nigeria, Benin, Cameroon, and Gabon: domestic servitude, market labor, vending, and possibly sexual exploitation Women from Cameroon, Benin, other neighboring countries, and China: sexual exploitation.
Gabon		Children from Benin, Nigeria, Togo, and Guinea, Sierra Leone, Burkina Faso, and Cameroon: forced labor. Girls: domestic servitude, forced market vending, forced restaurant labor, and sexual exploitation. Boys: forced street hawking and forced labor in small workshops. Young men and women from other African countries: domestic servitude and sexual exploitation.

(Continued)

Western Africa

Country	Internal Trafficking	Source (Trafficking to)	Destination (Trafficking from)
Benin	Girls: domestic servitude and sexual exploitation. Boys: plantation and construction labor, street hawking, and handicraft activities. Child sex tourism in northern Benin.	Children from Benin to other African countries: domestic servitude and sexual exploitation, plantation and construction labor, street hawking, handicraft activities, and forced labor in mines and stone quarries. Victims to Nigeria and Gabon, Cameroon, Togo, Côte d'Ivoire, Ghana, Congo, and Guinea-Bissau.	Children from Togo, Niger, and Burkina Faso to Benin.
Burkina Faso	Internal trafficking from rural areas to urban centers: domestic servitude, sexual exploitation, forced agricultural labor, and forced labor in gold mines and stone quarries.	Children to other West African countries (notably Côte d'Ivoire, Mali, Benin, Nigeria, Niger, and Togo): domestic servitude, sexual exploitation, forced agricultural labor, and forced labor in gold mines and stone quarries. Women to Europe: forced prostitution.	Children from West African countries to Burkina Faso: domestic servitude, sexual exploitation, and forced agricultural labor. Women from Nigeria, Togo, Benin, Ghana, and Niger to Burkina Faso: forced labor in bars or commercial sexual exploitation.
Côte d'Ivoire	Women and girls from northern areas to southern cities: domestic servitude, restaurant labor, and sexual exploitation. Boys: agricultural and service labor. Children: child soldiers (forced labor in a noncombat capacity).	Women to Europe: sexual exploitation.	Boys from Ghana, Mali, Burkina Faso, and Benin: forced agricultural labor. Boys from Guinea: forced mining. Boys from Togo: forced construction labor. Boys from Benin: forced carpentry work. Boys from Ghana and Togo: forced labor in fishing industry. Women and girls

172

			from other Western and Central African countries: domestic servitude and forced street vending. Women and girls from Ghana and Nigeria: sexual exploitation. Women from China, Ukraine, the Philippines, and North Africa: sexual exploitation.
Gambia, The	Women and children: domestic servitude, sexual exploitation, and sex tourism. Boys: forced begging by religious teachers and street vending.	Boys to Senegal: forced begging. Women and girls to Senegal: domestic servitude and sexual exploitation. Women and children to Europe.	Women, girls, and boys from Senegal, Mali, Sierra Leone, Liberia, Ghana, Nigeria, Guinea-Bissau, Guinea, and Benin: forced begging, street vending, domestic servitude, and sexual exploitation. Senegalese boys: forced begging.
Ghana	Boys: forced labor in agriculture and fishing industry, as porters, and street hawking. Girls: domestic servitude and sexual exploitation. Women: commercial sexual exploitation and child sex tourism.	Children to primarily Côte d'Ivoire, Togo, Nigeria, and The Gambia: forced domestic service labor and sexual exploitation.	Refugee children from Liberia: commercial sexual exploitation. Children from Côte d'Ivoire, Togo, Nigeria, and The Gambia: labor and sexual exploitation and domestic servitude.
Guinea	Girls: domestic servitude and sexual exploitation. Boys: forced agricultural labor, forced begging, street vendors, shoe shiners, and laborers in gold and diamond mines. Men: agricultural labor.	Women and girls to Nigeria, Côte d'Ivoire, Benin, Senegal, Greece, and Spain: domestic servitude and sexual exploitation.	Girls from Mali, Sierra Leone, Nigeria, Ghana, Liberia, Senegal, Burkina Faso, and Guinea-Bissau: domestic servitude and sexual exploitation. Chinese women: commercial sexual exploitation by Chinese men living in Guinea.

(Continued)

173

Western Africa (*Continued*)

Country	Internal Trafficking	Source (Trafficking to)	Destination (Trafficking from)
Guinea-Bissau	Children: forced begging and agricultural labor.	Boys to other West African countries (Senegal): forced begging.	
Liberia	Victims from rural to urban areas: domestic servitude, forced street vending, and sexual exploitation. Children: forced labor in diamond mining areas.	Children to Côte d'Ivoire, Guinea, and Nigeria: domestic servitude, street vending, sexual exploitation, and agricultural labor.	Children from Sierra Leone, Guinea, and Côte d'Ivoire: domestic servitude, street vending, sexual exploitation, and agricultural labor.
Mali	Women and girls: domestic servitude and sexual exploitation. Boys: forced begging and labor in agriculture and gold mines.	Victims to other West African countries (Burkina Faso, Côte d'Ivoire, Guinea, Senegal, and Mauritania). Women and girls: domestic servitude and sexual exploitation. Boys: forced begging and labor in agriculture and gold mines.	Victims from West African countries (Burkina Faso, Côte d'Ivoire, Guinea, Senegal, and Mauritania). Women and girls: domestic servitude and sexual exploitation. Boys: forced begging and labor in agriculture and gold mines.
Mauritania	Boys (trafficked by religious teachers): forced begging. Girls: domestic servitude and sexual exploitation. Children: forced agricultural and construction labor, herding, and forced labor in the fishing industry. Children by street gang leaders: forced to steal, beg, and sell drugs.		Boys from Mali and Senegal: (by religious teachers) forced begging. Girls from Senegal and Mali: domestic servitude. Women and girls from Senegal, Mali, Ghana, and Nigeria: sexual exploitation.

Niger	Children (trafficked by religious teachers): forced begging. Children: forced labor in gold mines, domestic servitude, sexual exploitation, agriculture, and stone quarries. Children: commercial sexual exploitation along the border with Nigeria.	Children to Nigeria and Mali: forced begging and manual labor. Women and children to North Africa, the Middle East, and Europe: domestic servitude and sexual exploitation.	Women and children from Benin, Burkina Faso, Gabon, Ghana, Mali, Nigeria, and Togo: domestic servitude, sexual exploitation, forced labor in mines and on farms, and as mechanics and welders.
Nigeria	Women and girls: domestic servitude and sexual exploitation. Boys: forced begging by religious teachers, as well as forced labor in street vending, agriculture, mining, stone quarries, and domestic servitude.	Women, girls, and boys to other Western and Central African countries (Gabon, Cameroon, Benin, Niger, The Gambia, and Ghana): sexual exploitation, forced labor in street vending, agriculture, mining, and domestic servitude. Women and girls to North Africa, Saudi Arabia, and Europe (Italy, Spain, the Netherlands, Belgium, Austria, Norway, and Greece): commercial sexual exploitation. Boys and girls to the United Kingdom: domestic servitude and forced labor in restaurants and shops.	Boys and girls from Benin: forced labor in granite quarries. Women, girls, and boys from Western and Central African countries (Gabon, Cameroon, Benin, Niger, The Gambia, and Ghana): forced labor in street vending, agriculture, mining, stone quarries, and domestic servitude.
Senegal	Boys (by religious leaders): forced begging. Women and girls: domestic servitude and sexual exploitation, including sex tourism.	Women and girls to neighboring countries, the Middle East, and Europe: domestic servitude and possibly sexual exploitation.	Boys from The Gambia, Mali, Guinea-Bissau, and Guinea: forced begging (by religious teachers). Women and girls from other Western African countries (Liberia, Ghana, Sierra Leone, and Nigeria): sexual exploitation and sex tourism.

(Continued)

Western Africa (*Continued*)

Country	Internal Trafficking	Source (Trafficking to)	Destination (Trafficking from)
Sierra Leone	Women and children from rural provinces to towns and mining areas: domestic servitude, sexual exploitation, and forced labor in diamond mines, petty trading, petty crime, and forced begging. Women and children: forced labor in agriculture and fishing industry.	Women and children to other Western African countries (Guinea, Côte d'Ivoire, Liberia, Nigeria, Guinea-Bissau, and The Gambia): domestic servitude, sexual exploitation, petty trading, petty crime, and forced begging. Women and children to North Africa, the Middle East, and Western Europe: domestic servitude and sexual exploitation.	Children from Nigeria and possibly from Liberia and Guinea: forced begging, forced labor in mines and as porters, and sexual exploitation.
Togo	Girls: domestic servitude, as market vendors, produce porters, and commercial sexual exploitation. Boys: market labor.	Girls to other African countries (Benin, Nigeria, Ghana, and Niger): domestic servitude, as market vendors, produce porters, and commercial sexual exploitation. Boys to other African countries (Nigeria, Côte d'Ivoire, Gabon, and Benin): forced work in agricultural labor. Women and girls to Lebanon and Saudi Arabia: domestic servitude and sexual exploitation. Women to Europe, primarily France and Germany: domestic servitude and sexual exploitation.	Children from Beninese and Ghanaian to Togo.

Southern Africa

Botswana*	Children: domestic servitude. Debt bondage.		Nurses and teachers from Zimbabwe: domestic labor and cattle herding.
Lesotho*	Boys: cattle herding and street vending. Girls: cattle herding, domestic servitude, or commercial sexual exploitation.	Women and girls to South Africa: domestic labor or commercial sexual exploitation.	
Namibia*	Children: prostitution, domestic servitude, forced agricultural labor, cattle herding, and possibly vending.		Children from Zambia and Angola: domestic servitude, agricultural labor, and livestock herding.
South Africa	Girls: commercial sexual exploitation and domestic servitude. Boys: street vending, food service, and agriculture. Child sex tourism.	Women to Ireland, the Middle East, and the United States: domestic servitude.	Women and girls from other African countries: commercial sexual exploitation, domestic servitude, and jobs in the service sector. Thai, Chinese, and Eastern European women: debt-bonded commercial sexual exploitation. Young men and boys from Mozambique, Zimbabwe, and Malawi: farm work.
Swaziland*	Girls, particularly orphans: commercial sexual exploitation and domestic servitude. Boys: forced labor in commercial agriculture and market vending.	Girls to South Africa and Mozambique: commercial sexual exploitation and domestic servitude. Women to South Africa and possibly Mozambique: forced prostitution.	Women from Mozambique: sexual exploitation. Boys from Mozambique: exploitation in low-skilled manual labor, such as car washing, livestock herding, and portering.

(Continued)

Northern Africa

Country	Internal Trafficking	Source (Trafficking to)	Destination (Trafficking from)
Algeria	Children: domestic servitude or street vending.		
Egypt, Arab Republic of	Children: commercial sexual exploitation, domestic servitude and agricultural work. Sex tourism.		
Libya			Men and women from Sub-Saharan Africa and Asia: forced labor and commercial sexual exploitation.
Morocco	Girls from rural areas to cities: involuntary servitude as child maids. Boys: involuntary servitude as apprentices in the artisan, construction, and mechanics industries. Boys and girls: prostitution and child sex tourism. Girls and women: commercial sexual exploitation.	Girls and women to Saudi Arabia, Qatar, Syria, United Arab Emirates, Cyprus, and European countries: commercial sexual exploitation.	Women from Sub-Saharan Africa, India, Bangladesh, Sri Lanka, and Pakistan: coerced into commercial sexual exploitation. Men: coerced into involuntary servitude.
Sudan	Men, women, and children: forced labor and sexual exploitation. Women and girls: domestic servitude. Children: child soldiers. Women: forced labor and sexual violence (by armed forces). Women and children: intertribal abductions and enslavement.	Women and girls to Middle Eastern countries (Qatar): domestic servitude. Children to Uganda and the Democratic Republic of Congo: child soldiers.	Women from Ethiopia: domestic servitude. Ugandan children: armed militias.
Tunisia	Children: commercial sexual exploitation and labor exploitation, such as domestic servitude.		

ASIA

Eastern Asia

China, People's Republic of China (P.R.C.)	Majority of trafficking occurs within the country's borders.	Chinese citizens to Africa, Asia, Europe, Latin America, the Middle East, and North America. Women to Taiwan, Thailand, Malaysia, and Japan: commercial sexual exploitation.	Women and children from Mongolia, Burma, North Korea, the Russian Federation, and Vietnam: forced labor, forced marriage, and prostitution.
Hong Kong Special Administrative Region of China			Women from Chinese mainland and Southeast Asia: forced prostitution and debt bondage. Indonesian workers: exploitation and involuntary servitude.
Japan	Women and girls: pornography or prostitution.		Women and children from the People's Republic of China, the Republic of Korea, Southeast Asia, Eastern Europe, Russia, and Latin America: commercial sexual exploitation and debt bondage. Male and female migrant workers: forced labor.
Korea, Republic of (South Korea)	Women and girls: commercial sexual exploitation.	Women and girls to the United States, Japan, Hong Kong (China), Guam, Australia, New Zealand,	Women from Russia, Uzbekistan, Kazakhstan, Mongolia, the People's Republic of China, North Korea, the Philippines, Thailand, Cambodia, and

(Continued)

179

Eastern Asia (*Continued*)

Country	Internal Trafficking	Source (Trafficking to)	Destination (Trafficking from)
		Canada, and Western Europe: commercial sexual exploitation.	other Southeast Asian countries: sexual exploitation and domestic servitude. Women from less-developed Asian countries: recruited for marriage (some subjected to conditions of sexual exploitation, debt bondage, and involuntary servitude).
North Korea		Women and girls sold as brides in China and forced into prostitution, marriage, or exploitative labor arrangements.	
Macao, Special Administrative Region of China			Women and girls from the Chinese mainland, Mongolia, Russia, the Philippines, Thailand, Vietnam, Myanmar, and Central Asia: commercial sexual exploitation.
Mongolia	Children: commercial sexual exploitation. Girls and women: kidnapped and forced to work in commercial sex trade. Child sex tourism increasing.	Women and girls to China, Macau, Malaysia, and the Republic of Korea: forced labor and sexual exploitation. Men to Kazakhstan: labor exploitation. Mongolian women (arranged marriages with mainly South Koreans): involuntary servitude.	North Korean workers: forced labor.

Taiwan, China	Women to Japan, Australia, the United Kingdom, and the United States.	Women and girls from the People's Republic of China and Southeast Asian countries: sexual exploitation and forced labor. Victims from rural areas of Vietnam, Thailand, Indonesia, and the Philippines: construction, fishing, and manufacturing industries, or domestic servants. Fraudulent marriages to facilitate labor and sex trafficking. Boys: forced prostitution.

Southern Asia

Afghanistan	Children: commercial sexual exploitation, forced marriage to settle debts or disputes, forced begging, debt bondage, service as child soldiers, and other forms of forced labor. Women: commercial sexual exploitation.	Women and children to Pakistan, Iran, Saudi Arabia, Oman, and elsewhere in the Gulf: commercial sexual exploitation. Men to Iran: forced labor.	Women and girls from China, Iran, and Tajikistan: commercial sexual exploitation.
Bangladesh	Girls and boys: commercial sexual exploitation, bonded labor, and other forms of forced labor. Some children sold into bondage by parents. Adults: commercial sexual exploitation, domestic servitude, and bonded labor.	Women and children to India and Pakistan: sexual exploitation. Men and women to Saudi Arabia, Bahrain, Kuwait, the United Arab Emirates, Qatar, Iraq, Lebanon, and Malaysia: domestic servants. Men and women to Malaysia, the Gulf, Jordan, and Finland: construction sector or garment industry.	

(Continued)

181

Southern Asia (*Continued*)

Country	Internal Trafficking	Source (Trafficking to)	Destination (Trafficking from)
India	Men, women, and children: debt bondage, forced to work in brick kilns, rice mills, agriculture, and embroidery factories. Women and girls: commercial sexual exploitation and forced marriage. Children: forced labor as factory workers, domestic servants, beggars, agriculture workers, and used as armed combatants by some terrorist and insurgent groups.	Women to the Middle East: commercial sexual exploitation. Victims to the Middle East, Europe, and the United States: forced labor as domestic servants and low-skilled laborers.	Women and girls from Nepal and Bangladesh: commercial sexual exploitation. Children from Nepal: forced labor in circus shows.
Iran, Islamic Republic of	Women: forced prostitution and forced marriages to settle debts. Children: forced marriages, commercial sexual exploitation, and involuntary servitude as beggars or laborers.	Women and girls to Pakistan, Turkey, Qatar, Kuwait, the United Arab Emirates, France, Germany, and the United Kingdom: commercial sexual exploitation.	Children from Afghanistan: forced marriages, commercial sexual exploitation, and involuntary servitude as beggars or laborers.
Nepal	Children: commercial sexual exploitation, forced marriage, involuntary servitude, child soldiers, domestic servants, and circus entertainment or factory workers. Child sex tourism. Children in indentured domestic servitude. Bonded labor a significant problem.	Children to India and the Middle East: commercial sexual exploitation or forced marriage, involuntary servitude and as child soldiers, domestic servants, and circus entertainment or factory workers. Women to India and to countries in the Middle East: commercial sexual exploitation. Men and women to Malaysia, Israel, the Republic of Korea, the United States, Saudi Arabia, the United Arab Emirates, Qatar, and other Gulf States: forced labor as domestic servants, construction workers, or other low-skill laborers. Victims to Iraq: forced labor.	

Pakistan	Women and children: sexual exploitation or domestic servitude to settle debts and disputes. Bonded labor is a problem.	Women and men to the Gulf States, Iran, Turkey, and Greece: involuntary servitude or debt bondage as domestic servants or construction workers. Girls to the Middle East: sexual exploitation.	Women and children from Bangladesh, India, Burma, Afghanistan, Sri Lanka, Nepal, Azerbaijan, Iran, Kazakhstan, Kyrgz Republic, Turkmenistan, Uzbekistan, and Tajikistan: commercial sexual exploitation and forced labor.
Sri Lanka	Children: commercial sexual exploitation and forced labor; child soldiers.	Men and women to Kuwait, Jordan, Saudi Arabia, Qatar, Lebanon, the United Arab Emirates, Singapore, Hong Kong (China), Malaysia, and the Republic of Korea: involuntary servitude as construction workers, domestic servants, or garment factory workers.	Women from Thailand, China, Russia, and other countries of the Newly Independent States: commercial sexual exploitation.

Southeastern Asia

*Brunei Darussalam**	Women: forced prostitution.		Men and women from Indonesia, Malaysia, the Philippines, Bangladesh, the People's Republic of China, and Thailand: involuntary servitude in domestic or low-skilled labor.

(Continued)

183

Southeastern Asia (*Continued*)

Country	Internal Trafficking	Source (Trafficking to)	Destination (Trafficking from)
Cambodia	Women and girls from rural to urban areas: forced prostitution. Child sex tourism.	Women and girls to Thailand and Malaysia: commercial sexual exploitation. Men to Thailand: fishing, construction, and agricultural industries. Women and girls to Thailand: exploitative labor as domestics. Children to Thailand and Vietnam: begging, streetwork selling candy, flowers, or shining shoes. Women to Taiwan: (brokered international marriages), prostitution.	Women and girls from Vietnam: prostitution.
Indonesia	Women and children: domestic servitude, commercial sexual exploitation, rural agriculture, mining, fishing, and cottage industries. Women and girls: commercial sexual exploitation throughout Indonesia. Sex tourism.	Women and girls to Malaysia and Singapore, Japan: commercial sexual exploitation. Young girls to Taiwan: as brides, forced prostitution. Men and women to Malaysia, Japan, Saudi Arabia, Iraq, Singapore, Taiwan, Hong Kong (China), United Arab Emirates, Jordan, Kuwait, Qatar, Syria, France, Belgium, Germany, and the Netherlands: forced labor and debt bondage in construction, agriculture, manufacturing, and domestic service sectors. Indonesian migrant workers to Malaysia and Saudi Arabia: domestic servitude, commercial sexual exploitation, and forced labor.	Women from the People's Republic of China, Thailand, and Eastern Europe: commercial sexual exploitation.

184

Laos	Young women and girls: commercial sexual exploitation in urban areas.	Women and girls to Thailand: commercial sexual exploitation and labor exploitation as domestics or factory workers. Subject to bonded labor or forced prostitution. Men exploited in Thai fishing and construction industry.
Malaysia	Women and girls from indigenous groups and rural areas: labor and commercial sexual exploitation.	Women, primarily of Chinese ethnicity trafficked abroad: commercial sexual exploitation. Men, women, and children from Indonesia, Nepal, Thailand, the People's Republic of China, the Philippines, Burma, Cambodia, Bangladesh, Pakistan, and Vietnam; involuntary servitude in the domestic, agricultural, construction, plantation, and industrial sectors. Female domestics from Indonesia, Thailand, the Philippines, Cambodia, Vietnam, Burma, Mongolia, and the People's Republic of China are forced into commercial sexual exploitation. Burmese refugees vulnerable to forced labor.
Myanmar (Burma)	Internal trafficking primarily from villages to urban centers: forced labor in industrial zones, agricultural estates, and commercial sexual exploitation. Urban poor and street children: child soldiers.	Women and children to Thailand, People's Republic of China, Bangladesh, India, Pakistan, Malaysia, the Republic of Korea, and Macau: commercial sexual exploitation, domestic servitude, and forced labor. Children to Thailand: hawkers, beggars, work in shops, agriculture, fish processing, and small-scale industries. Women to Malaysia and the People's Republic of China: commercial sexual exploitation. Some women to China as forced brides.

(Continued)

Southeastern Asia (*Continued*)

Country	Internal Trafficking	Source (Trafficking to)	Destination (Trafficking from)
Philippines	Women and children from poor communities to urban areas: commercial sexual exploitation, forced labor as domestic servants or factory workers. Child sex tourism.	Men and women to Bahrain, Canada, Cyprus, Hong Kong (China), Côte d'Ivoire, Japan, Kuwait, Malaysia, Palau, Qatar, Saudi Arabia, Singapore, South Africa, Turkey, and the United Arab Emirates: involuntary servitude. Women to Japan, Malaysia, Singapore, Hong Kong (China), South Korea, and countries in the Middle East and Western Europe: commercial sexual exploitation.	Women from the People's Republic of China, the Republic of Korea, and Russia: commercial sexual exploitation.
Singapore			Women from India, Thailand, the Philippines, and the People's Republic of China: sexual servitude.
Thailand	Ethnic minorities such as northern hill tribe peoples at high risk of trafficking.	Ethnic minorities at high risk of trafficking to Bahrain, Australia, South Africa, Singapore, Malaysia, Japan, Hong Kong (China), Europe, and the United States. Men to Taiwan, the Republic of Korea, Israel, the United States, and Gulf States: forced labor and debt bondage.	Women and children from Burma, Cambodia, Laos, the People's Republic of China, Vietnam, Russia, and Uzbekistan: commercial sexual exploitation. Men, women, and children from Myanmar: forced labor in agricultural work, factories, construction, commercial fisheries and fish processing, domestic work, and begging. Children from Myanmar, Laos, and Cambodia: forced begging and exploitative labor.

East Timor	Women and children from rural areas, camps or internally displaced persons: commercial sexual exploitation.	Women from Indonesia, the People's Republic of China, Thailand, Malaysia, and the Philippines: commercial sexual exploitation.
Vietnam (Viet Nam)	Women and children from rural areas to urban centers: commercial sexual exploitation and forced labor. Child sex tourism.	Women and children to the People's Republic of China, Cambodia, Thailand, the Republic of Korea, Malaysia, Taiwan, and Macau (China): sexual exploitation. Women to the China, Taiwan, and the Republic of Korea via misrepresented marriages into commercial sexual exploitation or forced labor. Men and women to Malaysia, Taiwan, China, Thailand, and the Middle East: forced labor or debt bondage in construction, fishing, or manufacturing sectors. Cambodian children to urban centers: forced labor or commercial sexual exploitation.

COMMONWEALTH OF INDEPENDENT STATES

Armenia	Women and girls to the United Arab Emirates and Turkey: commercial sexual exploitation. Men and women to Turkey and Russia: forced labor.

(Continued)

187

COMMONWEALTH OF INDEPENDENT STATES (*Continued*)

Country	Internal Trafficking	Source (Trafficking to)	Destination (Trafficking from)
Azerbaijan		Women and children to Turkey and the United Arab Emirates: sexual exploitation. Men and boys to Russia: forced labor. Men and women to Iran, Pakistan, the United Arab Emirates, and India: sexual exploitation and forced labor.	
Belarus	A small number of victims trafficked within country.	Men and women to Russia: forced labor.	
Georgia	Women and girls: commercial sexual exploitation. Men: forced labor.	Women and girls to Turkey and the United Arab Emirates: commercial sexual exploitation. Men to Turkey, Russia, Greece, and the Gulf States.	
Kazakhstan	Men and women: forced labor and sexual exploitation.	Men and women to the United Arab Emirates, Azerbaijan, Turkey, Israel, Greece, Russia, Germany, and the United States: forced labor and sexual exploitation.	Women, men and girls from Uzbekistan, Kyrgyzstan, Tajikistan, and Ukraine: commercial sexual exploitation and forced labor in the construction and agricultural industries.
Kyrgyz Republic (Kyrgyzstan)		Men and women to Kazakhstan: forced agricultural labor (mainly in tobacco fields), to Russia: forced construction work, and to China: bonded labor. Women to the United Arab Emirates, China, Kazakhstan, the Republic of Korea, Italy, Turkey, Greece, Cyprus, Thailand, Germany, and Syria: sexual exploitation.	Men and women from Uzbekistan, Tajikistan, and Turkmenistan: forced labor and commercial sexual exploitation.

188

Moldova	Girls and young women from rural areas to capital: sexual exploitation.	Women to Turkey, Russia, the United Arab Emirates, Ukraine, Israel, Cyprus, Greece, Albania, Romania, Hungary, Slovakia, the Czech Republic, Italy, France, Portugal, Austria, and other Western European countries. Children to neighboring countries: forced labor and begging. Men to Russia: construction, agriculture, and service sectors.	Children from Ukraine and Moldova: sexual exploitation and forced begging. Men and women from Kyrgyzstan, Tajikistan, Uzbekistan, Ukraine, Moldova, and Belarus: sexual exploitation and forced labor, including work in the construction industry; Men from Belarus: forced labor in the construction, textile, and food industries.
Russian Federation (Russia)	Children: sexual exploitation and forced begging. Men and women: sexual exploitation and forced labor, including work in the construction industry. Child sex tourism.	Men and women from the Russian Far East to China, Japan, the Middle East, and the Republic of Korea: sexual exploitation, debt bondage, and forced labor, including in the agricultural and fishing industries. Women to Turkey, Greece, Germany, Italy, Spain, Malta, the United States, Canada, Vietnam, Thailand, Australia, New Zealand, Costa Rica, and the Middle East: sexual exploitation.	
Tajikistan	Boys and girls: forced labor and forced begging.	Women to the United Arab Emirates, Turkey, and Russia: commercial sexual exploitation. Women to Pakistan: sexual exploitation and forced labor. Men to Russia and Kazakhstan: forced labor in the construction and agriculture industries.	

(Continued)

189

COMMONWEALTH OF INDEPENDENT STATES (*Continued*)

Country	Internal Trafficking	Source (Trafficking to)	Destination (Trafficking from)
*Turkmenistan**	Women from rural provinces to larger cities: sexual exploitation and involuntary servitude.	Women to Turkey, Algeria, Sudan, Tunisia, the United Kingdom, Thailand, the United Arab Emirates, Cyprus, Kazakhstan, Kyrgyzstan, Pakistan, Iran, and Israel: sexual exploitation. Women to Turkey: domestic servitude. Men to Turkey: forced labor in textile sweatshops.	
Ukraine	Men and women: labor exploitation in the agriculture and service sectors, commercial sexual exploitation, and forced begging. Children: commercial sexual exploitation, forced begging and involuntary servitude in the agriculture industry.	Women to Russia, Poland, Turkey, the Czech Republic, the United Arab Emirates, Austria, Italy, Portugal, Germany, Greece, Israel, Spain, Lebanon, Hungary, Slovak Republic, Cyprus, United Kingdom, Netherlands, Serbia, Argentina, Norway, and Bahrain. Men to Russia, the Czech Republic and Poland: in construction, as laborers, sailors, and factory and agriculture workers. Ukrainian children trafficked transnationally: commercial sexual exploitation and forced begging.	A destination for people from neighboring countries: forced labor and sexual exploitation.
Uzbekistan	Men and women: domestic servitude, forced labor in the agriculture and construction industries, and commercial sexual exploitation.	Women and girls to the United Arab Emirates, Kazakhstan, Russia, Thailand, Turkey, India, Israel, Malaysia, the Republic Korea, Japan, and Costa Rica: commercial sexual exploitation. Men to Kazakhstan and Russia: forced labor in the construction, cotton, and tobacco industries.	

190

EUROPE

Central Europe

Czech Republic	Roma women: sexual exploitation.	Roma women trafficked abroad: sexual exploitation.	Women from Russia, Ukraine, Romania, Belarus, Moldova, Slovakia, Bulgaria, China, and Vietnam: commercial sexual exploitation. Men and women from Ukraine, China, Vietnam, Moldova, and Belarus: labor exploitation.
Hungary	Roma women and girls: sexual exploitation.		Women and girls from Slovakia, Romania, Ukraine, Moldova, Poland, the Balkans, and China: commercial sexual exploitation.
Poland		Men and women to Italy, Austria, Germany, Belgium, France, Spain, Sweden, the Netherlands, and Israel: forced labor and sexual exploitation.	Women from Ukraine, Moldova, Romania, Belarus, Lithuania, Russia, Bulgaria, Cameroon, Somalia, Uganda, Kenya, Nigeria, and Vietnam: commercial sexual exploitation.
Slovak Republic (Sovakia)	Roma women and girls: sexual exploitation.		Women and girls from Moldova, Ukraine, Bulgaria, the Balkans, the Baltics, and China: commercial sexual exploitation. Men from Vietnam: forced labor.

(Continued)

Central Europe (*Continued*)

Country	Internal Trafficking	Source (Trafficking to)	Destination (Trafficking from)
Slovenia	Women: commercial sexual exploitation.	Women to countries in Western Europe: commercial sexual exploitation.	Men, women, and children from Ukraine, Slovakia, Romania, Moldova, Bulgaria, Colombia, the Dominican Republic, Turkey, Albania, and Montenegro: commercial sexual exploitation and forced labor, including in the construction industry. Disabled men from Slovakia trafficked to Slovenia: forced begging.

Southeastern Europe

Country	Internal Trafficking	Source (Trafficking to)	Destination (Trafficking from)
Albania	Women and children: commercial sexual exploitation and forced labor.	Albanian victims to Greece, Italy, Macedonia, and Kosovo, Western European countries (the United Kingdom, France, Belgium, Norway, Germany, and the Netherlands): commercial sexual exploitation and forced labor. Children to Greece: begging and other forms of child labor.	
Bosnia and Herzegovina	Minors trafficked. Romani children: forced labor.	Women and girls trafficked to Western Europe: commercial sexual exploitation.	Victims from Serbia, Ukraine, Moldova, Romania, and Russia: commercial sexual exploitation.

Bulgaria	Roma children: forced begging and petty theft. Bulgarian victims: commercial sexual exploitation.	Roma children to Austria, Italy, and other West European countries: forced begging and petty theft.
Croatia	Croatian girls and women: sexual exploitation.	Women and girls from Romania, Bulgaria, Serbia, Bosnia and Herzegovina, and other parts of Eastern Europe: sexual exploitation.
*Kosovo**	Children: forced begging.	Victims are young women from Eastern Europe: commercial sex industry.
Macedonia, former Yugoslav Republic of	Women and children from eastern rural areas to urban bars in western Macedonia: commercial sexual exploitation.	Victims primarily from Serbia and Albania: commercial sexual exploitation.
Montenegro	Children: forced begging.	
Romania	Men, women, and children: commercial sexual exploitation, forced labor, and forced begging.	Men, women, and children to Italy, Spain, Switzerland, the Czech Republic, Greece, Germany, France, the Netherlands, Turkey, Austria, and Israel: commercial sexual exploitation and forced labor in the agriculture, construction, and hotel industries.	Women from Moldova, Ukraine, and Russia: commercial sexual exploitation.
Serbia	Women and girls: commercial sexual exploitation. Children: forced labor or forced street begging.	Victims to South Central and Western Europe, including Bosnia, Serbia, Italy, and Sweden: commercial sexual exploitation.	Victims from Macedonia, Ukraine, Moldova, Bosnia and Herzegovina, Bulgaria, Romania, Croatia, Albania, and the People's Republic of China: commercial sexual exploitation.

(Continued)

Northern Europe

Country	Internal Trafficking	Source (Trafficking to)	Destination (Trafficking from)
Denmark			Women and girls from Russia, Latvia, Estonia, Lithuania, Ukraine, the Czech Republic, Thailand, Nigeria and other West African countries, Romania, and Bulgaria: commercial sexual exploitation.
Estonia		Women and girls to Sweden, Finland, Norway, Denmark, the United Kingdom, Spain, Belgium, Germany, and the Netherlands: sexual exploitation.	Men, women, and children from Russia: commercial sexual exploitation and forced labor.
Finland			Women from Russia, China, Estonia, Ukraine, Belarus, Moldova, the Caucasus, Lithuania, Latvia, and Thailand: sexual exploitation. Men and women from China, India, Pakistan, and Bangladesh: forced labor in the construction industry, restaurants, and as domestic servants.
Latvia	Women and teenage girls: commercial sexual exploitation.	Women to Cyprus, Denmark, Germany, Greece, Italy, the Netherlands, Norway, Spain, and the United Kingdom: commercial sexual exploitation. Men and women to the United Kingdom: forced labor.	Victims from Thailand: forced labor.

Lithuania	Women: commercial sexual exploitation.	Women to the United Kingdom, Germany, Spain, Italy, Denmark, Norway, and the Netherlands: commercial sexual exploitation.	Women from Belarus, Russia (the Kaliningrad region), and Ukraine: sexual exploitation.
Norway			Women and children from Nigeria, Russia, Albania, Ukraine, Latvia, Lithuania, Estonia, Brazil, and East Asian nations: commercial sexual exploitation.
Sweden			Women and children from Estonia, Russia, Poland, Albania, Slovakia, Nigeria, Hungary, Serbia, Montenegro, Macedonia, Venezuela, and Thailand: commercial sexual exploitation. Women and children from Romania and Bulgaria: forced begging and petty theft. Boys and young men from the United Kingdom: forced labor on construction sites and other forced work (laying asphalt, yard work, and odd jobs).
Southern Europe			
Greece			Women from Eastern Europe, the Balkans, and Africa (Romania, Bulgaria, Russia, Lithuania, Moldova, Ukraine, Albania, Nigeria, and

(Continued)

195

Southern Europe (*Continued*)

Country	Internal Trafficking	Source (Trafficking to)	Destination (Trafficking from)
			Sudan): commercial sexual exploitation and forced labor. Albanian men: forced labor. Children from Albania: forced labor, including forced begging and petty crimes; some sexual exploitation. Nigerian victims: sexual exploitation.
Italy			Women and children trafficked from Nigeria, Romania, Bulgaria, Moldova, Albania, Ukraine, Russia, South America, North and East Africa, the Middle East, China, and Uzbekistan: sexual exploitation. Chinese men and women: forced labor. Victims from Poland, Romania, Pakistan, Albania, and Côte d'Ivoire: forced labor, mostly in the agriculture sector. Roma children: sexual exploitation and forced begging.
Malta			Women from Russia, Ukraine, Romania, and other Eastern European countries: forced prostitution.

Portugal

Women, men, and children from Brazil, Ukraine, Moldova, Russia, Romania, and Africa: commercial sexual exploitation and forced labor. Male victims from Eastern European countries: forced labor in farming and construction industries.

Spain

Young women from Romania, Russia, Brazil, Colombia, and Nigeria, other areas of Latin America, Eastern Europe, and Africa: sexual exploitation. Men from same countries: forced labor, usually in agriculture. Chinese victims: labor exploitation.

Western Europe

Austria

Women from Romania, Bulgaria, Hungary, Moldova, Belarus, Ukraine, Slovakia, and Nigeria: commercial sexual exploitation and forced labor. Women from Africa: sexual exploitation. Children from Bulgaria and Romania: forced petty theft and sexual exploitation.

(Continued)

Western Europe (*Continued*)

Country	Internal Trafficking	Source (Trafficking to)	Destination (Trafficking from)
Belgium			Women and girls from Nigeria, Russia, Albania, Bulgaria, Romania, and the People's Republic of China: sexual exploitation. Male victims: labor exploitation in restaurants, bars, sweatshops, and construction sites.
France			Women from Romania, Bulgaria, Nigeria, Cameroon, other nations in Eastern Europe, Africa, South America, and Asia: sexual exploitation. Men from Romania and Bulgaria: sexual exploitation. Young women and girls also exploited in domestic work. French Guyana is a destination for women and children from Brazil: sexual exploitation.
Germany	German nationals: commercial sexual exploitation.		Men and women primarily from Central and Eastern Europe (the Czech Republic, Romania, Poland, and Russia) and Nigeria: commercial sexual exploitation and forced labor, including in the construction industry, in restaurants and ice cream parlors, and as domestic servants.

Country	Description
Ireland	Women from Eastern Europe, Nigeria, other parts of Africa, South America, and Asia: forced prostitution. Men and women from Bangladesh, Pakistan, Egypt, and the Philippines, South America, Eastern Europe, and other parts of Asia and Africa: labor exploitation in domestic labor, restaurant, and agriculture work.
Luxembourg	Women from Bulgaria, Poland, and Ukraine: commercial sexual exploitation. Women from Africa and Latin America engaged in prostitution, possible victims of trafficking.
Netherlands	Young women: prostitution. Women and girls from Nigeria, Bulgaria, China, Sierra Leone, and Romania and other countries in Eastern Europe: sexual exploitation and forced labor. Men from India, China, Bangladesh, and Turkey: forced labor and sexual exploitation.
Switzerland	Women from Romania, Hungary, Poland, Bulgaria, Slovakia, the Czech Republic, Slovenia, Ukraine, Moldova, Brazil, the Dominican Republic, Thailand, Cambodia, Nigeria, and Cameroon: commercial sexual exploitation, domestic servitude, and labor exploitation.

(Continued)

Western Europe (*Continued*)

Country	Internal Trafficking	Source (Trafficking to)	Destination (Trafficking from)
United Kingdom	Minors within the country: commercial sexual and labor exploitation.		Migrant workers from Lithuania, Russia, Albania, Ukraine, Malaysia, Thailand, the People's Republic of China, Nigeria, and Ghana: forced labor in agriculture, construction, food processing, domestic servitude, and food service. Women and girls from above countries: commericial sexual exploitation.

LATIN AMERICA AND THE CARIBBEAN

Caribbean

Country	Internal Trafficking	Source (Trafficking to)	Destination (Trafficking from)
*Bahamas**			Haitians: involuntary servitude, domestic servants, gardeners, construction workers, and agriculture laborers. Women and girls from Jamaica and other countries: commercial sexual exploitation.
*Barbados**	Children: prostitution, sex tourism.		Men, women, and children: commercial sexual exploitation and forced labor. Women and girls from Guyana, the Dominican Republic, and other Caribbean islands: sexual exploitation and domestic servitude. Men from China, India, and Guyana: forced labor in construction and other sectors.

Cuba	Women and children: commercial sexual exploitation. Children and adults: forced labor. Sex tourism destination (also children).	Women to Mexico, the Bahamas, and Western Europe, the United States: forced labor, sexual exploitation, and abuse.	
Dominican Republic	Women, boys, and girls: sexual exploitation and domestic servitude. Sex tourism and child sex tourism.	Women to Western Europe, Australia, Argentina, Brazil, Costa Rica, Panama, Haiti, and other Caribbean destinations: prostitution and sexual exploitation.	Haitian nationals: forced labor in the service, construction, and agriculture sectors. Haitian children: domestic servitude.
Haiti*	Children: domestic service. Girls: domestic servitude. Boys: agriculture servitude. Children: violent criminal gangs as fighters or thieves.	Haitians to the Dominican Republic, the Bahamas, the United States, and other Caribbean nations: forced labor on sugarcane plantations, and in agriculture and construction.	Dominican women and girls: commercial sexual exploitation.
Jamaica	Women and girls, and increasingly boys from rural to urban and tourist areas: commercial sexual exploitation. Children: domestic servants. Sex tourism in resort areas.	Women and girls to Canada, the United States, the Bahamas, and other Caribbean destinations: commercial sexual exploitation.	Women from the Dominican Republic, Russia, and Eastern Europe: sexual exploitation.

Central America

Belize	Young girls: sexual exploitation ("sugar daddy" phenomenon—poor families push their school-age daughters to provide sex to wealthy men in exchange for school fees, money, and gifts).		Central American men, women, and children: forced agriculture labor or prostitution.

Central America (*Continued*)

Country	Internal Trafficking	Source (Trafficking to)	Destination (Trafficking from)
Costa Rica	Women and children: sexual exploitation. Men, women, and children: forced labor in fishing, construction, and domestic service. Child sex tourism.	Women and children to El Salvador, Guatemala, Japan, and the United States: sexual exploitation.	Women and girls from Nicaragua, the Dominican Republic, Colombia, Panama, Russia, Uzbekistan, and the Philippines: sexual exploitation. Young men from Nicaragua and Chinese nationals: labor exploitation, mostly in agriculture and construction.
El Salvador	Women and girls from rural to urban areas: sexual exploitation.	Salvadorans to Guatemala, Mexico, and the United States: commercial sexual exploitation.	Women and children from Nicaragua and Honduras: prostitution or domestic servitude. Men and children from neighboring countries: forced agriculture labor.
Guatemala	Women and children: commercial sexual exploitation. Men, women, and children: forced labor. Child sex tourism. Men and women: exploited labor in agriculture.	Women and children to Mexico and the United States: commercial sexual exploitation. Men, women, and children to Mexico and the United States: forced labor. Children in the Mexican border area: forced labor and begging.	Victims from El Salvador, Honduras, and Nicaragua: commercial sexual exploitation.
Honduras	Children from rural to urban areas and tourist centers: commercial sexual exploitation and forced labor for violent criminal gangs.	Women and children to Guatemala, El Salvador, Mexico, and the United States: sexual exploitation.	Most foreign victims from neighboring countries: commercial sexual exploitation.

Mexico	Women, girls, and boys from poor rural regions to urban, border, and tourist areas: sexual exploitation. Sex tourism and child sex tourism. Men and boys from southern to northern Mexico: forced labor.	Women and girls by organized criminal networks to the United States: commercial sexual exploitation. Men, women, and boys into the United States: forced labor, particularly in agriculture.	Victims from Central America (Guatemala, Honduras, and El Salvador): sexual exploitation. Some Central American minors fall victim to traffickers, near Guatemalan border. Victims from South America, the Caribbean, Eastern Europe, and Asia: sexual or labor exploitation. Central Americans, especially Guatemalans: agriculture servitude and labor exploitation.
Nicaragua	Women and children: commercial sexual exploitation. Minors: prostitution and child sex tourism. Children: forced labor in construction, agriculture, and the fishing industry, and domestic servitude. Young males: forced labor in agriculture and construction from southern border areas to Costa Rica.	Women and children to Guatemala and El Salvador, and in smaller numbers to Costa Rica, Mexico, Honduras, Venezuela, Spain, and the United States: commercial sexual exploitation.	
Panama	Women and children: sexual exploitation. Rural children to urban areas: labor exploitation.	Women to Jamaica and Europe: sexual exploitation.	Women from Colombia, the Dominican Republic, and Central America: involuntary servitude and forced prostitution.

(Continued)

South America

Country	Internal Trafficking	Source (Trafficking to)	Destination (Trafficking from)
Argentina	Victims from rural to urban areas: exploitation in prostitution. Child sex tourism in the triborder area.	Women and girls to neighboring countries, Mexico, and Western Europe: sexual exploitation.	Women and children from Paraguay, Brazil, and the Dominican Republic: commercial sexual exploitation. Bolivians, Peruvians, and Para-guayans: forced labor in sweatshops, agriculture, and as domestic servants. Chinese migrants: labor exploitation into Chinese-owned supermarkets.
Bolivia	Young women and girls from rural to urban areas: commercial sexual exploitation. Members of indigenous communities at risk: domestic labor exploitation, particularly on sugar cane and Brazil nut plantations. Children: forced labor in mining, in agriculture, and as domestic servants.	Bolivians mainly to Argentina, Brazil, Peru, Chile, Spain, and the United States: forced labor in sweatshops, factories, and agriculture.	
Brazil	Men: forced labor and exploited on plantations, growing sugar cane. Women and children: prostitution. Child sex tourism.	Women and girls to destinations in South America, the Caribbean, Western Europe, Japan, the United States, and the Middle East: sexual exploitation.	Men, women, and children from Bolivia, Peru, and the People's Republic of China: forced labor in factories in major urban areas.
Chile	Women and girls: sex trafficking.	Chileans to neighboring countries such as Argentina, Peru, and Bolivia, in addition to Europe, Japan, and the United States: sexual and labor exploitation.	Victims from neighboring countries and Asian countries such as the People's Republic of China: forced prostitution. Migrants including children from Peru and Bolivia: involuntary servitude in agriculture.

Colombia	Women and children from rural to urban areas: commercial sexual exploitation. Men: forced labor. Children: child soldiers. Women and children forced by gangs and organized criminal networks: commercial sexual exploitation and compulsory labor, including forced begging and servitude in the illegal drug trade. Sex tourism in coastal cities.	Women and girls to countries throughout Latin America, the Caribbean, Western Europe, East Asia, the Middle East, and North America, including the United States: commercial sexual exploitation and involuntary servitude.	
Ecuador	Children from coastal and border areas to urban centers: sexual exploitation. Children: hazardous forms of labor, domestic servitude, forced begging, work in the hospitality and commercial sectors, and hard labor in mines.	Children to neighboring countries and to European countries, including Spain and Italy. Women to Colombia, Peru, Venezuela, and Western Europe, particularly Spain and Italy: commercial sexual exploitation.	Colombian women and adolescent girls: sexual exploitation.
Guyana	Amerindian girls: sexual exploitation and domestic servitude near the mining camps and coastal areas. Young Amerindian men: forced labor conditions in mining and logging camps.	Women and girls to Barbados, Trinidad and Tobago, Brazil, Suriname, and Venezuela: sexual exploitation. Men and boys to same countries: labor exploitation in construction and agriculture.	Women and girls from northern Brazil: commercial sexual exploitation in the interior.
Paraguay	Adults and children: domestic servitude. Indigenous persons: labor exploitation. Children from rural to urban centers: sexual exploitation and domestic servitude. Underage males ("taxi boys"): transgendered prostitution.	Victims to Argentina, Brazil, Bolivia, Spain, and Italy. Underage males to Italy: transgendered prostitution.	Paraguayan and Brazilian women and girls, and increasingly boys in the Brazil-Paraguay-Argentina triborder area: sexual exploitation.

(Continued)

205

South America (*Continued*)

Country	Internal Trafficking	Source (Trafficking to)	Destination (Trafficking from)
Peru	Women and children: commercial sexual exploitation. Children and adults: forced labor as domestic servants and in mining, logging, agriculture, fishing, and brick-making sectors. Child sex tourism in the Amazon region.	Peruvians to Ecuador, Spain, Japan, Italy, and the United States: sexual exploitation.	
Suriname	Girls and boys: sexual exploitation near gold mines.		Girls and women from Guyana, Brazil, the Dominican Republic, Colombia: commercial sexual exploitation. Chinese men: debt bondage and forced labor in supermarkets and the construction sector. Chinese women: sexual exploitation. Haitian migrants: forced labor in agriculture.
Uruguay	Women, girls, and boys to border and tourist areas: sexual exploitation. Children: domestic and agriculture servitude in rural areas.	Women to Spain and Italy: sexual exploitation.	
Venezuela	Women and girls from poor regions in the interior to urban and tourist areas: labor or sexual exploitation. Children: prostitution and child sex tourism.	Women and girls to Western Europe and Mexico and to Caribbean destinations such as Trinidad and Tobago, Aruba, and the Dominican Republic: commercial sexual exploitation.	Men, women, and children from Colombia, Peru, Ecuador, Brazil, the Dominican Republic, and the People's Republic of China: commercial sexual exploitation and forced labor.

MIDDLE EAST (WESTERN ASIA)

Country	Internal Trafficking	Source (Trafficking to)	Destination (Trafficking from)
Bahrain			Men and women from India, Pakistan, Nepal, Sri Lanka, Bangladesh, Indonesia, Thailand, the Philippines, Ethiopia, and Eritrea. Women from Thailand, Morocco, Eastern Europe, and Central Asia: commercial sexual exploitation.
Cyprus			Women from the Philippines, Russia, Moldova, Hungary, Ukraine, Greece, Vietnam, Uzbekistan, the Dominican Republic, Colombia, Romania, Belarus, Bulgaria, and the United Kingdom: commercial sexual exploitation.
Iran, Islamic Republic of	Women: forced prostitution and forced marriages. Children: forced marriages, commercial sexual exploitation and involuntary servitude as beggars or laborers.	Women and girls to Pakistan, Turkey, Qatar, Kuwait, the United Arab Emirates, France, Germany, and the United Kingdom: commercial sexual exploitation.	Children from Afghanistan: forced marriages, commercial sexual exploitation, and involuntary servitude as beggars or laborers.
Iraq	Girls: commercial sexual exploitation. Young boys: criminal gangs. Women: commercial sexual exploitation.	Women to Syria, Jordan, Kuwait, Qatar, United Arab Emirates, Turkey, and Iran: commercial sexual exploitation.	Men and women from Georgia, India, Pakistan, Indonesia, Nepal, Philippines, and Sri Lanka: involuntary servitude as construction workers, cleaners, and handymen. Women from the Philippines and Indonesia: involuntary servitude as domestic servants in Kurdish territory.

(Continued)

MIDDLE EAST (WESTERN ASIA) (*Continued*)

Country	Internal Trafficking	Source (Trafficking to)	Destination (Trafficking from)
Israel	Women: commercial sexual exploitation.	Women to Canada, Ireland, and England.	Workers from China, Romania, Jordan, Turkey, Thailand, the Philippines, Nepal, Sri Lanka, and India: debt bondage and exploitation in the construction, agriculture, and health care industries. Women from Russia, Ukraine, Moldova, Uzbekistan, Belarus, China, and the Philippines: sexual exploitation. African asylum seekers also vulnerable: forced labor or prostitution.
Jordan			Women and men from South and Southeast Asia: forced labor. Women from Bangladesh, Sri Lanka, Indonesia, and the Philippines: forced labor as domestic servants. Men and women from China, Bangladesh, India, Sri Lanka, and Vietnam: forced labor in several factories.
Kuwait			Men and women from Bangladesh, India, Pakistan, Sri Lanka, Nepal, Indonesia, and the Philippines: domestic servants or low-skilled laborers. Women: commercial sexual exploitation.

Lebanon	Children: commercial sexual exploitation and forced labor in the metal works, construction, and agriculture sectors.	Asian and African women: domestic servitude. Eastern European and Syrian women: commercial sexual exploitation. Women from Sri Lanka, the Philippines, and Ethiopia: forced labor.
Oman		Men and women from India, Pakistan, Bangladesh, Sri Lanka, the Philippines, and Indonesia: involuntary servitude as domestic servants or low-skilled workers. Women from China, India, the Philippines, Morocco, and Eastern Europe: commercial sexual exploitation.
Qatar		Men and women from India, Pakistan, Bangladesh, Nepal, the Philippines, Indonesia, Vietnam, Sri Lanka, Ethiopia, Sudan, Thailand, Egypt, Syria, Jordan, and China: involuntary servitude as laborers and domestic servants. Women from China, Indonesia, the Philippines, Morocco, Sri Lanka, Lebanon, India, Africa, and Eastern Europe: prostitution.

(Continued)

MIDDLE EAST (WESTERN ASIA) (*Continued*)

Country	Internal Trafficking	Source (Trafficking to)	Destination (Trafficking from)
Saudi Arabia			Men and women from Bangladesh, India, Sri Lanka, Nepal, Pakistan, the Philippines, Indonesia, Vietnam, Kenya, Nigeria, and Ethiopia: involuntary servitude as domestic servants or other low-skilled laborers. Women from Yemen, Morocco, Pakistan, Nigeria, Ethiopia, Tajikistan, and Thailand: comercial sexual exploitation. Children from Nigeria, Yemen, Pakistan, Afghanistan, Chad, and Sudan: involuntary servitude as forced beggars and street vendors.
Syrian Arab Republic (Syria)			Iraqi refugee women and children: commercial sexual exploitation. Women from Somalia and Eastern Europe: commercial sexual exploitation. Women from Indonesia, Sri Lanka, the Philippines, Ethiopia, and Sierra Leone: involuntary servitude as domestic servants.
Turkey			Women and girls from Moldova, Russia, Ukraine, Belarus, Bulgaria, Kyrgyzstan, Turkmenistan, Uzbekistan, Azerbaijan, Georgia, and Romania: sexual exploitation. Men from Turkmenistan: forced labor.

210

United Arab Emirates		Women from India, Sri Lanka, Bangladesh, Indonesia, Ethiopia, Eritrea, and the Philippines: involuntary servitude as domestic servants. Men from India, Sri Lanka, Bangladesh, and Pakistan: coercive labor and debt bondage in the construction industry. Women from Uzbekistan, Kyrgyzstan, Ukraine, Russia, Kazakhstan, Armenia, Azerbaijan, Ethiopia, Eritrea, Somalia, Uganda, India, Pakistan, Afghanistan, China, the Philippines, Iraq, Iran, and Morocco: commercial sexual exploitation.
Yemen, Republic of	Children, mostly boys: forced begging, forced unskilled labor, forced street vending. Women and girls: commercial sexual exploitation.	Children across northern border into Saudi Arabia: forced begging. Women and girls to Saudi Arabia: commercial sexual exploitation. Women from Ethiopia, Eritrea, Somalia, and the Philippines to Yemen.

NORTH AMERICA

Canada	Girls and women, many of whom are aboriginal: commercial sexual exploitation.	Women and children primarily from Asia (Thailand, Cambodia, Malaysia, Vietnam, and the Republic of Korea), Eastern Europe (Russia and Ukraine), Africa, and Latin America: sexual exploitation.

(Continued)

North America (*Continued*)

Country	Internal Trafficking	Source (Trafficking to)	Destination (Trafficking from)
United States of America	American citizens and legal residents: sexual servitude and forced labor.		Men, women, and children from East Asia, Mexico, and Central America: sexual and labor exploitation, involuntary servitude or debt bondage.

OCEANIA

Australia and New Zealand

Country	Internal Trafficking	Source (Trafficking to)	Destination (Trafficking from)
Australia			Women from Southeast Asia, the Republic of Korea, Taiwan (China), and the People's Republic of China: commercial sexual exploitation. Men and women from India, the People's Republic of China, the Republic of Korea, the Philippines, and Ireland: forced labor.
New Zealand	Minors: commercial sexual exploitation.		Women from Malaysia, Hong Kong (China), the People's Republic of China, and other countries in Asia: commercial sexual exploitation.

Melanesia

Fiji	Children: commercial sexual exploitation.	Women from the People's Republic of China and India: forced labor and commercial sexual exploitation.
Papua New Guinea	Women and children: sexual exploitation and involuntary domestic servitude. Women: sold as brides. Children: indentured servitude to pay family debt.	Women and children from Malaysia, the Philippines, Thailand, and the People's Republic of China: commercial sexual exploitation.
*Solomon Islands**	Girls and women: commercial sexual exploitation. Child sex tourism.	Women from Southeast Asian countries (Indonesia, the People's Republic of China, the Philippines, and Malaysia): commercial sexual exploitation.

Micronesia

*Kiribati**	Girls: commercial sexual exploitation.	
*Palau**		Women from the Philippines and the People's Republic of China: commercial sexual exploitation in karaoke bars. Men and women from the Philippines, the People's Republic of China, and Bangladesh: involuntary servitude as domestics, in agriculture, or in construction.

Appendix 3 —————————————————————

Human Trafficking Indicators[1]

Children or adults who have been trafficked into various markets of exploitation exhibit a variety of characteristics.

GENERAL INDICATORS

General indicators include the following:

- Have acted on the basis of false promises
- Believe that they must work against their will
- Be unable to leave their work environment
- Show signs that their movements are being controlled
- Feel that they cannot leave their situation
- Show fear or anxiety
- Be subjected to violence or threats of violence against themselves or against their family members or loved ones
- Suffer injuries or impairments typical of certain jobs or control measures
- Be distrustful of the authorities
- Be threatened with being handed over to the authorities
- Be afraid of revealing their immigration status
- Have false identity or travel documents
- Not be in possession of their passport other travel or identity documents, as those documents are held by someone else
- Be found in or connected to a type of location likely to be used for exploiting people
- Be unfamiliar with the local language
- Not know their home or work address
- Allow others to speak for them when addressed directly
- Act as if they were instructed by someone else
- Be forced to work under certain conditions

---

[1]These human trafficking indicators were described in the brochure *Human Trafficking Indicators* produced by the United Nations Office on Drugs and Crime and distributed at the UN.GIFT Conference, February, 13–15, 2008.

- Be disciplined through punishment
- Be unable to negotiate working conditions
- Receive little or no earnings
- Have no access to their earnings
- Work excessively long hours over long periods
- Not have any days off
- Live in poor or substandard accommodations
- Have no access to medical care
- Have limited or no social interaction
- Have limited contact with their families or with people outside of their immediate environment
- Be unable to communicate freely with others
- Be under the perception that they are bonded by debt
- Be in a situation of dependence
- Come from a place known to be a source of human trafficking
- Have had the fees for their transport to the country of destination paid for by facilitators, whom they must pay back by working or providing services in the destination

CHILDREN

Children may exhibit the following:

- Have no access to their parents or guardians
- Look intimidated and behave in a way that does not correspond with behavior typical of children their age
- Have no friends of their own age outside of work
- Have no access to education
- Have no time for playing
- Live apart from other children in the family and in substandard accommodations
- Eat apart from the other members of the "family"
- Be given only leftovers to eat
- Be engaged in work that is not suitable for children
- Travel unaccompanied by adults
- Travel in groups with persons who are not their relatives

The following may also indicate that children have been trafficked:

- The presence of child-sized clothing typically worn for doing manual or sex work
- The presence of toys, beds, and children's clothing in inappropriate places such as brothels and factories
- The claim made by an adult that he or she has "found" an unaccompanied child

- The finding of unaccompanied children carrying telephone numbers for calling taxis
- The discovery of cases involving illegal adoption

DOMESTIC SERVITUDE

Adults and children forced into domestic servitude may exhibit the following:

- Live with a family not their own
- Not eat with the rest of the family
- Have no private space or sleep in a shared or inappropriate space
- Be reported missing by their employer even though they are still living in their employer's house
- Never or rarely leave the house for social reasons
- Never leave the house without their employer
- Be given only leftovers to eat
- Be subjected to insults, abuse, threats, or violence

SEXUAL EXPLOITATION

Children or adults who are being sexually exploited may exhibit the following:

- Be of any age, although the age may vary according to the location and the market
- Move from one brothel to the next or work in various locations
- Be escorted whenever they go to and return from work and other outside activities
- Have tattoos or other marks indicating "ownership" by their exploiters
- Work long hours or have few if any days off
- Sleep where they work
- Live or travel in a group, sometimes with other women who do not speak the same language
- Have very few items of clothing
- Have clothes that are mostly the kind typically worn for doing sex work
- Only know how to say sex-related words in the local language or in the language of the client group
- Have no cash of their own
- Be unable to show an identity document
- Do not smile

The following may also indicate sexual exploitation:

- Evidence that suspected victims can not refuse or have had unprotected and/or violent sex

- Evidence that victim or groups of women or children are under the control of others
- Evidence that a person has been bought and sold
- Advertisements for brothels or similar places offering the services of women of a particular ethnicity or nationality

LABOR EXPLOITATION

Children or adults who are being exploited for their labor may exhibit the following:

- Live in groups in the same place where they work and leave those premises infrequently, if at all
- Live in degraded, unsuitable places, such as in agriculture or industrial buildings
- May not be dressed adequately for the work they do: they may lack protective equipment or warm clothing
- Be given only leftovers to eat
- Have no access to their earnings
- Have no labor contract
- Work excessively long hours
- Multiple dependency on their employer for number of services, including work, transportation, and accommodation
- Have no choice of accommodation
- Never leave the premises without their employer
- Are unable to move freely
- Be subject to security measures designed to keep them on the work premises
- Be disciplined through fines
- Be subjected to insults, abuse, threats, or violence
- Lack basic training

The following may also indicate labor exploitation:

- Evidence that workers must pay for tools, food, or accommodation or that those (unreasonable) costs are being deducted from their wages
- Evidence that equipment has been designed or modified so that it can be operated by children
- The employer is unable to show documents required for employing workers (from other countries) or records of wages paid
- Lack of health and safety notices, and evidence that labor laws are being breached

BEGGING AND PETTY CRIME

Children or adults who are trafficked for begging or petty crime may exhibit the following:

- Be children, elderly persons, or disabled migrants who tend to be in public places and on public transport
- Be children carrying or selling illicit drugs
- Have physical impairments that appear to be the result of mutilation
- Be children of the same nationality or ethnicity who move in large groups with only a few adults
- Be unaccompanied minors who have been "found" by an adult of the same nationality or ethnicity
- Participate in the activities of organized criminal gangs
- Be part of large groups of children who have the same adult guardian
- Be punished if they do not collect or steal enough
- Live with members of their gang or with adults who are not their parents or family
- Travel with members of their gang to the country of destination
- Move daily in large groups and over considerable distances

The following might also indicate that people have been trafficked for begging or for committing petty crimes:

- New forms of gang-related crime appear
- Evidence that the group of suspected victims has moved over a period of time, through a number of countries
- Evidence that suspected victims have been involved in begging or in committing petty crimes in another country

Notes

Preface

1. Miller, J. R. "On-the-Record Briefing by Ambassador John R. Miller, Ambassador-at-Large on International Slavery, on Release of the Sixth Annual Trafficking in Persons Report," U. S. Department of State (2006). http://www.state.gov/r/prs/ps/2006/67559.htm.

2. U.S. Department of State (2008a).

Chapter 1

1. United Nations (2000a).
2. United Nations (2000a).
3. Kovalev (2007).
4. Kelly and Regan (2000); Aronowitz (2001).
5. Ojomo (1999).
6. The interview was held with Anna Yakovleva, a representative of a St. Petersburg human rights organization, Stellit, and reported in Kovalev (2007).
7. Weissbrodt and Anti-Slavery International (2002).
8. ILO (2002a, 5).
9. United Nations (2000b).
10. Adnkronosinternational (2006).
11. Wynter (2006).
12. Morgan, Marcus (2007).
13. CNN International (2007b).
14. Rodriguez (2006).
15. All Africa (2006).

16. The victim reports that the group included young Nigerian boys and girls. It is unclear whether the boys were also being trafficked or whether the criminals were using the same routes to traffic some and smuggle other persons.

17. Aronowitz (2001).

18. Aronowitz (2003b).

19. Free the Slaves (2005), citing, Bureau of Democracy, Human Rights, and Labor (2003) and Asian Development Bank, *Combating Trafficking in Women and Children in South Asia: India Country Paper* (New Delhi) (Asian Development Bank, July 2002).

20. The problem of internal trafficking is discussed in the following reports: Aronowitz (2006); UNICEF (2003); Innocenti Research Centre/UNICEF (2003, 21).

21. BNRM (2002).

22. Information provided to the author during an interview with IOM Director Mr. Mauricio Busetti and Deputy Director Ms. Anita Santiago, Tirana, Albania, January 30, 2003.

23. Aronowitz (2003a).

24. Europol (2000).

25. Aronowitz and Peruffo (2003).

26. Aronowitz (2003b).

27. Okojie et al. (2003, 63).

28. Anderson and O'Connel Davidson (2002, 16).

29. Anti-Slavery International (2003); Heyzer (2002).

30. Anti-Slavery International (2003).

31. Gunnatilleke (1996).

32. Aronowitz (2001).

33. According to the United Nations, another 1.6 million people have been displaced within Iraq (Walt 2007).

34. Bales (1999a).

35. Bales (1999a).

36. IOM (2000).

37. IOM (2000) links this to use of the local knowledge, key locations, or weaknesses in border or migration control, whereas Kelly and Regan (2000) relate this to the ease in crossing borders.

38. Kelly and Regan (2000).

39. Okojie et al. (2003, 49).

Chapter 2

1. Sections of this chapter correspond to a study prepared for and owned by the United Nations Division for the Advancement of Women (see Aronowitz 2005). The United Nations has authorized the publication of portions of that study in this book.

2. International Human Rights Law Institute (2002, 6).

3. Dutch women forced into prostitution in the Netherlands are considered victims of human trafficking and statistics on this group of victims is included in the rapports of the Dutch National Rapporteur (BNRM, *Bureau National Rapporteur Mensenhandel*).

4. In July 2003, Nigeria enacted the Trafficking in Persons (Prohibition) Law Enforcement and Administration Act, making the offense of trafficking in persons a federal crime. Research conducted in Nigeria within the framework of the United

Nations Office on Drugs and Crime (UNODC) project "Measures to combat trafficking in human beings in Benin, Nigeria and Togo" found that one year after the passage of the law, not one single case of trafficking had been prosecuted under this new law (Okojie et al. 2003).

5. BNRM (2003).

6. Limanowska (2002).

7. Aronowitz (2005).

8. U.S. Department of State (2008a).

9. U.S. Department of State (2004, 23).

10. Estimates broken down by geographic region provide the following picture: 3,500 to 5,500 trafficked victims from Europe and Eurasia; 3,500 to 5,500 from Latin America; 5,000 to 7,000 from East Asia and the Pacific; 200 to 700 from Africa; 200 to 600 from South Asia; 0 to 200 from the Near East (U.S. Mission to the European Union 2005).

11. Webber and Shirk (2005).

12. Free the Slaves and Human Rights Center (2004).

13. For a description of how these estimates were derived, see the ILO (2005).

14. Forced labor, as different from trafficking, may be perpetrated by the state (as was the case in Chinese and Russian labor camps). Vulnerable groups such as caste and tribal minorities in Asia, or indigenous people from Latin America are also at risk of becoming victims of forced labor (ILO 2005).

15. More on the UNESCO Trafficking Statistics Project can be found at their Web site http://www.unescobkk.org/index.php?id=1022.

16. Organizations that provide information on trafficked victims and included in UNESCO's data comparison sheet include the United Nations, UNIFEM, UNICEF, UNDCP, IOM, the U.S. government, USAID, the FBI, the Protection Project, South East Asian Women's Conference, and Terre des Hommes. A comparison sheet with estimates from these various organizations can be downloaded from the UNESCO Web site at http://www.unescobkk.org/fileadmin/user_upload/culture/Trafficking/project/Graph_Worldwide_Sept_2004.pdf.

17. Makkai (2003).

18. Lehti (2003); Makkai (2003).

19. Lehti (2003).

20. Joint Committee on Human Rights (2006, 29).

21. Polaris Project (2003).

22. Kelly and Regan (2000).

23. Hughes (2002, 7).

24. Lehti and Aromaa (2007).

25. Makkai (2003).

26. UNESCO (2003).

27. Both of these conflicting figures can be found in Gupta (n.d.) and Hughes et al. (1999).

28. Limanowska (2002).

29. The United Nations *Protocol to Prevent, Suppress and Punish Trafficking in Persons, Especially Women and Children* (2000a), does not require that the exploitation take place but that the recruitment, transportation, transfer, harboring, or reception of persons occurs (by means of threat or use of force, coercion, abduction, fraud,

deception, abuse of power or vulnerability, or giving payments or benefits to a person in control of the victim) *for the purpose of exploitation.*

30. Nigeria Immigration Service (2004).

31. UNICEF (2003, 19).

32. Netwerk (2005).

33. Limanowska (2002).

34. The T-visa is provided to victims of severe forms of trafficking, allowing them to remain in the United States. To quality for a T-visa, a victim must meet the following criteria (1) be physically present in the United States; (2) have complied with any reasonable request for assistance to officials in the investigation or prosecution of acts of trafficking (at a minimum, the victim must either report the crime or respond to inquiries made by investigators or prosecutors), or be under the age of 18; and (3) be likely to suffer extreme hardship involving unusual and severe harm upon removal. Webber and Shirk (2005, 8) report that "[t]he large discrepancy between the number of trafficking victims estimated to be present in the United States and the total number of victims receiving protection under the TVPA is the result of several factors: (1) the imperfect nature of trafficking estimates; (2) misidentification of victims by law enforcement; (3) the conditional nature of victim protections; and (4) overly restrictive eligibility requirements for the T-visa." For a further discussion on the restrictions of the T-visa, see Wetmore (2002).

35. The Bundeskriminalamt registered 775 victims in 2006 and 642 in 2005 (BKA 2008).

36. BKA (2004).

37. BNRM (2005). In the Rapporteur's latest report from 2008, the NGO Comensha (the former Foundation against Trafficking in Women) reported 579 (suspected) victims of trafficking (BNRM 2008).

Chapter 3

1. Anti-Slavery International (2003).

2. Webber and Shirk (2005, 4).[0]

3. Omelaniuk (2005).

4. Omelaniuk (2005); Limanowska (2002, 2005).

5. Dottridge (2002).

6. Dottridge (2002); IOM (2005a).

7. Salt (2000, 35).

8. Escaler (1998, 16).

9. Savona et al. (1995).

10. Transnational Criminal Organizations are defined as those that have a home base in one state but that operate in one or more host states where there are favorable market opportunities. The term was coined by Phil Williams (cited in Savona et al. 1995).

11. Aronowitz (2001).

12. O'Neill Richard (1999).

13. Aronowitz (2001).

14. Heyzer (2002).

15. Anderson and O'Connel Davidson (2002, 41).

16. Newman (2006, 16).

17. Goward (2003).

18. Heyzer (2002).

19. Heyzer (2002).

20. Shelley (2006).

21. A report on slavery in the twenty-first century in the United Kingdom claims that the U.K. government has tended to address trafficking as an issue of migration control rather than one of human rights (Craig et al. 2007).

22. Europol (2001).

23. Shelley (2006).

24. See the following reports for more information on the types of crimes into which traffickers force their victims: Europol (2001); Gunnatilleke (1996); O'Neill Richard (1999); Kendall (1999).

25. Webber and Shirk (2005).

26. See the following reports for the link between human trafficking and other criminal activities: Savona et al. (1995); Jantsch (1998): Kendall (1999).

27. Aronowitz (2001).

28. These include but are not limited to the 1949 U.N. Convention for the Suppression of the Traffic in Persons and of the Exploitation of the Prostitution of Others; The Supplemental Convention on the Abolition of Slavery, the Slave Trade, and Institutions and Practices Similar to Slavery; the ILO Convention 182 Concerning Prohibition and Immediate Action for the Elimination of the Worst Forms of Child Labour and the ILO Convention 29 Concerning Forced Labour.

29. Gallagher (2001, 1004).

30. O'Neill Richard (1999).

31. Heyzer (2002, 11).

32. United Nations General Assembly. 1948. The Universal Declaration of Human Rights. http://www.un.org/overview/rights.html.

33. Descent slavery refers to the form of slavery into which people are born because they belong to a group discriminated against by their society. The rights of these persons are ignored and they are treated as property. Department for International Development (2006).

34. Craig et al. (2007).

35. Bales and Robbins (2001). See also Bales (2004).

36. Bales and Lize (2005, 10).

37. U.S. Department of State (2008a).

38. Farrior (1997).

39. Bales (1999b, 102).

Chapter 4

1. The stories of these victims were reported in different sources. For more detail, see Akofa (2001): U.S. Department of State (2006a): Zakaryan (2007); *Pattaya Daily News* (2007); Mayoyo (2007).

2. Aronowitz (2001).

3. Prostitution is not an illegal activity in all countries. In the Netherlands, for example, prostitution by adult women, if voluntary, is not an offense. It is, however, a criminal offense to live off of the proceeds of a prostitute, thus pimping is illegal.

4. Ateneo Human Rights Center (1999); Ould (1999).

5. O'Neill Richard (1999, 3).

6. Ruggiero (1996, 1997).

7. See Aronowitz (2001) citing Ould (1999).

8. Espino (2006).

9. FBI (2004).

10. Information obtained from an article in the Italian newspaper *La Stampa*, September 22, 1994 (cited in Ruggiero 1996, 1997).

11. Business Week (2000).

12. American Civil Liberties Union (2007).

13. The Calimlims were convicted by a Milwaukee federal jury of forced labor, sentenced to four years in prison, and ordered to pay the victim $900,000 in restitution (see *United States v. Calimlim* (Wisconsin), cited in U.S. Department of Justice 2007b).

14. Based on the dialect that the child spoke, the police suspected that she came from Benin and the child was turned over to personnel at the Embassy of Benin for assistance. Interviews with the child took place at the Embassy of Benin in Lagos, Nigeria, November 2000.

15. Ruggiero (1996).

16. Pomodoro and Stefanizzi (1996).

17. U.S Department of State (2005).

18. Webber and Shirk (2005).

19. Makkai (2003).

20. Ann Jordan, the director of the Initiative Against Trafficking in Persons, International Human Rights Law Group, and currently Initiative Against Trafficking in Persons, Global Rights, in an e-mail to Stop Traffic listserv, May 2003.

21. UNODC (2006a).

22. The data contained in the U.N. Trafficking database were generated largely from reports produced by different organizations (intergovernmental, NGO, governmental, and research institutes) in different parts of the world. The report registers a country as a source, transit, or destination if it is mentioned in one of the reports included in the database. Certain areas of the world (Latin America, the Caribbean, and the Commonwealth of Independent States are underrepresented). For more on the data contained in the report, the analysis, and findings, see UNODC (2006a, 2006b).

23. UNODC (2006a, 2006b).

24. Most of the cases in the database were referrals to IOM by NGOs, law enforcement agencies, embassies, and international organizations.

25. Omelaniuk (2005).

26. UNODC (2006a, 2006b).

27. Lagon (2007).

28. Portions of this section correspond to a study prepared for and owned by the United Nations Division for the Advancement of Women (see Aronowitz 2005). The United Nations has authorized the publication of portions of that study in this book.

29. ILO-IPEC (2003).

30. UNDP (n.d.), "Trafficking."

31. Innocenti Research Centre (2003).

32. ILO (2005).

33. UNDP (n.d.), "Trafficking."

34. Okojie et al. (2003); ILO-IPEC (2003); Djisseanou (2003).

35. Heinrich (2007)

36. The study by Girls Power Initiative (2002), an NGO operating in Edo State, was cited in Okojie (2003, 14).

37. U.S. Department of State (2008a).

38. Save the Children (2005).

39. This may be due to the fact that stories abound of children succumbing to thirst or drowning on long and unsafe voyages to foreign countries. Children being sent to live or work in a city within their own country are subjected less frequently to these dangers (Aronowitz 2006).

40. Aronowitz and Peruffo (2003).

41. Akofa (2001).

42. ILO-IPEC (2007).

43. Balch (2006).

44. ILO-IPEC (2007).

45. U.S. Department of State (2008a). In Nigeria, for example, young boys from the age of five or six may be entrusted by their families to serve a religious leader, or *marabout*. In addition to performing various household tasks, the child is often, as part of the learning process, forced to beg (Anti-Slavery International 1994).

46. ILO-IPEC (2007).

47. UNICEF (n.d.), "Factsheet: Child Trafficking."

48. Surtees (2006).

49. ILO-IPEC (2007).

50. *Pattaya Daily News* (2007).

51. ILO-IPEC (2007).

52. RTL Nieuws (2007).

53. UNICEF (n.d.), "Trafficking Violates the Entire Spectrum of Children's Rights."

54. For a description of the dangers to which these children are exposed, see U.S. Department of State (2005). On May 8, 2005 the United Arab Emirates, in partnership with UNICEF, established a program to identify child camel jockeys, compensate them financially for their work, repatriate them to their countries of origin at the government's expense, and provide programs for their training and education (see UAE-UNICEF Program 2008).

55. This was told to the author by NGOs working with trafficked child victims in Togo, Benin, and Nigeria during visits to these countries in September and November 2000.

56. UNICEF (n.d.), "Trafficking Violates the Entire Spectrum of Children's Rights."

57. U.S. Department of State (2006a, 15).

58. UNICEF (n.d.), "Trafficking Violates the Entire Spectrum of Children's Rights."

59. Limanowska (2002).

60. Limanowska (2002); International Human Rights Law Institute (2002).

61. Wijers and Lap-Chew (1999).

62. International Human Rights Law Institute (2002, 40).

63. Vocks and Nijboer (1999, 2000).

64. Because of the large number of victims repatriated to Benin City and the intensive prevention campaigns in the city and nearby areas, it is said to be highly unlikely that victims are unaware of the work they will be performing when traveling abroad. This information was provided to the author during a visit to Benin City, Nigeria, November 2003. *Transcrime* also reports that many Nigerian victims trafficked to Italy know beforehand that they will be working in prostitution but are unaware of the conditions to which they will be subjected.

65. Mayoyo (2007).

66. Savona et al. (2003, 168).

67. IOM (2007c).

68. Free the Slaves and Human Rights Center (2004).

69. Savona et al. (2003).

70. U.S. Department of State (2006a).

71. CNN International (2007a).

72. These projects are being funded by the U.S. Department of State (U.S. Department of Justice 2008a).

73. U.S. Department of Justice (2008a).

74. The Trans Bay Steel Corp. of Napa settled for $1.4 million dollars and Sathaporn Pornsrisirisak, and a number of other men, were allowed to remain and work in the U.S. (*Napa Valley Register* 2006).

75. Baskakova, Tiurukanova, and Abdurazakova (2005).

76. *The Nation* (2007).

77. Galnor (2007).

78. *United States v. Baicu and Baicu* (New York), reported in U.S. Department of Justice (2008a).

79. U.S. Department of State (2008a).

80. OSCE (2006).

81. Free the Slaves and Human Rights Center (2004).

82. Information provided to the author during trafficking assessments to Nigeria in November 2000 and 2003.

83. UNDP (n.d.), "Trafficking and HIV/AIDS."

84. Personal communication with Ms. Talens and Mr. Murat, June 2, 2007.

85. IOM (n.d.), "Human Trafficking in Persons: Moldova."

86. CBC News (2006).

87. AMFAR (n.d.).

88. Zimmerman (2003).

89. At the end of 2005, an estimated 24.5 million people were living with HIV and approximately 2.7 million additional people were infected with HIV during that year. In 2006, the AIDS epidemic in Africa claimed the lives of an estimated 2 million people (UNAIDS 2006).

90. This is also supported by UNIFEM studies in Zimbabwe that show that girls "are increasingly pulled out of school to take on the burden of health care" resulting in a decrease in school enrollment of girls. Of the children removed from school, 70 percent were female children (Fokus n.d.).

91. Djisseanou (2003).

92. McDonald and Timoshkina (2007).
93. Navis (2008).
94. Brunovskis and Surtees (2007).

Chapter 5

1. BKA (2007, 2008).
2. BNRM (2007).
3. Surtees (2008).
4. Maxwell and Skelly (2006).
5. IOM (2004); Europol (2007).
6. Surtees (2008).
7. Tomiuc (2008).
8. Undercover film and interview with Chris Rogers on CNN International, aired on 31 January 2008. The video clips can be accessed at http://edition.cnn.com/video/#/video/world/2008/01/30/rogers.czech.sex.trafficking.part3.itn.itn?iref=24hours and http://edition.cnn.com/video/#/video/world/2008/01/30/rogers.czech.sex.trafficking.part3.itn.itn?iref=24hours
9. (USICE 2007a).
10. Kouri (2007); U.S. Department of Justice (2007c); Krikorian (2007).
11. This is particularly true in Italy.
12. See Okojie et al. (2003); Aronowitz and Peruffo (2003).
13. Siegel (2007).
14. BNRM (2008).
15. Kangaspunta (2008).
16. BNRM (2008).
17. BKA (2008).
18. Kangaspunta (2008).
19. Free the Slaves and Human Rights Center (2004).
20. This was found in a study conducted by the Albanian Ministry of Public Order (2003) and cited in Aronowitz (2004).
21. Interview with staff at the Swiss NGO Terre des Hommes, Elbasan, Albania, February 2003 (Aronowitz 2003b).
22. U.S. Department of State (2005).
23. Aronowitz (2003, a and b).
24. The author of this paper was a member of the delegation. This information was also provided to Okojie et al. (2003) who carried out research in Nigeria on trafficking of women to Italy and other destinations.
25. Aronowitz (2003, a and b).
26. Aronowitz (2005). Stories of children drowning while en route to a destination country have also been documented by Human Rights Watch. The organization documented a boat trip from Nigeria to Gabon in which nine Togolese girls drowned off the coast of Cameroon when their boat capsized. According to a Nigerian newspaper, *This Day*, about 20 percent of children bound for Gabon from Nigeria die in open seas due to boat mishaps, about 150 children in the year 2001 alone (Human Rights Watch 2003).
27. Okojie et al. (2003).

28. The U. S. dollar fluctuates against other currencies. Where the original currency was reported, that is the amount given in the text.

29. Van Dongen (2007a).

30. Police and Italian NGOs in a study of Nigerian women trafficked into Italy reported that women incur debts ranging from US $50,000 to $60,000 (Aronowitz 2006).

31. Savona et al. (2003, 168).

32. Savona et al. (2003, 168).

33. U.S. Department of State (2006c).

34. Russel (2008).

35. Human Rights Watch (1995, 1).

36. See Karr (2005) who reports on studies conducted by the IOM on women trafficked from Tajikistan and another on women trafficked from Kosovar as well as a study by the Coalition Against Trafficking in Women (CATW) of women trafficked to the United States.

37. Spector (1998).

38. Fidler (1998).

39. Van Dongen (2007a, 2007b). The names Halit and Nejat are fictitious names used by the newspaper to protect the privacy of the suspects who are identified by the Public Prosecution Department in press reports as Hasan and Saban B.

40. Van Dongen (2007b).

41. Bovenkerk and Pronk (2007); BNRM (2004).

42. Kristof (2008).

43. Okojie et al. (2003); Aghatise (2005); Skogseth (2006).

44. Aghatise (2005). This may also be an indication of the fact that women are working as freelance prostitutes rather than as trafficked victims.

45. Surtees (2007a).

46. IOM (2004).

47. Kleemans et al. (1998).

48. Savona et al. (2003).

49. Tully (2008).

50. Geest (2007).

51. Undercover film and interview with Chris Rogers on CNN International, aired on January 31, 2008. The video clips can be accessed at http://edition.cnn.com/video/#/video/world/2008/01/30/rogers.czech.sex.trafficking.part3.itn.itn?iref=24hours

52. The women were not interviewed; this information was obtained by other women who were interviewed for the study (Aronowitz 2003b).

53. Free the Slaves and Human Rights Center (2004).

54. Council of Europe (2002).

55. Human Rights Watch (2002).

56. Ibid.

57. Radio Free Europe (2006).

58. Aronowitz (2003b), citing Wong and Saat (2002), *Coalitions against Trafficking in Human Beings in the Philippines: Country Report on Malaysia/Sabah*, Universiti Kebangsaan Malaysia Bangi, Kuala Lumpur, Malaysia, unpublished report submitted to the United Nations Interregional Crime and Justice Research Institute, 2002.

59. U.S. Department of State (2008).

60. Van Dongen (2007c); Openbaar Ministerie (2007).

61. These figures are fairly consistent for studies ranging from exploited Mexican women involved with the Cadena family who were forced to provide sexual services to 25 to 30 men per night; Eastern European women forced to have sex with 20 to 30 customers a day in London; Ukrainian women trafficked to Brussels and forced to have sex with 20 men a day; trafficked women in Tel Aviv reporting having to have sex with 15 men a day; and studies on Cambodian brothels in which women report having sex with as many as 15 customers a day (see Karr 2005, 36).

62. Undercover film and interview with Chris Rogers on CNN International, aired on January 31, 2008. The video clips can be accessed at http://edition.cnn.com/video/#/video/world/2008/01/30/rogers.czech.sex.trafficking.part3.itn.itn?iref=24hours and http://edition.cnn.com/video/#/video/world/2008/01/30/rogers.czech.sex.trafficking.part3.itn.itn?iref=24hours

63. Pallister (2006); Maxwell and Skelly (2006).

64. Pallister (2006).

65. EITB (2007).

66. Van Dongen (2007a).

67. Tully (2008).

68. Europol (2005).

69. Profits were calculated by taking the total economic value-added minus total wage payments.

70. Belser (2005).

71. One of the cases mentioned in the ILO report dated back to 1998. If inflation and increased earnings are taken into account, this figure would be higher. For more see Belser (2005).

72. A group of Pakistanis who had been smuggled from Pakistan via Turkey to Cairo were joined by a larger group of Sri Lankans. After boarding a ship in Alexandria and reaching the Malta-Sicily Channel, they were to transfer to a smaller ship—one operated by a legitimate shipping company. The ship, which could carry approximately 100 passengers floundered and sunk, resulting in the death of almost 300 passengers (Ruggiero 1997).

73. Ruggiero (1996) reports that Albanians wishing to reside in Italy are offered a "package" that includes transport and illegal entry into Italy as well as a variety of job opportunities.

74. Staring et al. (2004); CNN International (2001).

75. Iselin (2003, 5).

76. Vocks and Nijboer (1999).

77. Scholoenhardt (1999).

78. CrimProf Blog (2007).

79. O'Neill Richard (1999).

80. Sentence is pending. The defendant faces a maximum sentence of up to 20 years in prison, a $250,000 fine, and restitution payments (U.S. Department of Justice 2006c).

81. O'Neill Richard (1999).

82. Maxwell and Skelly (2006).

83. Adamoli et al. (1998); Schloenhardt (1999).

84. BNRM (2004).

85. Bajrektarevic (2000a, 2000b).

86. Bajrektarevic (2000a, 2000b).

87. Aronowitz (2001); Europol (2007); Schloenhardt (1999).

88. Reporter Chris Rogers identifies another function that he calls the "gate-keeper." This individual is responsible for checking the legitimacy of an organization wishing to do business with the gang selling women. Undercover film and interview with Chris Rogers on CNN International, aired on January 31, 2008. The video clips can be accessed at http://edition.cnn.com/video/#/video/world/2008/01/30/rogers.czech.sex.trafficking.part3.itn.itn?iref=24hours

89. Sipaviciene (2000), cited in IOM (2000).

90. Europol (2001).

91. Centre for Equal Opportunity and Opposition to Racism (2005).

92. Van Dongen (2007b).

93. Case 10b describes the organized criminal network involved in human trafficking to the Netherlands. For more cases, see Kleemans et al. (1998).

94. *Staats courant* (2000).

95. Kleemans et al. (2002).

96. Council of Europe (2005, 18). The United Nations Convention Against Transnational Organized Crime entered into force in September 2003. As of January 2008, 138 member states were parties to the Convention; 147 were signatories. For more information on the Convention and its Signatories, see the United Nations website at http://www.unodc.org/unodc/en/treaties/CTOC/signatures.html

97. Farr (2005).

98. Glenny (2008).

99. Farr (2005,108,109).

100. Farr (2005) refers to work done on organized criminal groups in Nigeria by Phil Williams, director of the Center for International Security Studies, University of Pittsburg.

101. For a more extensive description of the involvement of these organized crime groups, see chapter 4 in Karr (2005).

102. Staring (2007) refers to DiMaggio's study of business organizations.

103. Ibid.

104. Europol (2007).

105. Shelley (2003a) reports that these are ideal types and not every crime group from a particular region will fit a model.

106. Abandoned by smugglers attempting to evade the U.S. Border Patrol, 14 undocumented immigrants died in a remote area of the Arizona desert in 2001 (*Democracy Now* 2001).

107. Between August 1996 and February 1998, Hugo Cadena-Sosa lured women and girls from Mexico to Florida promising them good jobs and better lives. Instead, they were forced into prostitution and held as sexual slaves in brothel houses in Florida and the Carolinas. The victims were forced to work at the Cadena's brothel houses as prostitutes until they paid the Cadena family a $2,000 smuggling fee. In some cases, the victims were locked in a room with no windows and given no money and were threatened with beatings and reprisal attacks against their families in Mexico. Those who attempted to escape were hunted down, returned to

the brothels, beaten, and subjected to confinement (U.S. Department of Justice 2002).

108. Shelley (2003a), citing Europol (2000), "European Union Organised Crime Situation Report." The report can be downloaded from http://www.europol.eu.int/index.asp?page=EUOrganisedCrimeSitRep2000.

Chapter 6

1. U.S. Department of State (2007).

2. Countries were examined as source, transit, and origin countries and then placed on a scale of Very High, High, Medium, Low, and Very Low. Eleven countries were ranked very high as origin countries (Albania, Belarus, Bulgaria, China, Lithuania, Nigeria, Republic of Moldova, Romania, the Russian Federation, Thailand, and Ukraine), while 10 ranked very high as destination countries (Belgium, Germany, Greece, Israel, Italy, Japan, the Netherlands, Thailand, Turkey, and the United States). See UNODC (2006a, 2006b).

3. The report profiles countries that are origin, transit, or destination countries determined to have a "significant number of victims of severe forms of trafficking" and places them in Tier 1, Tier 2, Tier 2 Watch List, or Tier 3—depending upon concrete measures governments have taken to fight trafficking. Tier rating is based upon three criteria: "(1) the extent to which the country is a country of origin, transit or destination for severe forms of trafficking; (2) The extent to which the government of the country does not comply with the Trafficking Victims Protection Act's minimum standards including, in particular, the extent of the government's trafficking-related corruption; and (3) the resources and capabilities of the government to address and eliminate severe forms of trafficking in persons." (U.S. Department of State (2007, 11). See Appendix 2 of this book and the 2008 report for the most recent descriptions of the trafficking problem in individual countries.

4. Laczko (2005).

5. This appears to be the case in the Middle East where hundreds of thousands of migrants work, are abused, and are trafficked. Countries in the region have been slow to respond to the problem.

6. Omelaniuk (2005).

7. See UNODC (2006b, appendixes 3 and 4).

8. The United Nations defines Western Asia and Turkey as the region comprising what has been dealt with in this report as the Middle East (UNODC 2006a, 2006b).

9. UNODC (2006, a and b).

10. Human Rights Watch (2003): UNICEF (2001).

11. Innocenti Research Centre/UNICEF (2003).

12. Protection Project (n.d.), "Human Rights Report: Nigeria."

13. Innocenti Research Centre/UNICEF (2003).

14. Aronowitz (2005).

15. UNICEF (n.d.), "Trafficking Violates the Entire Spectrum of Children's Rights."

16. ILO (2001b).

17. Innocenti Research Centre/UNICEF (2003).

18. Aronowitz (2005).

19. UNODC (2008d).

20. U.S. Department of State (2007).

21. Watchlist on Children and Armed Conflict (n.d.): United Nations (2005).

22. Watchlist on Children and Armed Conflict (2006).

23. Human Rights Watch (2003).

24. UNODC (2008d).

25. UNODC (2008d).

26. Employers seize the girl's documents and they are subjected to physical and sexual abuse (IOM 2002).

27. Surtees (2005).

28. UNODC (2008d, 44), citing studies carried out by UNICEF and the ILO-IPEC.

29. UNODC (2008d, 44), citing studies by UNICEF and Federation of Kenya Employers.

30. IOM (2007c).

31. UNICEF (2005).

32. The trafficking is said to be controlled by organized criminal groups from Bulgaria, China, Nigeria, the Russian Federation, and Thailand (Fitzgibbon 2003), citing a report by Molo Songolo, Cape Town, South Africa (2000, 1).

33. IOM (2003).

34. UNICEF (2005).

35. Senta (2003), citing a report by UNICEF.

36. Senta (2003), citing IOM, Combating trafficking in South-East Asia (Geneva, 2000).

37. Senta (2003) citing the Congressional Research Service Report: Trafficking in Women and Children, the US and International Response (U.S. Department of State, 2002b).

38. United Nations (2008b).

39. Senta (2003) citing Mr. Farooq Azam, Chief of Mission/Regional Representative, IOM Bangkok.

40. UNDP (n.d.).

41. UNODC (2006a, 2006b).

42. Interview with an activist who works with trafficked women in Thailand, in Tomiuc (2008).

43. UNIAP (n.d.), "Human Trafficking in the GMS."

44. Rivers (2007).

45. Rivers (2007).

46. UNICEF (n.d.), "Trafficking Violates the Entire Spectrum of Children's Rights."

47. Rosenberg (2003).

48. Masud Ali (2005).

49. Senta (2003); UNODC (2008b).

50. UNDP (n.d.), Trafficking: You and Aids."

51. UNODC (2008b).

52. For more information on the girls and women trafficked from Nepal and Bangladesh, see National Human Rights Commission (2004b).

53. UNODC (2008b).

54. UNICEF (n.d.), "Trafficking Violates the Entire Spectrum of Children's Rights."

55. UNODC (2008b), citing Nepal, National Human Rights Commission, Office of National Rapporteur on Trafficking in Women and Children, 2005 National Report: Trafficking in Person Especially on Women and Children in Nepal (Lalitpur, Nepal, September 2006), 8.

56. The number of children recruited as child soldiers is thought to be much higher (Watchlist on Children and Armed Conflict 2008).

57. Molina (n.d.).

58. The report by UNODC and UNICRI highlights, in detail, the plight of Filipina women trafficked to Japan for work in the sex industry (Aronowitz 2003a, 2003b).

59. U.S. Department of State, Bureau of Democracy, Human Rights, and Labor (2008c).

60. ILO-IPEC (2003).

61. U. S. Department of State, Bureau of Democracy, Human Rights, and Labor (2008d).

62. CNN International (2007a).

63. UNODC (2006, a and b); Lehti and Aromaa (2007).

64. Baskakova, Tiurukanova, and Abdurazakova (2005, 3–4).

65. Kovalev (2007).

66. Anti-Slavery International (n.d.), "Trafficking in Russia"; U.S. Department of State (2007).

67. Kovalev (2007).

68. Anti-Slavery International (n.d.), "Trafficking in Russia"; U.S. Department of State (2007).

69. U.S. Department of State (2008a).

70. IOM (n.d.), "Human Trafficking in Persons: Moldova."

71. Schepper-Hughes (2004).

72. IOM (2008d).

73. Anti-Slavery International (n.d.), "Trafficking in Russia Case Study: Sergey's Story."

74. Because of the huge geographic spread of countries formerly categorized as CIS countries, Moldova and other countries are now frequently included in other geographic groups. The countries of Kazakhstan, Kyrgyzstan, Tajikistan, Turkmenistan, and Uzbekistan are classified by the United Nations as belonging to Central Asia, and Belarus and Moldova as belonging to Eastern Europe. Limanowska (2002, 2005) includes Moldova in a study on Southeastern Europe.

75. UNODC (2006a, 2006b).

76. The Western Balkans include the countries of Albania, Bosnia and Herzegovina, Croatia, Republic of Macedonia, Montenegro, and Serbia. Bulgaria, Moldova, Romania, Slovenia, Greece, and Turkey are included in discussions of the Balkan peninsula.

77. Aronowitz (2005); Lehti and Aromaa (2007).

78. Serious Organised Crime Agency (2006).

79. HEUNI (2003). The report presented by HEUNI used primary data from the reports of the IOM, STOP, and STOP II research projects (the Stop Programme of the European Commission funds research projects on trafficking in human beings), reports

of national and regional research programs, U.S. State Department Human Rights reports, and national crime and court statistics.

80. Lehti and Aromaa (2007).

81. Europol (2007).

82. Lehti and Aromaa (2007).

83. Lehti and Aromaa (2007, 129 and 130). This statement reveals the attitude of many law enforcement and immigration officials in their failure to recognize that women working as prostitutes in their own countries can be trafficked victims at home or abroad.

84. UNICEF (n.d.), "Child Trafficking: Sexual Exploitation."

85. Lehti and Aromaa (2007).

86. Aronowitz (2003b).

87. Lehti and Aromaa (2007).

88. Limanowska (2005).

89. IOM (2004).

90. For more detail on new travel routes in individual countries in South Eastern Europe, see Rahmani (2006).

91. Lehti and Aromaa (2007).

92. U.S. Department of State (2008a).

93. Lehti and Aromaa (2007).

94. U.S. Department of State (2007).

95. Lehti and Aromaa (2007).

96. The U.S. Department of State (2008a) has placed Austria, Belgium, France, Germany, Luxembourg, the Netherlands, Switzerland, and the United Kingdom on Tier 1.

97. Espino (2006); AGI (2006).

98. In Germany, see reports produced by the Federal Criminal Police Office (BKA); in the Netherlands, see reports produced by the Bureau of the National Rapporteur on Trafficking in Human Beings (BNRM).

99. U.S. Department of State (2007).

100. U.S. Department of State (2007).

101. Human Rights Without Frontiers International (2008).

102. U.S. Department of State (2007).

103. BKA (2007, 2008).

104. United Kingdom Human Trafficking Centre (2007).

105. BNRM (2008).

106. United Kingdom Human Trafficking Centre (2007); U.S. Department of State (2007).

107. U.S. Department of State (2007).

108. IADB (2006); Ribando (2007).

109. ILO (2005).

110. Coffey (2004).

111. UNODC (2008c).

112. Coffey (2004).

113. UNODC (2006a).

114. U.S. Department of State (2007).

115. International Human Rights Law Institute (2002).

116. Coffey (2004).

117. UNICEF (n.d.), "Trafficking Violates the Entire Spectrum of Children's Rights."

118. Phinney (2001) citing Calcetas-Santos, Report on the mission to Guatemala. Report of the Special Rapporteur on the sale of children, child prostitution and child pornography (United Nations Commission on Human Rights, E/CN.4/ 2000/73/Add.2, 2000) and Dimenstein, *Meninas da Noite: a Prostituição de Meninas-escravas no Brasil,* ed. Ática S.A. (São Paulo, 1992); Center for Reference, Studies, and Action for Children and Adolescents (CECRIA) (2000), Tráfico de Mulheres, Criancas, e Adolescentes para Fins de Exploração Sexual no Brasil." Brasilia, Brazil.

119. Phinney (2001), citing Pratt, "Sex Slavery Racket a Growing Concern in Latin America," *The Christian Science Monitor,* January 11, 2001.

120. Coffey (2004); Ribando (2007).

121. It is unclear whether these are all trafficked women or freelance sex workers and these numbers were not documented by European police officials (Ribando 2007).

122. Toneto (2004).

123. U.S. Department of State (2008a).

124. U.S. Department of State (2007, 28).

125. U.S. Department of State (2007).

126. ILO (2005).

127. IADB (2006), citing the Brazilian Center for Childhood and Adolescence.

128. Phinney (2001), citing Harris, B., Presentation to the Inter American Commission on Human Rights on the Subject of the Commercial Sexual Exploitation of Children in Costa Rica, March 3, 2000.

129. IADB (2006), citing the Center for Childhood and Adolescence.

130. IADB (2006), citing a study by the Latin American Institute for Education and Communication (ILPEC 2006) pertaining to Guatamala and the (IOM/OAS 2004) in Bolivia.

131. IADB (2006), citing a report by the United Nations High Commissioner for Human Rights (2003).

132. Ribando (2007).

133. It is unclear whether these are all trafficked women or freelance sex workers and these numbers were not documented by European police officials (Ribando 2007).

134. U.S. Department of State (2007); IOM (2008a).

135. These countries (along with Armenia, Azerbaijan, and Georgia) are classified by UNDP as Western Asia.

136. The U.S. State Department places countries with a significant trafficking problem in various tiers. Bahrain, Kuwait, Oman, Qatar, and Saudi Arabia have been placed in Tier 3, while Cyprus and the United Arab Emirates have been placed on Tier 2 Watch. Countries that fail to make significant efforts to comply with the minimum standards eliminating human trafficking receive a Tier 3 rating.

137. U.S. Department of State (2008a).

138. Human Rights Watch (2007b) reports that of the more than 660,000 Sri Lankan women who work abroad as domestic workers, nearly 90 percent work in Kuwait, Lebanon, Saudi Arabia, and the United Arab Emirates.

139. IOM (2005b).

140. Berg (2007).

141. Osava (2004).

142. Human Rights Watch (2007a).

143. Since 2005, the government of the United Arab Emirates has worked closely with UNICEF to repatriate child victims.

144. At the time of the research, trafficking in humans had been identified in more than 20 states.

145. Coalition against Trafficking in Women (2001).

146. Protection Project (2002).

147. U.S. Department of State, "International Narcotics and Law Enforcement," 2000, *cited in* the Protection Project, country report, United States.

148. McMahon (1999).

149. FBI (2008a).

150. Tully (2008), citing Louise Shelley.

151. Shared Hope International (2007), citing Estes, Richard J., and Neil Alan Weiner, "The Commercial Sexual Exploitation of Children in the U.S., Canada, and Mexico" (University of Pennsylvania School of Social Work: Philadelphia, 2001, revised 2002).

152. Shared Hope International (2007).

153. FBI (2008b).

154. FBI (2008d).

155. FBI (2008a); U.S. Department of Justice (2008b).

156. The Department of Health and Human Services' Office of Refugee Resettlement issues "certifications" to trafficked victims under the TVPA. Certified victims are eligible for federally funded services and benefits to include medical care, food stamps, housing, and cash assistance (U.S. Department of Justice 2007b).

157. U.S. Department of Justice (2008a). For comparison, in fiscal year 2006, the government supplied 234 certification letters to victims in 20 states and the District of Colombia, the Northern Mariana Islands, and Guam. The majority of victims were from El Salvador (28 percent) and Mexico (20 percent) with another 12 percent of the victims coming from other Latin American countries. Certified victims came from countries in Africa, Europe, and the Pacific Islands (U.S. Department of Justice 2007a).

158. U.S. Department of Justice (2007a).

159. *U.S. v. Maddox and deMaddox* (Texas), cited in U.S. Department of Justice (2007b).

160. *United States v. Zheng and Liu* (Northern Mariana Islands), cited in U.S. Department of Justice (2007b).

161. Rayman (2001a).

162. U.S. Department of State (2007).

163. Rayman (2001a, 2001b).

164. Fournier (2008).

165. U.S. State Department (2007).

166. Graycar and McCusker (2007).

167. U.S. Department of State (2008a).

168. U.S. Department of State (2008a).

Chapter 7

1. This definition is based on the 'Cape Town Principles', 1997 (UNICEF n.d., "Factsheet Child Soldiers").

2. UNODC (2008e).

3. UNICEF (n.d.) "Factsheet Child Soldiers"; Coalition to Stop the Use of Child Soldiers (2008).

4. Wessells (2007).

5. Human Rights Watch (n.d.), "Facts About Child Soldiers."

6. Valentine (2003).

7. Even though the Democratic Republic of Congo is at peace, UNICEF estimates that 12,000 chidren are still serving as soldiers (War Child 2007).

8. War Child (2007).

9. Coalition to Stop the Use of Child Soldiers (2008).

10. Waging Peace (2008); Borger (2008).

11. War Child (2007).

12. Coalition to Stop the Use of Child Soldiers (2008); War Child (2007).

13. Watchlist on Children and Armed Conflict (2008) citing studies of UNICEF and Human Rights Watch.

14. War Child (2007).

15. IRIN (2008d).

16. War Child (2007); Coalition to Stop the Use of Child Soldiers (2008).

17. Coalition to Stop the Use of Child Soldiers (2008).

18. War Child (2007, 300.011)

19. Human Rights Watch (n.d.) "Facts About Child Soldiers."

20. Coalition to Stop the Use of Child Soliders (n.d.), "Some Facts"; Human Rights Watch (n.d.), "Facts About Child Soldiers."

21. Interview with Brigadier General, Chadian National Army, Human Rights Watch (2007a, 19).

22. War Child (2007).

23. Human Rights Watch (n.d.), "Facts About Child Soldiers."

24. IRIN (2003).

25. Tiefenbrun (2007).

26. United Nations (n.d.), "Child Soldier's Stories."

27. Brown-brown is a form of powdered cocaine, cut with gunpowder and commonly given to child soldiers in West African armed conflicts. The drug is inhaled. It is reported to have no different effects from regular cocaine, but the addition of gunpowder largely serves to add to an aura of toughness (Beah 2007).

28. Ishmael was rescued by UNICEF in 1995 when the organization hand-picked him for rehabilitation. It took medical staff one year to weed him off of the drugs and hatred. In 1996 Ishmael was invited to speak to the United Nations. He now lives in the United States. Ishmael was adopted by an American journalist, graduated from the United Nations High School in 2000, and completed college in New York State (CNN International 2007c). Ishmael has written about his experience in the book, *A Long Way Gone*. See also Beach (2007).

29. Coalition to Stop the Use of Child Soldiers (2008).

30. Wessells (2007).

31. IRIN (2003).

32. Tiefenbrun (2007).

33. IRIN (2003).

34. IRIN (2003).

35. U.S. Department of State (2008, 23a).

36. IRIN (2003).

37. IRIN (2008a).

38. Human Rights Watch (1997).

39. Derluyn et al. (2004).

40. IRIN (2008b).

41. Coalition to Stop the Use of Child Soldiers (2008).

42. Coalition to Stop the Use of Child Soldiers (2008).

43. On December 18, 2006, the United Nations launched the Integrated Disarmament, Demobilization and Reintegration Standards (IDDRS), a set of policy and guidelines for carrying out disarmament, demobilization, and reintegration (DDR) programmes in postconflict situations around the world (UNICEF, 2006b).

44. UNICEF (2006a).

45. IRIN (2008c).

46. IRIN (2008a).

47. United Nations (2006b).

48. UN.GIFT (2008a), citing Scheper-Hughes, Nancy, "Illegal Organ Trade: Global Justice and the Traffic in Human Organs" (forthcoming).

49. Council of Europe (2003); and Tomiuc (2003a).

50. Rothman and Rothman (2003).

51. Rothman and Rothman (2003).

52. Scheper-Hughes (2004).

53. Scheper-Hughes (2004).

54. Scheper-Hughes (2003).

55. GTZ (2004).

56. Matas and Kilgour (2007).

57. Paddock (2008).

58. Saletan (2007).

59. Reuters (2007a).

60. Shimazono (2007).

61. Srinivasan (2008).

62. GTZ (2004).

63. Saletan (2007).

64. Gagalac (2008).

65. GTZ (2004); Scheper-Hughes (2003).

66. Scheper-Hughes (2004).

67. Council of Europe (2003).

68. GTZ (2004).

69. Reuters (2007b).

70. GTZ (2004).

71. GTZ (2004): Scheper-Hughes (1999).

72. UN.GIFT (2008a).

73. Scheper-Hughes (2004).

74. Paddock (2008).

75. Information obtained from http://www.liver4you.org/ (accessed June 17, 2008).

76. Kumar (2003).

77. United Nations (2006b), Economic and Social Council.
78. Gentleman (2008).
79. Information based on the World Health Organization estimates (Saletan 2007).
80. Scheper-Hughes (2003).
81. Goyal et al. (2002).
82. GTZ (2004).
83. Scheper-Hughes (2003).
84. Council of Europe (2003).
85. United Nations (2006b, paragraph 82).
86. Scheper-Hughes (1999).
87. GTZ (2004).
88. Scheper-Hughes (2001, 36).
89. Scheper-Hughes (2003).
90. Scheper-Hughes (2004, 47).
91. GTZ (2004).
92. Scheper Hughes (2003).
93. These prices were quoted in Scheper-Hughes (2003). A more recent article from 2008 states that a kidney in Manila sold on the black market brings only $760 (Paddock 2008).
94. Scheper-Hughes (2005a).
95. Scheper-Hughes (2005a).
96. Eyadat (2007).
97. Organs Watch is a human rights oriented documentation center at the University of California, Berkeley, which investigates complaints, conducts research, and issues reports on the global trade in organs.
98. Schepper-Hughes (2003).
99. Goyal et al. (2002).
100. Scheper-Hughes (2003).
101. Paddock (2008).
102. Goyal et al. (2002).
103. Scheper-Hughes (2004, 52); BBC News (2001).
104. Scheper-Hughes (2003).
105. Kumar (2003).
106. Paddock (2008).
107. Scheper-Hughes (2003, 2004).
108. Human Organ Transplant Act (1989, Chapter 31).
109. The Transplantation of Human Organs Act (1994, Section 9.3).
110. Paddock (2008).
111. Scheper-Hughes (2007).
112. Shimazono (2007).
113. Council of Europe (2003).
114. Tomesen (2008).
115. Srinivasan (2008).
116. GTZ (2004).
117. Scheper-Hughes (2004).
118. Davis (2006).

119. Bielke (2004).

120. Scholes and Phataralaoha (n.d.).

121. BBC News (2007b).

122. Omelaniuk (2005), citing Coomaraswamy, "Report of the Special Rapporteur on violence against women: trafficking in women and forced prostitution" UNHCR, Geneva. 2003).

123. Clarke (2004).

124. Clarke (2004).

125. U.S. Department of State (2007, 17).

126. U.S. Department of State (2007).

127. Yousafzai et al. (2008).

128. Yousafzai et al. (2008).

129. Aronowitz (2003b).

130. Clarke (2004).

131. U.S. Department of State (2007).

132. BBC News (2007a)

133. USCIS (2006).

134. U.S Department of State (2007).

135. Philippine Government (1990).

136. U.S. Department of State (2007).

137. Dottridge (2004).

138. Europol (2005, 16).

139. UNIAP (n.d.).

140. Netwerk (2008).

141. Estrada (2008).

142. IHT (2008).

143. For a full listing of countries of origin for U.S. couples internationally adopting, see the U.S. Department of State, Immigrant Visas Issued to Orphans Coming to U.S. at http://travel.state.gov/family/adoption/stats/stats_451.html (2008).

Chapter 8

1. Drob-Hiestien (2004).

2. Ilani (2007).

3. Internet World Stats (2008).

4. Council of Europe (2007).

5. Council of Europe (2007, 32).

6. Council of Europe (2007).

7. Council of Europe (2007).

8. Other experts put the number much higher. According to Europol, a Google search yields 10.2 million hits on Web sites that offer such services (Council of Europe 2007). It is probable that Europol conducted the search in the languages of the member states. It is also possible that these sites are listed more than once.

9. Council of Europe (2007, 40).

10. The tour reservation form with information on tours and prices to various destinations can be accessed at http://www.loveme.com/tour/order/order.shtml.

11. Morgan, Karen (2007).

12. See Frantana's amputee gallery at http://www.frantana.ru/amp-gallery.html.

13. Testimony of Dr. Donna Hughes before the U.S. Senate on Human Trafficking: Mail Order Bride Abuses (2004).

14. Clark (2004).

15. Testimony of Dr. Donna Hughes before the U.S. Senate on Human Trafficking: Mail Order Bride Abuses (2004).

16. Chon (2007).

17. Ilani (2007).

18. Tomiuc (2003b).

19. Wolak, Finkelhor, and Mitchell (2005).

20. FBI (2008c).

21. Council of Europe (2007).

22. In October 2008, Perverted Justice claimed 300 convictions for Internet predators due to the work of the organization since 2004. See http://www.perverted-justice.com/.

23. Protection Project (2007).

24. U.S. Department of Justice (n.d.), "Child Exploitation and Obscenity Section."

25. U.S. Department of State (2008a).

26. ECPAT USA, Shared Hope International, The Protection Project (2006).

27. U.S. Department of Justice (n.d.), "Child Exploitation and Obscenity Section."

28. U.S. Department of State (2008a).

29. Protection Project (2007).

30. Child Wise Tourism (2007).

31. Song (2005).

32. Information obtained from the Protection Project (2007), citing Luc Ferran, ECPAT International, presentation at the National Workshop: Child Sex Tourism: Overview of World Situation, Presentation Phnom Penh, Cambodia (December 7, 2005).

33. U.S. Department of Justice (n.d.), "Child Exploitation and Obscenity Section."

34. Protection Project (2007), citing Luc Ferran, ECPAT International, presentation at the National Workshop: Child Sex Tourism: Overview of World Situation, Presentation Phnom Penh, Cambodia (December 7, 2005).

35. Protection Project (2007).

36. This trend was noted in the ASEAN region (Association of Southeast Asian Nations) comprising Brunei Darussalam, Cambodia, Indonesia, Laos, Malaysia, Myanmar, Philippines, Singapore, Thailand, and Vietnam.

37. Child Wise Tourism (2007).

38. Protection Project (2007), citing Luc Ferran, ECPAT International, presentation at the National Workshop: Child Sex Tourism: Overview of World Situation, Presentation Phnom Penh, Cambodia (December 7, 2005).

39. Both of the mothers were arrested, as was the woman who found the children for Pepe and taught them how to have sex.

40. Child Wise Tourism (2007, 13), citing "U.S. 'pedophile' arrested for rape, torture in Cambodia." *Tapei Times,* Wednesday, June 21, 2006, 4.

41. U.S. Department of Justice (n.d.), "Child Exploitation and Obscenity Section."

42. U.S. Department of State (2008a).

43. Svensson (2006).

44. Protection Project (2007).

45. Child Wise Tourism (2007).

46. World Vision (n.d.).

47. Crimes (Child Sex Tourism) Amendment Act 1994 No. 105, 1994, http://www.comlaw.gov.au/ComLaw/Legislation/Act1.nsf/framelodgmentattachments/332EE746136 CDDF6CA256F720018338C.

48. UK Sexual Offences Act, 2003, article 72, http://www.opsi.gov.uk/Acts/acts2003/ukpga_20030042_en_5#pt1-pb19-l1g72.

49. Svensson (2006).

50. Farrell (2004).

51. U.S. Department of State (2008a).

52. UNICRI (2006).

53. UNICRI (2006, 25).

54. Allred (2005, 64).

55. Omelaniuk (2005).

56. Allred (2005, 65).

57. Johnston (2004).

58. Allred (2006a).

59. UNICRI (n.d.).

60. Johnston (2004, 41).

61. For a complete list of U.N. Missions, see the Web site of the U.N. Department of Peacekeeping Operations at http://www.un.org/Depts/dpko/dpko/currentops.shtml#africa and http://www.un.org/Depts/dpko/list/list.pdf.

62. Allred (2006a) citing reports from the following newspapers: Maggie Farley, "150 Cases Found in U.N. Sex Abuse Inquiry in Congo," *Los Angeles Times*, Home Edition, November 23, 2004; and Colum Lynch, "U.N. Sexual Abuse Alleged in Congo," *Washington Post*, December 15, 2004.

63. Allred (2006a), citing Graca Machel, *The Impact of War on Children: A Review of Progress Since the 1996 United Nations Report on the Impact of Armed Conflict on Children* (New York: Palgrave, 2001).

64. U.S. Department of State (2008a).

65. Allred (2006a), quoting David Lamb, U.N. Human Rights Investigator in Bosnia during 2000 and 2001.

66. Testimony of Martina Vandenburg of Human Rights Watch (U.S. House Committee on International Relations 2002).

67. Shelley (2003b).

68. Mendelson (2005, ix).

69. UNDPKO (n.d.), "DPKO's Comprehensive Strategy."

70. Johnston (2004).

71. UNDPKO (n.d.), "Statistics."

72. U.S. Department of State (2008a).

73. The courses involved 35 participants from 17 countries (Austria, the Czech Republic, Denmark, Finland, France, Germany, Italy, Malta, Poland, Portugal, Romania, the Slovak Republic, Slovenia, Spain, Sweden, the Netherlands, and the United Kingdom).

74. Allred (2006b).

75. U.S. Department of State (2007).

76. U.S. Department of Defense (n.d.).

77. U.S. Department of State (2007).

78. As of 2008, these countries included Australia, Austria, Bangladesh, Belgium, Benin, Bosnia and Herzegovina, Burundi, Cameroon, Canada, Chile, Croatia, the Czech Republic, Ethiopia, Fiji, Finland, France, Georgia, Germany, Greece, Hungary, Indonesia, Ireland, Italy, Malawi, Malaysia, the Netherlands, New Zealand, Nigeria, Norway, Philippines, Poland, Romania, Rwanda, Slovenia, South Africa, Spain, Sweden, Switzerland, Tanzania, Togo, Turkey, Ukraine, United Kingdom, United States, and Uruguay (U.S. State Department 2008a).

79. IOM (2007b).

80. Council of the European Union (2007b).

81. IOM (2008c).

82. Brown (2008).

83. Nishiyama (2005).

Chapter 9

1. UN.GIFT (n.d.), "About UN.GIFT."

2. UN.GIFT (n.d.), "The Vienna Forum."

3. This list is not comprehensive but is a starting point to obtain more information on the projects implemented by these and other agencies and organizations.

4. Video viewed by the author at IOM office in Tirana, Albania, during a trafficking assessment mission in 2003.

5. IOM (n.d.), "Support Activities for MTV's No Exit Pan-European Anti-trafficking Campaign."

6. "MTV Networks in Asia and Pacific and MTV Europe Foundation Launch Youth-Focused Anti-Human Trafficking Campaign," August 12, 2007; http://human-trafficking.org.

7. Exchange 4 Media (2007).

8. The film *Human Trafficking* was subtitled in French, Portuguese, Mandarin, Russian, Romanian, Spanish, Thai, Turkish, and Ukrainian. Three documentaries (*Dreams Die Hard, Freedom and Beyond,* and *The Silent Revolution*) produced by the Washington-based NGO Free the Slaves portray labor trafficking in India and the United States (Green 2007).

9. U.S. Department of Health and Human Services (2004).

10. Meld Misdaad Anoniem (n.d.).

11. Business Travelers against Human Trafficking (2006).

12. UN.GIFT (2008d).

13. UNODC (2008a).

14. UN.GIFT (2008b).

15. U.S. Department of State (2008a).

16. For other initiatives, see also End Human Trafficking Now! Campaign (2007).

17. Stop the Traffik (n.d.); U.S. Department of State (2007).

18. Stop the Traffik (n.d.).

19. BBC News (2007b).

20. Information obtained from Microsoft at the UN.GIFT conference, Vienna, February 13–15, 2008 (Kangaspunta 2008).

21. Microsoft (2007).

22. For a complete list of coalition partners, see the ICMEC Web site at http://208.254.21.185/missingkids/servlet/PageServlet?LanguageCountry=en_X1&PageId=3064.

23. BBC News (2006).

24. USAID (2008).

25. IOM (2007a).

26. Mackay (2006).

27. Kralis (2006).

28. Van Dongen (2007a). The two Turkish-German brothers were given sentences of 2.5 and 7.5 years in prison.

29. U.S. Department of Justice (2008b).

30. UNODC (2006c).

31. UNDP (n.d.), "Anti-trafficking Manual."

32. UNODC (2007).

33. Miles (2007).

34. U.S. Department of Justice (2006b).

35. CNN (2007).

36. U.S. Department of Justice (2007d).

37. Maxwell and Skelly (2006).

38. Half of the women were from EU countries. Some voluntarily returned home without making a complaint; the others were referred to specialist agencies for the provision of services (Pallister 2006).

39. Pallister (2006).

40. These include the Salvation Army, the Poppy Project, Eaves Housing, and CHASTE.

41. Maxwell and Skelly (2006).

42. ACPO (2007).

43. ACPO (2008).

44. USICE (2007a).

45. U.S. Department of State (2007).

46. U.S. Department of State (2008a).

47. IJM's Sex Trafficking Factsheet and Story can be downloaded from http://www.ijm.org/ourwork/whatwedo. For a more personal account of their work, see Batstone (2007).

48. Information presented at the UN.GIFT workshop "Technology and Human Trafficking," Vienna, February 14, 2008e. See also http://www.ibixtranslate.com/.

49. UN.GIFT (2008c).

50. Meeting with OSCE representative in Tirana, Albania, February 2003.

51. National Human Rights Commission (2004).

52. Information on *the Hearth* reported in ILPA (2006).

53. Information obtained in an e-mail from IOM's Counter Trafficking Focal Point and IOM's "Development fo Guidelines for the Collection of Data on Trafficking in Human Beings, Including Comparable Indicators," IOM (2008b) A similar project, "Trafficking in Human Beings: Data Collection and Harmonised Information Management Systems-DCIM EU," is being launched by the Ministry of Internal Affairs of Portugal, in cooperation with ICMPD. The Dutch National Rapporteur as well as the

Ministries of Interior of the Czech Republic, Poland, and the Slovak Republic are participating in the project (project description obtained from ICMPD).

54. IOM (2008c).

55. IOM (n.d.), "IOM's Activities on Migration Data: An Overview."

56. For a list of countries signing and ratifying the Protocol, see http://www.unodc.org/unodc/en/treaties/CTOC/countrylist-traffickingprotocol.html.

57. OSCE (2003).

58. For a list of States that ratified and signed the convention, see the Council of Europe (http://www.coe.int/t/dg2/trafficking/campaign/default_en.asp).

59. U.S. Department of State (2008a).

60. According to Dr. Mattar, only 19 countries have yet to join the international community in legislating against trafficking in persons (Mattar 2008).

61. For a brief description of the Philippines National Action Plan Against Trafficking In Human Beings, launched on October 24, 2001, see UNIS (2001).

62. La Strada International (2008).

References

ACPO (Association of Chief Police Officers) of England, Wales and Northern Ireland. 2008. "Major Police Probe Into Trafficking Leads To 528 Arrests." Press release, July 2. http://www.ukhtc.org/includes/75__Operation_Pentameter_2_Results.pdf.

ACPO (Association of Chief Police Officers) of England, Wales and Northern Ireland). 2007. "Pentameter 2 Starts Today." Press release, October 3. http://www.ukhtc.org/includes/104%20Operation%20Pentameter.pdf.

Adamoli, S. A. Di Nicoli, E. Savona, and P. Zoffi. 1998. *Organized Crime Around the World.* Helsinki: European Institute for Crime Prevention and Control (HEUNI).

Adnkronosinternational. 2006. "Italy: Hundreds of Would-Be Immigrants Land In Lampedusa." October 23. http://www.adnki.com/index_2Level_English.php?cat=Security&loid=8.0.352068902&par=0 (accesed October 25, 2006).

Aghatise, Esohe. 2005. "Women Trafficking from West Africa to Europe: Cultural Dimensions and Strategies." *Mozaic* 1. http://www.koed.hu/mozaik15/esohe.pdf.

AGI. 2006. "Human Trafficking: Marzano, Immigrants Like Slaves." AGI online, July 20. http://www.agi.it/english/news.pl?doc=200607181828-1228-RT1-CRO-0-NF51&page=0&id=agionline-eng.arab.

Akofa, Henriette. 2001. *Een slavin in Parijs.* Arena: Amsterdam.

Albania, Ministry of Public Order, 2003. "Study on Trafficking in Human Beings in Albania (1992–2002). Tirana, Albania.

All Africa. 2006. "Nigeria: Human Trafficking—a Tale of Sorrow, Tears and Death." December 13, 2006; http://allafrica.com/stories/200612130687.html?viewall=1.

Allred, Keith. 2006a. "Peacekeepers and Prostitutes: How Deployed Forces Fuel the Demand for Trafficked Women and New Hope for Stopping It." *Armed Forces and Society* 33 (1): 5–23.

Allred, Keith. 2006b. "Invocation of Article 5: Five Years On." *NATO Review* (Summer). http://www.nato.int/docu/review/2006/issue2/english/Analysis.html.

Allred, Keith. 2005. "Human Trafficking: Breaking the Military Link." *Partnership for Peace Consortium Quarterly Journal* (Winter): 63–72.

American Civil Liberties Union. 2007. "Trapped in the Home: Global Trafficking and Exploitation of Migrant Domestic Workers." January 17. http://www.aclu.org/womensrights/humanrights/28031res20070117.html.

AMFAR (American Foundation for AIDS Research). n.d. http://www.amfar.org/cgi-bin/iowa/news/record.html?record=114.

Anderson, B., and J. O'Connel Davidson. 2002. *Trafficking—a Demand-Led Problem?* Stockholm: Save the Children.

Anti-Slavery International. 2003. "The Migration-Trafficking Nexus." United Kingdom. http://www.antislavery.org/homepage/resources/the%20migration%20trafficking%20nexus%202003.pdf.

Anti-Slavery International. 1994. "Forced Begging in West Africa. Child Workers in Asia." October-December.

Anti-Slavery International. n.d. "Trafficking in Russia." United Kingdom. http://www.antislavery.org/homepage/antislavery/traffickingrussia.htm.

Anti-Slavery International. n.d. "Trafficking in Russia, Case Study: Sergey's Story." United Kingdom. ttp://www.antislavery.org/homepage/antislavery/traffickingrussia.htm#sergey.

Aronowitz, A. A. 2006. "Measures to Combat Trafficking in Human Beings in Benin, Nigeria and Togo." United Nations Office on Drugs and Crime, Vienna, Austria. http://www.unodc.org/pdf/publications/ht_research_report_nigeria.pdf.

Aronowitz, A. A. 2005. "Expert Brief Data on Trafficking in Women." Unpublished report, United Nations Division for the Advancement of Women, New York.

Aronowitz, A. A. 2004. "Trafficking in Human Beings: The Albanian Situation." *CIROC Newsletter* (Centre for Information and Research on Organised Crime) 1 (August): 2–3.

Aronowitz, A. A. 2003a. "Coalitions Against Trafficking in Human Beings in the Philippines." United Nations Office on Drugs and Crime and the United Nations Interregional Crime and Justice Research Institute, Vienna, Austria. http://www.unodc.org/pdf/crime/human_trafficking/coalitions_trafficking.pdf

Aronowitz, A. A. 2003b, "Coalitions Against Trafficking in Human Beings in the Philippines." Unpublished report, United Nations Office on Drugs and Crime and the United Nations Interregional Crime and Justice Research Institute, Vienna, Austria.

Aronowitz, A. A. 2003c. "Assessment of Trafficking in Human Beings in Albania, Report on Meetings Conducted: 29 January–11 February 2003." Unpublished report, February 18, Management Systems International, Washington, D.C.

Aronowitz, A. A. 2001. "Smuggling and Trafficking in Human Beings: The Phenomenon, the Markets That Drive It and the Organisations That Promote It." *European Journal on Criminal Policy and Research* 9: 163–195.

Aronowitz, A. A., and M. Peruffo. 2003. "Trafficking of Human Beings and Related Crimes in West Africa." In *The Blackwell Companion to Criminology*, ed. Colin Sumner, Editor, 394–414. Malden, MA: Blackwell Publishers.

Ateneo Human Rights Center. 1999. *The Philippine-Beligan Pilot Project Against Trafficking in Women.* G/F Ateneo Professional Schools, Rockwell Center, Makati City, Philippines.

Bajrektarevic, A. 2000a. "Trafficking in and Smuggling of human Beings—Linkages to Organized Crime—International Legal Measures." Statement Digest, International Centre for Migration Policy Development, Vienna, Austria.

Bajrektarevic, A. 2000b. "Trafficking in and Smuggling of Human Beings—Linkages to Organized Crime—International Legal Measures." Presentation Outline, International Centre for Migration Policy Development, Vienna, Austria.

Balch, Oliver. 2006. "Latin America's Secret Slave Trade." *Guardian Unlimited*, December 20. http://www.guardian.co.uk/argentina/story/0,,1976028,00.html?gusrc=rss&feed=12.

Bales, K. 2004. *Disposable People: New Slavery in the Global Economy.* Berkeley: University of California Press.

Bales, K. 1999a. "What Predicts Global Trafficking?" Paper presented at the International Conference on New Frontiers of Crime: Trafficking in Human Beings and New Forms of Slavery, Verona, Italy, October 22–23.

Bales, K. 1999b. "Globalization and Slavery." *International Dialogue* I (Summer): 102–113.

Bales, K., and S. Lize. 2005. *Trafficking in Persons in the United States.* Washington, DC: U.S. Department of Justice.

Bales K., and P. T. Robbins. 2001. "No One Shall Be Held in Slavery or Servitude: A Critical Analysis of International Slavery Agreements and Concepts of Slavery." *Human Rights Review* 2 (2).

Baskakova, Marina, Elena Tiurukanova, and Dono Abdurazakova. 2005. "Human Trafficking in the CIS." *Development and Transition*, no. 2: 3–6. http://www.developmentandtransition.net/uploads/issuesAttachments/13/DevelopmentAnd Transition2.pdf.

Batstone, David. 2007. *Not for Sale.* New York: Harper Collins Publishers.

BBC News. 2007a. "Vietnam Jails Six For Human Trafficking of Women." July 27. http://news.bbc.co.uk/2/hi/asia-pacific/6918952.stm.

BBC News. 2007b. "'Slavery' behind Easter Chocolate." April 6. http://news.bbc.co.uk/2/hi/uk_news/6533405.stm.

BBC News. 2006. "Selling Child Porn Targeted." March 16. http://news.bbc.co.uk/2/hi/technology/4812962.stm.

BBC News. 2001. "Europe's Poorest Country Supplying Organs to Its Neighbours." July 9. http://news.bbc.co.uk/2/hi/events/newsnight/1437345.stm.

Beah, Ishmael. 2007. "The Making, and Unmaking, of a Child Soldier." *The International Herald Tribune*, January 14. http://www.iht.com/articles/2007/01/14/america/web.0113soldier.nytMAG.php?page=3.

Belser, Patrick. 2005. *Forced Labour and Human Trafficking: Estimating the Profits.* Geneva: International Labour Organization. http://www.ilo.org/wcmsp5/groups/public/—ed_norm/—declaration/documents/publication/wcms_081971.pdf.

Berg, Raffi. 2007. "Israel's Fight against Sex Trafficking." BBC News, November 6. http://news.bbc.co.uk/2/hi/middle_east/7070929.stm.

Bielke, Audra. 2004. "Illegal Migration in China and Implications for Governance." *The National Review* 14 (26).http://www.csis.org/china/040630bielke_ni.pdf.

BKA (Bundeskriminalamt). 2008. *Bundeslagebild Menschenhandel 2007.* Bundeskriminalamt, Wiesbaden, Germany. http://www.bka.de/lageberichte/mh/2007/bundeslagebild_mh_2007.pdf.

BKA (Bundeskriminalamt). 2007. *Bundeslagebild Menschenhandel 2006*. Bundeskriminalamt, Wiesbaden, Germany. http://www.bka.de/lageberichte/mh/2006/mh2006.pdf.

BKA (Bundeskriminalamt). 2004. Lagebild Menschenhandel 2003. Bundeskriminalant, Wiesbaden, Germany. http://www.bka.de/lageberichte/mh/2003/mh2003.pdf.

BNRM (*Bureau National Rapporteur Mensenhandel*, National Rapporteur on Trafficking in Human Beings). 2008. *Mensenhandel, Aanvullende kwantitatieve gegevens, Zesde Rapportage van de Nationaal Rapporteur*. BNRM, den Haag. http://www.bnrm.nl/Images/6de%20rapportage%20Nationaal%20Rapporteur%20Mensen handel_%202008_tcm63-111370.pdf.

BNRM (*Bureau National Rapporteur Mensenhandel*, National Rapporteur on Trafficking in Human Beings). 2007. *Mensenhandel, Vijfde Rapportag*. BNRM, den Haag.

BNRM (*Bureau National Rapporteur Mensenhandel*, National Rapporteur on Trafficking in Human Beings). 2005b. "Trafficking in Human Being: Supplementary figures, Fourth report of the Dutch National Rapporteur." BNRM, The Hague. http://rechten.uvt.nl/victimology/national/NL-NRMEngels4.pdf.

BNRM (*Bureau National Rapporteur Mensenhandel*, National Rapporteur on Trafficking in Human Beings). 2004. *Mensenhandel, Derde Rapportage van de Nationaal Rapporteur*. BNRM, den Haag.

BNRM (*Bureau National Rapporteur Mensenhandel*, National Rapporteur on Trafficking in Human Beings). 2003. *Mensenhandel, Aanvullende kwantitatieve gegevens, Tweede Rapportage van de Nationaal Rapporteur*. BNRM, den Haag.

BNRM (*Bureau National Rapporteur Mensenhandel*, National Rapporteur on Trafficking in Human Beings). 2002. "Trafficking in Human Beings, First report of the Dutch National Rapporteur." BNRM, the Hague.

Borger, Julian. 2008. "Darfur's Child Refugees Being Sold to Militias." *The Guardian*, June 6. http://www.guardian.co.uk/world/2008/jun/06/sudan.humanrights.

Bovenkerk, Frank, and G. J. Pronk. 2007. *"Over de bestrijding van loverboy methoden." Mensenhandel, Justitiële Verkeningen*, no. 7.

Brown, Alan. 2008. "Burma Cyclone: British Aid Reaching Rangoon." *The Telegraph*, May 13. http://www.telegraph.co.uk/news/worldnews/asia/burmamyanmar/1952685/Myanmar-cyclone-British-aid-supplies-reaching-Rangoon.html.

Brunovskis, Annette, and Rebecca Surtees. 2007. *Leaving the Past Behind? When Victims of Trafficking Decline Assistance*. Oslo, Norway: Fafo.

Business Travelers against Human Trafficking. 2006. "Anti-Trafficking Hotline in Azerbaijan." January 20. http://www.businesstravellers.org/archives/anti-trafficking-hotline-in-azerbaijan/.

Business Week. 2000. "Workers in Bondage." November 27, 57–68.

CBC News. 2006. "Human Trafficking Victims Face Immigration Barriers." October 26. http://www.cbc.ca/canada/story/2006/10/26/human-trafficking.html#skip300x250.

Centre for Equal Opportunity and Opposition to Racism. 2005. *Belgian Policy on Trafficking in and Smuggling of Human Beings: Shadows and Lights*. Brussels, Belgium. http://www.diversiteit.be/NR/rdonlyres/4DCB2177-A42D-439D-A81B-B45FE7BAE244/0/05_reporttrafficking.pdf.

Child Wise Tourism. 2007. *2007 ASEAN Child-Sex Tourism Review*. Melbourn, Australia.

Chon, Katherine. 2007. "Children for Sale Online." *Global Eye on Human Trafficking* 1 (December): 6. International Organization for Migration.

Clarke, Michele. 2004. "Mail-Order Brides: Exploited Dreams." Testimony to the U.S. Senate Committee on Foreign Relations, July 13. http://foreign.senate.gov/testimony/2004/ClarkTestimony040713.pdf.

Coalition to Stop the Use of Child Soldiers. 2008. "Child Soldiers Global Report 2008." London. http://www.childsoldiersglobalreport.org/files/country_pdfs/FINAL_2008_Global_Report.pdf.

Coffey, Pamela. 2004. *Literature Review of Trafficking in Persons in Latin America and the Caribbean.* Development Alternatives, Inc., U.S. Agency for International Development. http://www.oas.org/atip/Regional%20Reports/USAID%20LAC%20TIP%20Literature%20Review.pdf.

Council of Europe. 2007. "Trafficking in Human Beings: Internet Recruitment." Strasbourg, France.

Council of Europe. 2005. "Organised Crime Situation Report 2005." Strasbourg, France.

Council of Europe. 2003. "Trafficking in Organs in Europe." Parliamentary Assembly, Document No. 9822, June 3. http://assembly.coe.int/documents/workingdocs/doc03/edoc9822.htm.

Council of Europe. 2002. "Trafficking in Human Beings and Corruption." Programme against Corruption and Organised Crime in South-eastern Europe (PACO), Report on the regional seminar, Portoroz, Slovenia, June 19–22. http://www.coe.int/t/e/legal_affairs/legal_co-operation/combating_economic_crime/3_technical_cooperation/PACO/PACOTP28rev(PortorozFinal).pdf.

Council of the European Union. 2007. "Experience Report on Human Trafficking for the Purpose of Sexual Exploitation and Forced Prostitution in Connection with the 2006 Football World Cup in Germany." No. 5006/1/07, January 19. http://register.consilium.europa.eu/pdf/en/07/st05/st05006-re01.en07.pdf.

CNN International. 2007a. "China: Worker Abuse Boss Caught." June 17. http://edition.cnn.com/2007/WORLD/asiapcf/06/17/china.slaves.reut/index.html.

CNN International. 2007b. "29 Dead as Refugees Forced Overboard." March 26. http://edition.cnn.com/2007/WORLD/europe/03/26/yemen.deaths.ap/index.html.

CNN International. 2007c. "Report on Former Child Soldier Ishmael Beah." February 20.

CNN International. 2001. "Traffickers Jailed for Chinese Deaths." May 11. http://edition.cnn.com/2001/WORLD/europe/05/11/dutch.verdict.02/.

CNN. 2007. "U.S. Intensifies Fight against Human Trafficking." February 1. http://edition.cnn.com/2007/LAW/02/01/us.human.trafficking/index.html.

Coalition against Trafficking in Women. 2001. "Sex Trafficking of Women in the United States." March.

Coalition against Trafficking in Women. n.d. "United States." http://www.catwinternational.org/factbook/usa1.php.

Coalition to Stop the Use of Child Soldiers. 2008. "Child Soldiers Global Report 2008." London. http://www.childsoldiersglobalreport.org/files/country_pdfs/FINAL_2008_Global_Report.pdf.

Coalition to Stop the Use of Child Soldiers. n.d. "Some Facts." http://www.child-soldiers.org/childsoldiers/some-facts.

Craig, G., A. Gaus, M. Wilkinson, K. Skrivankova, and A. McQuade. 2007. *Comtemporary Slavery in the UK.* York, UK: Joseph Rowntree Foundation. http://www.jrf.org.uk/bookshop/eBooks/2016-contemporary-slavery-UK.pdf.

CrimProf Blog. 2007. "Problems Prosecuting Diplomats with Immunity and Domestic Slavery." March 4. http://lawprofessors.typepad.com/crimprof_blog/2007/03/problems_prosec.html.

Davis, Kathleen. 2006. "Brides, Bruises and the Border: The Trafficking of North Korean Women into China." *SAIS Review* XXVI (1): 131–141.

Democracy Now. 2001. "Death of 14 Immigrants in Arizona Desert Spotlights Human Costs of the Militarization Of U.S.-Mexico Border." May 25. http://www.democracynow.org/article.pl?sid=03/04/07/023235.

Department for International Development. 2006. "Breaking the Chains, Eliminating Slavery, Ending Poverty." DfID, London. http://www.dfid.gov.uk/pubs/files/slavery-brochure.pdf.

Derluyn, I., E. Broekaert, G. Schuyten, E. Temmerman. 2004. "Post-traumatic Stress in Former Ugandan Child Soldiers." *The Lancet* 363 (9412): 861–863.

Djisseanou, K. 2003. *Borderline Slavery: Child Trafficking in Togo.* Human Rights Watch. http://www.hrw.org/reports/2003/togo0403/togo0403.pdf.

Dottridge, Mike. 2004. *Kids as Commodities? Child Trafficking and What To Do About It.* Terre des Hommes. Lausanne, Switzerland. http://www.terredeshommes.org/pdf/commodities.pdf.

Dottridge, Mike. 2002. "Trafficking in Children in West and Central Africa." *Gender and Development* 10 (1): 38–49.

Drob-Hiestien, Gili. 2004. "The Responsibility of Newspaper Publishers for Sex Advertisements." *The Seventh Eye Journal* 53 (November). Israel Democracy Institute. http://www.idi.org.il/sites/english/ResearchAndPrograms/Communications AndDemocracy/TheSeventhEyeJournal/Pages/TheSeventhEye4.aspx.

ECPAT USA, Shared Hope International, The Protection Project. 2006. "U.S. Mid-Term Review on the Commercial Sexual Exploitation of Children in America." September. http://www.ecpatusa.org/pdfs/FinalReportfromtheUSMidTermReview withcoverart.pdf.

EITB. 2007. "Police Arrest 60 People in Crackdown on Human Trafficking Ring." EITB, April 19. http://www.eitb24.com/new/en/B24_45095/life/SPANISH-REGION-ANDALUSIA-Police-arrest-60-people-in/.

End Human Trafficking Now! Campaign. 2007. "Progress Report 2006." http://www.endhumantraffickingnow.com/public/content/documents/173/EHTN2006PROGRESS-REPORT_FINAL.pdf.

Escaler, N. 1998. "Keynote Address." *Report of the U.S.-EU Trafficking in Women Seminar*, 15–20. L'Viv, Ukraine, July 9–10.

Espino, Nathaniel. 2006. "Polish Slave Laborers Freed by Italian Police; Traffickers Held." July 18. http://www.bloomberg.com/apps/news?pid=20601085&sid=axhj GYBfJM6M&refer=europe.

Estrada, Rodrigo. 2008. "Guatemalan Held in Illegal Adoption Case." *USA Today*, May 7. http://www.usatoday.com/news/topstories/2008-05-07-492777574_x.htm.

Europol. 2008. "Child Abuse in Relation to Trafficking in Human Beings." January, The Hague. http://www.europol.europa.eu/publications/Serious_Crime_Overviews/Child_abuse_2008.pdf.

Europol. 2007. "Trafficking Human Beings in the European Union: A Europol Perspective." May, The Hague. http://www.europol.europa.eu/publications/Serious_Crime_Overviews/THB_FactSheet2007.pdf.

Europol. 2005. "European Union Organised Crime Report 2005." October, The Hague. http://www.europol.europa.eu/publications/Organised_Crime_Reports-in_2006_ replaced_by_OCTA/EU_OrganisedCrimeReport2005.pdf.

Europol. 2001. "Crime Assessment Trafficking of Human Beings into the European Union." The Hague.

Europol. 2000. "Europol Situation Report THB 1999." The Hague.

Exchange 4 Media. 2007. "MTV Networks and MTV Europe Foundation Launch Anti-Human Trafficking Campaign." August 11. http://www.exchange4media.com/e4m/news/newfullstory.asp?section_id=6&news_id=27211&tag=22110&pict=11.

Eyadat, Fadi. 2007. "Two Haifa Men Sentenced to Jail for Organ Trafficking." *Haaretz*, December 18. http://www.haaretz.com/hasen/spages/935092.html.

Farr, Kathryn. 2006. *Sex Trafficking*. New York: Worth Publishers.

Farrell, Michael. 2004. "Global Campaign to Police Child Sex Tourism." *The Christian Science Monitor*, April 22. http://www.csmonitor.com/2004/0422/p11s01-wogi.html.

Farrior, Stephanie. 1997. "The International Law on Trafficking in Women and Children for Prostitution: Making It Live Up to its Potential." *Harvard Human Rights Journal* 10. http://ssrn.com/abstract=886444.

FBI (Federal Bureau of Investigation). 2008a. "Human Trafficking: Today's Slave Trade." May 9. http://www.fbi.gov/page2/may08/humantrafficking_050908.html.

FBI (Federal Bureau of Investigation). 2008b. "Innocence Lost Sting." June 25. http://www.fbi.gov/page2/june08/innocence_lost062508.html.

FBI (Federal Bureau of Investigation). 2008c. "Major Child Porn Ring Busted." March 6. http://www.fbi.gov/page2/march08/innocentimages_030608.html.

FBI (Federal Bureau of Investigation). 2008d. "Innocence Lost Initiative." October 2008. http://www.fbi.gov/innolost/innolost.htm.

FBI (Federal Bureau of Investigation). 2004. "The Case of the Florida Fruit-Pickers Slave Ring." March 9. http://www.fbi.gov/page2/march04/florida030904.htm.

Fidler, Eric. 1998. "Two Charged for Enslaving Stripper." Associated Press, September. Reported in Coalition Against Trafficking in Women. http://www.catwinternational.org/factbook/usa1.php.

Fitzgibbon, Kathleen. 2003. "Modern-day Slavery? The Scope of Trafficking in Persons in Africa." *African Security Review* 12 (1): 81–89.

Fokus (Forum for Women and Development). n.d. "Fakta og statistikk om kvinner og hiv/aids fra UNIFEM." http://www.fokuskvinner.no/Temasider/Hiv_Aids/Fakta/823.

Fournier, Suzanne. 2008. "U.S. Slams Canada's Record on Sex Trafficking." *Canwest News Service*, June 5. http://www.canada.com/topics/news/national/story.html?id=3242587b-1804-49c3-90a5-9f58d6ab67e7.

Free the Slaves. 2005. *Recovering Childhoods*. Washington, D.C.

Free the Slaves and Human Rights Center, University of California, Berkely. 2004. "Hidden Slaves: Forced Labor in the United States." September, Washington, D.C. http://www.hrcberkeley.org/download/hiddenslaves_report.pdf.

Gagalac, Ron. 2008. "NBI Raises Alarm on Child-Organ Trafficking." ABS-CBN News, August 24. http://www.abs-cbnnews.com/storypage.aspx?StoryId=129159.

Gallagher, Anne. 2001. "Human Rights and the New UN Protocols on Trafficking and Migrant Smuggling: A Preliminary Analysis." *Human Rights Quarterly* 23 (4): 975–1004.

Galnor, Matt. 2007. "Labor Camp Owner Given 30 Years in Prison." *The Times-Union*, January 27. http://www.jacksonville.com/tu-online/stories/012707/met_7605933.shtml.

Geest, van der, Thea. 2007. "De zak 'Handel in Letlandse vrouwen'." *Opportuun*, March 2007. http://www.om.nl/mensenhandel/_mensenhandel_smokkel_documenten/31380/.

Gentleman, Amelia. 2008. "Kidney Thefts Shock India." *New York Times*, January 30. http://www.nytimes.com/2008/01/30/world/asia/30kidney.html?ex=1359349200& en=b4c62469af7d7c0f&ei=5088&partner=rssnyt&emc=rss.

Glenny, Misha. 2008. "The New Gangsterism." *Time*, May 19, 43–45.

Goward, P. 2003. "Stop the Traffic 2." Conference paper. Presented October 23–24, 2003. Melbourne, Australia.

Goyal, Madhav, L. Mehta Ravindra, Lawrence J. Schneiderman, and Ashwini R. Sehgal. 2002. "Economic and Health Consequences of Selling a Kidney in India." *Journal of the American Medical Association* 288 (13): 1589–1593.

Graycar, Adam, and Rob McCusker. 2007. "Transnational Crime and Trafficking in Persons: Quantifying the Nature, Extent and Facilitation of a Growing Phenomenon." *International Journal of Comparative and Applied Criminal Justice* 31 (2): 147–165.

Green, Eric. 2007. "State Department Offers Film Program on Trafficking in Persons." June 8. http://www.america.gov/st/washfile-english/2007/June/20070608130830X1 eneerg0.3753168.html.

GTZ (Deutsche Gesellschaft für Technische Zusammenarbeit GmbH). 2004. *Coercion in the Kidney Trade?* April, GTZ, Eschborn. http://www.gtz.de/de/dokumente/ en-svbf-organ-trafficking-e.pdf.

Gunnatilleke, G. 1996. "Summary of the Report of the Rapporteur, International Cooperation in Fighting Illegal Immigration Networks," International Organization for Migrants (IOM) Seminar on International Responses to Trafficking in Migrants and the Safeguarding of Migrant Rights, Geneva, October 26–28. *Trends in Organized Crime* (Winter): 65–67.

Gupta, Ruchira. n.d. "Trafficking of Children for Prostitution and the UNICEF Response." Asian Social Issues Program. http://www.asiasource.org/asip/gupta.cfm.

Heyzer, N. 2002. "Combating Trafficking in Women and Children: A Gender and Human Rights Framework." Paper presented at the conference, The Human Rights Challenge of Globalization: Asia-Pacific-U.S., Honolulu, Hawaii, 2002, UNIFEM. http://www.hawaii.edu/global/projects_activities/Trafficking/Noeleen.pdf.

Heinrich, Mark. 2007. "U.N. Anti-Trafficking Drive Hits Culture Barriers." *The Scotsman*, April 23. http://news.scotsman.com/latest.cfm?id=625492007.

HEUNI (European Institute for Crime Prevention and Control). 2003. "Europe: The Regional Report on Trafficking in Women and Children." Paper presented at the 12th Session of the Commission on Crime Prevention and Criminal Justice, Vienna, May 15. http://www.unicri.it/annual_workshop_2003.htm.

Hughes, Donna. 2002. "Trafficking for Sexual Exploitation, The Case of the Russian Federation. IOM, Geneva, Switzerland. http://www.uri.edu/artsci/wms/hughes/ russia.pdf.

Hughes, Donna M., Laura Joy Sporcic, Nadine Z. Mendelsohn, and Vanessa Chirgwin. 1999. "India." In *The Factbook on Global Sexual Exploitation*, Coalition Against Trafficking in Women. http://www.uri.edu/artsci/wms/hughes/india.htm.

Human Rights Watch. 2007a. "Exported and Exposed Abuses against Sri Lankan Domestic Workers in Saudi Arabia, Kuwait, Lebanon, and the United Arab Emirates." *Human Rights Watch* 19 (16C). http://hrw.org/reports/2007/srilanka1107/srilanka1107web.pdf.

Human Rights Watch. 2007b. "Early to War, Child Soldiers in the Chad Conflict." *Human Rights Watch* 19 (9A). http://hrw.org/reports/2007/chad0707/chad0707 webwcover.pdf.

Human Rights Watch. 2003. "Borderline Slavery: Child Trafficking in Togo." *Human Rights Watch* 15 (8A).

Human Rights Watch. 2002. *HOPES BETRAYED: Trafficking of Women and Girls to Post-Conflict Bosnia and Herzegovina for Forced Prostitution.* New York: Human Rights Watch. http://www.hrw.org/reports/2002/bosnia/Bosnia 1102.pdf.

Human Rights Watch. 1997. "The Scars of Death: Children Abducted by the Lord's Resistance Army in Uganda." Human Rights Watch Report. http://www. hrw.org/reports97/uganda/1ra.htm.

Human Rights Watch. 1995. "Rape for Profit, Trafficking of Nepali Girls and Women to India's Brothels." Human Rights Watch Asia Report. http://www.hrw.org/reports/pdfs/c/crd/India957.pdf.

Human Rights Watch n.d. "Facts About Child Soldiers." Fact sheet. http://www. hrw.org/campaigns/crp/fact_sheet.html.

Human Rights Without Frontiers International. 2008. "Human Rights in Belgium." March. http://www.hrwf.net/pdf/Human%20Rights%20in%20Belgium%202008% 20PTL.doc.

Humantrafficking.org. n.d. "China." http://www.humantrafficking.org/countries/china.

Humantrafficking.org. August 12, 2007. "MTV Newtworks in Asia and Pacific and MTV Europe Foundation Launch Youth-Focused Anti-Human Trafficking Campaign." Http://www.humantrafficking.org/updates/690.

Human Organ Transplants Act. 1989. Chapter 31, Office of Public Sector Information, U.K. Government. http://www.opsi.gov.uk/acts/acts1989/ukpga_19890031_en_1.

IBIX Translate. (n.d.) http://www.ibixtranslate.com.

ICMEC (International Coalition of Missing and Exploited Children). n.d. Financial Coalition against Child Pornography. http://208.254.21.185/missingkids/servlet/PageServlet?LanguageCountry=en_X1&PageId=3064.

IHT (*International Herald Tribune*). 2008. "US Report Alleges Baby-Selling, Corruption in Adoptions from Vietnam." April 25. http://www.iht.com/articles/ap/2008/04/25/asia/AS-GEN-Vietnam-Adoptions.php?page=2.

Ilani, Ofri. 2007. "Virtual Pimps May Pay the Price." *Haaretz*, July 6. http://www.haaretz.com/hasen/spages/877530.html.

ILO (International Labour Organization). 2005. "A Global Alliance against Forced Labour." ILO, Geneva. http://www.ilo.org/wcmsp5/groups/public/—ed_norm/—declaration/documents/publication/wcms_081882.pdf.

ILO (International Labour Organization). 2002b. "Yunnan Province, China, Situation of Trafficking in Children and Women: A Rapid Assessment." August, ILO, Geneva. http://www.oit.org/public/english/region/asro/bangkok/child/trafficking/downloads/final-yunnan-ra-2003.pdf.

ILO (International Labour Organization). 2001a. *World of Work Magazine*, no. 39.

ILO-IPEC (International Labour Organization/International Programme on the Elimination of Child Labour). 2007. "Child Trafficking: The ILO's Response through IPEC." December, ILO-IPEC, Geneva.

ILO-IPEC (International Labour Organization/International Programme on the Elimination of Child Labour). 2003. "Combating Child Labour and HIV/AIDS in Sub-Saharan Africa." *News Update: Archive*, October.

ILPA (Immigration Law Practitioners' Association). 2006. "ILPA Response to Tackling Human Trafficking—Consultation on Proposals for a UK Action Plan." April 5. http://www.ilpa.org.uk/submissions/tacklinghumantrafficking.htm.

Innocenti Research Centre/UNICEF (United Nations Children's Fund). 2003. "Trafficking in Human Beings, Especially Women and Children, in Africa." UNICEF, Geneva.

IADB (Inter-American Development Bank). 2006. "Human Trafficking's Dirty Profits and Huge Costs." November 2. http://www.iadb.org/news/articledetail.cfm?language=English&ARTID=3357.

International Human Rights Law Institute. 2002. "In Modern Bondage: Sex Trafficking In The Americas: Central America and the Caribbean." October, DePaul University College of Law.

Internet World Stats. 2008. http://www.internetworldstats.com/stats.htm.

IOM (International Organization for Migration). 2008a. "Child Trafficking and Abuse in Haiti." *Global Eye on Human Trafficking*, no. 2: 8. http://www.iom.int/jahia/webdav/site/myjahiasite/shared/shared/mainsite/projects/showcase_pdf/global_eye_second_issue.pdf.

IOM (International Organization for Migration). 2008b. *Guidelines for the Collection of Data on Trafficking in Human Beings, Including Comparable Indicators.* Vienna: IOM.

IOM (International Organization for Migration). 2008c. "Sporting Events and Human Trafficking." *Global Eye on Human Trafficking*, no. 2: 4.

IOM (International Organization for Migration). 2008d. "Tajikistan's Artists Unite Against Human Trafficking." April 15. http://www.iom.int/jahia/Jahia/pbnAS/cache/offonce?entryId=16936.

IOM (International Organization for Migration). 2007a. "Efforts to Engage Clergy in Counter Trafficking Reaches New High." October 2. http://www.iom.int/jahia/Jahia/pbnEU/cache/offonce?entryId=15471.

IOM (International Organization for Migration). 2007b. "Trafficking in Human Beings and the 2006 World Cup in Germany." http://www.iom.int/jahia/webdav/site/myjahiasite/shared/shared/mainsite/published_docs/serial_publications/mrs29.pdf.

IOM (International Organization for Migration). 2007c. "Research on Trafficking of Men for Labour Exploitation." December 18. http://www.iom.int/jahia/Jahia/pbnAF/cache/offonce?entryId=16263.

IOM (International Organization for Migration). 2005a. *World Migration 2005: Costs and Benefits of International Migration.* Geneva: IOM.

IOM (International Organization for Migration). 2005b. *Data and Research on Human Trafficking: A Global Survey.* Geneva: IOM. http://www.nswp.org/pdf/IOM-GLOBALTRAFFICK.PDF.

IOM (International Organization for Migration). 2004. *Changing Patterns and Trends of Trafficking in Persons in the Balkan Region.* Geneva: IOM. http://www.iom.md/materials/balkans_trafficking.pdf.

IOM (International Organization for Migration). 2003. "Seduction, Sale and Slavery: Trafficking of Women and Children for Sexual Exploitation in Southern Africa." May. http://www.iom.org.za/site/media/docs/TraffickingReport3rdEd.pdf.

IOM (International Organization for Migration). 2002. "Addis Ababa, Ethiopia Focus on Trafficking in Women." Integrated Regional Information Network, U.N. Office for the Co-ordination of Humanitarian Affairs, October 21.

IOM (International Organization for Migration). 2000. *Migrant Trafficking and Human Smuggling in Europe: A Review of the Evidence with Case Studies from Hungary, Poland and Ukraine.* Geneva: IOM.

IOM (International Organization for Migration). n.d. "Human Trafficking in Persons: Moldova." http://www.iom.md/faq_ht.html.

IOM (International Organization for Migration). n.d. "Support Activities for MTV's Exit Pan-European Anti-trafficking Campaign 'No Exploitation and Trafficking'." http://www.iom.int/jahia/Jahia/eventEU/cache/offonce?entryId=9700.

IOM (International Organization for Migration). n.d. "Development of Guidelines for the Collection of Data on Trafficking in Human Beings, Including Comparable Indicators." http://www.iomvienna.at/index.php?module=Content&func=display&id=249&folder=.

IOM (International Organization for Migration). n.d., "IOM's Activities on Migration Data: An Overview." http://www.iom.int/jahia/webdav/shared/shared/mainsite/policy_and_research/policy_documents/iom_data_infosheet.pdf.

IRIN (Integrated Regional Information Network). 2008a. "Côte d'Ivoire: Former Child Soldiers Still at Risk." February 13. http://www.irinnews.org/Report.aspx?ReportId=76729.

IRIN (Integrated Regional Information Network). 2008b. "Former Child Soldiers at Risk of HIV." February 15. http://www.plusnews.org/Report.aspx?ReportId=76781.

IRIN (Integrated Regional Information Network). 2008c. "Nepal: Reintegration of Child Soldiers 'Taking Too Long'." May 27. http://www.irinnews.org/report.aspx?ReportId=78422.

IRIN (Integrated Regional Information Network). 2008d. "Pakistan: Child Soldiers in Swat Valley." May 26. http://www.irinnews.org/report.aspx?ReportID=78400.

IRIN (Integrated Regional Information Network). 2003. "Africa: Too Small To Be Fighting in Anyone's War." Indepth: Child Soldiers, December. http://www.irinnews.org/IndepthMain.aspx?IndepthId=24&ReportId=66280.

Iselin, Brian. 2003. "Trafficking in Human Beings: New Patterns of an Old Phenomenon." Paper presented at Trafficking in Persons: Theory and Practice in Regional and International Cooperation, Bogota, Colombia, November 19–21. http://www.iselinconsulting.com/Downloads/New_Patterns_Colombia.pdf.

Jantsch, H. 1998. "Law Enforcement: Germany's Perspective." *Report of the U.S.-EU Trafficking in Women Seminar*, 51–54, L'Viv, Ukraine, July 9–10.

Johnston, Nicola. 2004. "Peace Support Operations." *Inclusive Security, Sustainable Peace: A Toolkit for Advocacy and Action*, Hunt Alternatives Fund (November): 33–50.

Joint Committee on Human Rights. 2006. "Human Trafficking." Twenty-sixth Report of Session 2005–2006. http://www.publications.parliament.uk/pa/jt200506/jtselect/jtrights/245/245.pdf.

Kangaspunta, Kristiina. 2008. "Women Traffickers." United Nations Office on Drugs and Crime, UN.GIFT Forum, Vienna, February 13–15. http://www.ungift.org/docs/ungift/pdf/vf/traffickerworkshop/women%20traffickers.pdf.

Kelly, Liz, and L. Regan. 2000. "Stopping Traffic: Exploring the Extent of, and Responses to, Trafficking in Women for Sexual Exploitation in the UK." Policing and Reducing Crime Unit, Research, Development and Statistics Directorate, Home Office, London.

Kendall, R. 1999. "Recent Trends in International Investigations of Trafficking in Human Beings." Paper presented at the International Conference on New Frontiers of Crime: Trafficking in Human Beings and New Forms of Slavery, Verona, Italy, October 22–23.

Kleemans, E. R., M. E. I. Brienen, and H. G. van de Bunt. 2002. *Georganiseerde criminaliteit in Nederland: Tweede rapportage op basis van de WODC-monitor*. Den Haag: Wetenschappelizk Onderfoeks en Documentatiecentrum.

Kleemans, E. R., E. A. I. M. van den Berg, H. G. van de Bunt, M. Brouwers, R. F. Kouwenberg, and G. Paulides. 1998. *Georganiseerde criminaliteit in Nederland; rapportage op basis van de WODC-monitor*. Ministry of Justice, The Hague. http://www.wodc.nl/onderzoeksdatabase/w00173-georganiseerde-criminaliteit-in-nederland-rapportage-op-basis-van-de-wodc-monitor.aspx.

Kralis, Barbara. 2006. "Catholic Church Fights Human Trafficking & Slavery." *Renew America*, August 4. http://www.renewamerica.us/columns/kralis/060804.

Krikorian, Greg. 2007. "9 Indicted in L.A. on Sex-Trafficking Charges." *L.A. Times*, August 10. http://www.latimes.com/news/printedition/california/la-me-sexring10aug10,1,599384.story?coll=la-headlines-pe-california&ctrack=1&cset=true.

Kouri, Jim. 2007. "Nine Guatemalans Charged with Sex Trafficking of Minors." *Renew America*, September 6. http://www.renewamerica.us/columns/kouri/070906.

Kovalev, Vladimir. 2007. "EU Presses Russia on Human Trafficking." *Business Week*, February 24. http://www.businessweek.com/globalbiz/content/feb2007/gb20070223_311905.htm?chan=globalbiz_europe_more+of+today's+top+stories.

Kristof, Nicholas. 2008. "The Pimps' Slaves." *The New York Times*, March 16. http://www.nytimes.com/2008/03/16/opinion/16kristof.html?_r=3&th&emc=th&oref=slogin&oref=slogin&oref=slogin.

Kumar, Sanjay. 2003. "Police Uncover Large Scale Organ Trafficking in Punjab." *British Medical Journal*, no. 326 (January 25): 180. http://bmj.bmjjournals.com/cgi/content/full/326/7382/180/b.

Laczko, Frank. 2005. "Data and Research on Human Trafficking." *International Migration* 43 (1–2): 5–16.

Lagon, Mark P. 2007. "Remarks at Swearing-in Ceremony." U.S. Department of State, July 9. http://www.state.gov/g/tip/rls/rm/07/88003.htm.

La Strada International. 2008. "Violation of Women's Rights: A Cause and Consequence of Trafficking in Human Beings." Amsterdam. http://www.lastradainternational.org/lsidocs/431%20LSI-%20violation%20of%20womens%20rights.pdf.

Lehti, Martti, and Kauko Aromaa. 2007. "Trafficking in Human Beings for Sexual Exploitation in Europe." *International Journal of Comparative and Applied Criminal Justice* 21 (2): 123–145.

Lehti, Martti. 2003. "Trafficking in Women and Children in Europe." HEUNI, No. 18, 2003.

Limanowska, B. 2005. *Trafficking in Human Beings in South Eastern Europe.* Geneva: UNICEF, UNOHCHR, and OSCE. http://www.unicef.org/ceecis/Trafficking. Report.2005.pdf.

Limanowska, B. 2002. *Trafficking in Human Beings in South Eastern Europe.* Genva: UNICEF, UNOHCHR, and OSCE.

Mackay, Maria. 2006. "Church of Bangladesh Raises Thousands for Anti-Trafficking Work." *Christian Today*, December 20. http://www.christiantoday.co.uk/article/church.of.bangladesh.raises.thousands.for.antitrafficking.work/8795.htm.

Makkai, Toni. 2003. "Thematic Discussion on Trafficking in Human Beings." Workshop on trafficking in human beings, especially women and children, 12th Session of the Commission on Crime Prevention and Criminal Justice, Vienna, May 15.

Masud Ali, A. K. M. 2005. "Treading along a Trecherous Trail: Research on Trafficking in Persons in South Asia." *International Migration* 43 (1/2): 141–164.

Matas, David, and David Kilgour. 2007. "Bloody Harvest: Revised Report into Allegations of Organ Harvesting of Falun Gong Practitioners in China." January 31. http://organharvestinvestigation.net/report0701/report20070131-eng.pdf.

Mattar, Mohammed. 2008. "The Vienna Forum to Combat Human Trafficking." Presented at the Panel on the Effectiveness of the Legal Frameworks and Anti-Trafficking Legislation, February 13–15, 2008. Vienna, Austria. http://www.protectionproject.org/news/The%20Vienna%20Forum%20to%20Combat%20Human%20Trafficking.

Maxwell, Grahame, and Bill Skelly. 2006. "Pentameter Final Conference 21 June 2006, Speech." United Kingdom Human Trafficking Centre. http://www.ukhtc.org/includes/speech2.pdf.

Mayoyo, Patrick. 2007. "Bold Woman's Tale of Life as Sex Slave Overseas." *Daily Nation Online*, February 20. http://www.nationmedia.com/dailynation/nmg contententry.asp?category_id=39&newsid=92179.

McDonald, Lynn, and Natalya Timoshkina. 2007. "The Working Life of Women Trafficked from the Eastern Bloc." *International Journal of Comparative and Applied Criminal Justice* 31 (2): 234–244.

McMahon, Kathryn. 1999. "Trafficking of Women: A Report from Los Angeles." Paper presented at the 1999 Berkshire Conference on the History of Women, June 3–6.

Meld Misdaad Anoniem. n.d. "M. Calls Prove Their Worth in Human Trafficking Investigations." http://www.meldmisdaadanoniem.nl/ArticleSub.aspx?id=106.

Mendelson, Sarah. 2005. "Barracks and Brothels." February, Center for Strategic and International Studies, Washington, D.C. http://www.csis.org/media/csis/pubs/0502_barracksbrothels.pdf.

Microsoft. 2007. "Human Trafficking in Asia," April 17. http://www.microsoft.com/about/corporatecitizenship/citizenship/giving/programs/up/casestudies/asia.mspx.

Miles, Darla 2007. "On Alert for Human Trafficking." WFAA-TV, August 18. http://www.wfaa.com/sharedcontent/dws/wfaa/latestnews/stories/wfaa070817_wz_slavetrade.451ca65b.html.

Miller, John R. 2006. Ambassador at Large. "Briefing on International Slavery on Release of the Sixth Annual Trafficking in Persons Report." http://wwww.hrwf.net/trafficking/ext/Briefing%20by%20Ambassador%20John%20R.pdf.

Molina, Fanny Polanía. n.d. "Japan, the Mecca for Trafficking in Colombian Women." http://www.december18.net/web/general/paper30ColombiaJapan.pdf.

Morgan, Karen. 2007. "Here Comes the Mail-Order Bride: Three Methods of Regulation in the United States, The Philippines, and Russia." *The George Washington International Law Review.* http://findarticles.com/p/articles/mi_qa5433/is_200701/ai_n21296630">FindArticles - HERE COMES THE MAIL-ORDER BRIDE: THREE METHODS OF REGULATION IN THE UNITED STATES, THE PHILIPPINES, AND RUSSIA.

Morgan, Marcus. 2007. "More Migrant Deaths as Europe Tightens Border Controls." *UKWatch*, October 13. http://www.ukwatch.net/article/more_migrant_deaths_as_europe_tightens_border_controls.

Napa Valley Register. 2006. "Napa Firm Pays $1.4 Million Settlement in Human Trafficking Case." December 9. http://www.napavalleyregister.com/articles/2006/12/09/news/local_top_story/iq_3723241.txt.

Nation, The. 2007. "Beggar Kings Are the Real Choosers." February 18. http://www.no-trafficking.org/content/Press_Rooms/05%20-%20beggar%20kings%20are%20the%20real%20choosers.doc.

National Human Rights Commission. 2004a. *Action Research on Trafficking in Women and Children in India 2002–2003.* http://nhrc.nic.in/Publications/ReportOnTrafficking.pdf.

National Human Rights Commission 2004b. *A Report on Human Trafficking in Women and Children in India*; http://nhrc.nic.in/Publications/ReportOnTrafficking.pdf.

Navis, Jan Willem. 2008. "Spong: Rechtbank partijdig." *Spits* (May 29): 8.

Netwerk. 2008. "Adopties uit China." March 11. http://www.netwerk.tv/weblog/index.php?itemid=92.

Netwerk. 2005. "Kinderhandel in Nederland." April 10.

Newman, G. 2006. *The Exploitation of Trafficked Women.* COPS, U.S. Department of Justice. http://www.cops.usdoj.gov/mime/open.pdf?Item=1699.

Nigeria Immigration Service. 2004. "Record of Deportations 2001–2004." Anti-Human Trafficking Unit, Abuja.

Nishiyama, George. 2005. "UNICEF Confirms Tsunami Child Trafficking Case." *The Tribune*, January 7. http://www.tribuneindia.com/2005/20050108/world.htm#1.

Ojomo, A. 1999. "Trafficking in Human Beings: Nigerian Law Enforcement Perspective." Paper presented at the International Conference on New Frontiers of Crime: Trafficking in Human Beings and New Forms of Slavery, Verona, Italy, October 22–23.

Okojie, C. E. E., O. Okojie, K. Eghafona, G. Vincent-Osaghae, and V. Kalu. 2003. *Trafficking of Nigerian Girls to Italy, Report of Field Survey in Edo State, Nigeria.* United Nations Interregional Crime and Justice Research Institute, Turin. http://www.unicri.it/wwd/trafficking/nigeria/docs/rr_okojie_eng.pdf.

Omelaniuk, Irena. 2005. "Trafficking in Human Beings." United Nations Expert Group Meeting on International Migration and Development, New York, UN/POP/MIG/2005/15, July 8. http://www.un.org/esa/population/meetings/ittmigdev2005/P15_IOmelaniuk.pdf.

O'Neill Richard, A. 1999. "International Trafficking in Women to the United States: A Contemporary Manifestation of Slavery and Organized Crime." Center for the Study of Intelligence, U.S. State Department. http://www.vawnet.org/Intersections/OtherViolenceTypes/Trafficking/ciatraffic.pdf.

Openbaar Ministerie. 2007. "Internationale actie tegen handel in minderjarige Nigeriaanse asielzoekers." News report. http://www.om.nl/mensenhandel/_mensenhandel_smokkel_nieuwsberichten/32448/.

Osava, Mario. 2004. "Brazil: Poor Sell Organs to Trans-Atlantic Trafficking Ring." Inter Press Service News. http://ipsnews.net/interna.asp?idnews=22524.

OSCE (Organization for Security and Cooperation in Europe). 2006. *Human Trafficking for Labour Exploitation, Forced and Bonded Labour: Identification, Prevention and Prosecution.* Vienna: OSCE. http://www.osce.org/publications/cthb/2008/05/31148_1143_en.pdf.

OSCE (Organization for Security and Cooperation in Europe). 2003. "OSCE Action Plan To Combat Trafficking in Human Beings." July 24. http://www.osce.org/documents/pc/2005/07/15591_en.pdf.

Ould, D. 1999. "Cross Border Trafficking and New Forms of Slavery." Paper presented at the International Conference on New Frontiers of Crime: Trafficking in Human Beings and New Forms of Slavery, Verona, Italy, October 22–23.

Paddock, Catherine. 2008. "Philippine Government Bans Organ Transplants For Foreigners." *Medical News Today*, May 1. http://www.medicalnewstoday.com/articles/105980.php.

Pallister, David. 2006. "Police to Launch Intelligence Unit to Target Human Trafficking." *The Guardian*, June 22. http://www.guardian.co.uk/news/2006/jun/22/crime.immigrationandasylum.

Pattaya Daily News. 2007. "Human Trafficking Racket Being Operated in Southern Thailand." March 22. http://www.pattayadailynews.com/shownews.php?IDNEWS=0000002594.

Philippine Government. Republic Act No. 6955. 1990. http://www.filipinawives.com/6955.htm.

Phinney, Alison. 2001. "Trafficking of Women and Children for Sexual Exploitation in the Americas." Inter-American Commission of Women (Organization of American States) and the Women, Health and Development Program (Pan American Health Organization). http://www.paho.org/english/hdp/hdw/TraffickingPaper.pdf.

Polaris Project. 2003. "Very Low Number of Police Reporting Trafficking in Women." January 21. http://www.humantrafficking.com/humantrafficking/client/view.aspx?ResourceID=1892.

Pomodoro, L., and S. Stefanizzi. 1996. "Traffico Degli Eseri Umani: Donne E Minori: Un'analisi esplorativa." Paper presented at "The New Slaves: Trafficking in Women and Minors" conference, Milan, Italy, October 19, 1995. *Trends in Organized Crime* (Winter): 90.

Protection Project. 2007. "International Child Sex Tourism." January. http://www.kmk-studio.com/JHU/JHU_Report.pdf.

Protection Project 2002. "An Excerpt From the Human Rights Report on Trafficking of Persons, Especially Women and Children, United States of America." http://www.protectionproject.org/programs/us_training/us_snapshot.htm.

Protection Project. n.d. "Human Rights Report: Nigeria." http://www.protectionproject.org/human_rights_reports/report_documents/nigeria.doc.

Protection Project. n.d. "Trafficking in the United States, U.S. Country Report." http://www.protectionproject.org/country_reports/united_states.htm.

Radio Free Europe 2006. "Albanian Corruption Fuels Human Trafficking." June 27. http://www.rferl.org/featuresarticle/2006/06/34E5049C-CA53-41EC-847F-908B847CE997.html.

Rahmani, Ladan. 2006. "Invisible Routes: An Exploratory Study of Changing Patterns and Trends in Routes of Trafficking in Persons in the Balkan Region." In *Trafficking in Persons in South East Europe—a Threat to Human Security*, Austrian Federal Ministry of Defense, 65–93. National Defence Academy and Bureau for Security Policy.; http://www.isn.ethz.ch/pubs/ph/details.cfm?lng=en&id=25160.

Rayman, Graham. 2001a. "Queens Mom Indicted in Buffalo; Linked to Ring Importing Sex Workers." *Newsday*, March 27.

Rayman, Graham. 2001b. "Toronto Targets Trafficking: Task Force Is Model for Law Enforcement Organizations." *Newsday*, March 14.

Reuters. 2007a. "IOM Says Alarmed over Rising Trade in Human Organs." June 7. http://in.reuters.com/article/worldNews/idINIndia-30192020070607.

Reuters. 2007b. "Five Organ Trafficking Hotspots." August 6. http://www.reuters.com/article/healthNews/idUSL0142628820070806?src=080707_0948_FEATURES_lifestyle.

Ribando, Clare. 2007. "Trafficking in Persons in Latin America and the Caribbean." CRS Report for Congress, January 8. http://www.humantrafficking.org/uploads/publications/RL33200.pdf.

Rivers, Dan. 2007. "Girl, 6, Embodies Cambodia's Sex Industry." CNN, January 26. http://edition.cnn.com/2007/WORLD/asiapcf/01/23/sex.workers/index.html.

Rodriguez, O. 2006. "Smuggling Deaths Likely to Rise with Fence." *Adelante*, October 16. http://x.adelantesi.com/news/story.php?ID=279.

Rosenberg, Ruth. 2003. "Trafficking of Women and Children in Indonesia." International Catholic Migration Commission (ICMC), Jakarta, Indonesia. http://www.solidaritycenter.org/content.asp?contentid=502.

Rothman, David, and Sheila Rothman. 2003. "The Organ Market." *The New York Times Book Review* 50 (16).

RTL Nieuws. 2007. "Dwangarbeiders Bevrijd." June 15. http://www.rtl.nl/actueel/rtlnieuws/.

Ruggiero, V. 1997. "Criminals and Service Providers: Cross-National Dirty Economies." *Crime, Law and Social Change*, no. 28: 27–38.

Ruggiero, V. 1996. "Trafficking in Human Beings - Slaves in Contemporary Europe." Paper presented at the Law and Society Association and Research Committee on the Sociology of Law of the International Sociological Association Joint Meetings, University of Strathclyde, Glasgow, Scotland, July 10–13. *Trends in Organized Crime* (Winter): 81–85.

Russel, Andy. 2008. "'Callous' Human Trafficker Jailed." *Manchester Evening News*, June 11. http://www.manchestereveningnews.co.uk/news/s/1053507_callous_human_traffickers_jailed_.

Saletan, William. 2007. "The Organ Market." *The Washington Post*, April 15, B02. http://www.washingtonpost.com/wp-dyn/content/article/2007/04/13/AR2007041302066_pf.html.

Salt, John. 2000. "Trafficking and Human Smuggling: A European Perspective." *International Migration*, Special Issue, 2no. 1: 31–56.

Save the Children. 2005. "Development of a Child Rights Methodology to Identify and Support Child Victims of Trafficking; Summary of Research Findings."

JLS/2005/AGIS/045. http://www.savethechildren.it/download/Summary_of_research_findings.pdf.

Savona, Ernest, Roberta Belli, Federica Curtol, Silvia Decarli, and Andrea Di Nicola. 2003. "Trafficking in Persons and Smuggling of Migrants into Italy." November, Transcrime, Trento, Italy.

Savona, E., S. Adamoni, P. Zoffi, and M. DeFeo. 1995. *Organized Crime across the Border.* Helsinki: European Institute of Crime Prevention and Control, HEUNI.

Scheper-Hughes, Nancy. 2007. "In Defense of the Body from the Queen of Hearts to the Knave of Hearts." *Journal of Medical Ethics*, April 23. http://jme.bmj.com/cgi/eletters/33/4/201.

Scheper-Hughes, Nancy. 2005a. "Black Market Organs." *Lip Magazine*, June 3. http://www.lipmagazine.org/articles/featscheperhughes.htm.

Scheper-Hughes, Nancy. 2005b. "Organs Without Borders." *Foreign Policy*, no. 146 (Jan/Feb): 26–27. http://www.foreignpolicy.com/Ning/archive/archive/146/PN146.pdf.

Scheper-Hughes, Nancy. 2004. "Parts Unknown: Undercover Ethnography of the Organs-Trafficking Underworld." *Ethnography* 5 (1): 29–73.

Scheper-Hughes, Nancy. 2003. "Keeping an Eye on the Global Traffic in Human Organs." *The Lancet* 361 (May 10): 1645–1648.

Scheper-Hughes, Nancy. 2001. "Commodity Fetishisms in Organ Trafficking." *Body and Science* 7 (2–3): 31–62.

Scheper-Hughes, Nancy. 1999. "Bodies of Apartheid: the Ethics and Economics of Organ Transplantation in South Africa." Center for African Studies, September 28. http://sunsite.berkeley.edu/biotech/organswatch/pages/bodiesapart.html.

Schloenhardt, A. 1999. "Organized Crime and the Business of Migrant Trafficking." *Crime, Law and Social Change*, no. 32: 203–233.

Scholes, Robert J., and Anchalee Phataralaoha. n.d. "The Mail Order Bride Industry and Its Impact on US Immigration." Appendix A, U.S. Citizenship and Immigration Service. http://www.uscis.gov/files/article/MobRept_AppendixA.pdf.

Senta, K. 2003. "Trafficking in Human Beings in the Asia-Pacific Region." Asia and Far East Institute for the Prevention of Crime and the Treatment of Offenders (UNAFEI), 12th Session of the Commission on Crime Prevention and Criminal Justice, Vienna, May 15. http://www.unicri.it/wwk/related/pni/docs/2003/unafei_wkshp.doc.

Serious Organised Crime Agency. 2006. "United Kingdom Threat Assessment of Serious Organised Crime 2006–2007." http://www.soca.gov.uk/assessPublications/downloads/threat_assess_unclass_250706.pdf.

Shared Hope International. 2007. *Demand: A Comparative Examination of Sex Tourism and Trafficking in Jamaica, Japan, the Netherlands and the United States.* https://www.sharedhope.org/files/demand.pdf.

Shelley, Louise. 2006. "The Globalization of Crime and Terrorism." *EJournal*, February. http://usinfo.state.gov/journals/itgic/0206/ijge/shelley.htm.

Shelley, Louise. 2003a. "Trafficking in Women: The Business Model Approach." *The Brown Journal of World Affairs* X (I): 119–131.

Shelley, Louise. 2003b. Statement to the Subcommittee on European Affairs United States Senate Committee on Foreign Relations Hearing on "Combating

Transnational Crime and Corruption in Europe," October 30, Washington, DC. http://foreign.senate.gov/testimony/2003/ShelleyTestimony031030.pdf.

Shimazono, Yosuke. 2007. "The State of the International Organ Trade: A Provisional Picture Based on Integration of Available Information." *World Health Organization* 85 (12): 955–962. http://www.who.int/bulletin/volumes/85/12/06-039370.pdf.

Siegel, Dina. 2007. "Nigeriaanse madams in de mensenhandel in Nederland." *Justitiële Verkenning* 33 (7): 39–49.

Skogseth, Geir. 2006. "Trafficking in Women." Fact-finding trip to Nigeria (Abuja, Lagos and Benin City), March 12–26, Landinfo, Oslo, Norway. http://www.landinfo.no/asset/224/1/224_1.pdf.

Song, Susan. 2005. "Global Child Sex Tourism: Children as Tourist Attractions." Youth Advocate Program International. http://www.yapi.org/rpchildsextourism.pdf.

Spector, Michael. 1998. "Traffickers' New Cargo: Naive Slavic Women." *The New York Times*, January 11. Reprinted on Brama. http://www.brama.com/issues/nytart.html.

Srinivasan, Sandhya. 2008. "'Dr Kidney' Arrest Exposes Indian Organ Traffic." *Asia Times Online*, February 22. http://www.atimes.com/atimes/South_Asia/JB22Df03.html.

Staats courant. 2000. "Europol: criminele groepen zijn op meer terreinen tegelijk actief." December 18, 5.

Staring, Richard. 2007. "Handelaars in vrouwen: achtergronden en werkwijze." *Justitiële Verkenningen* 33 (7): 50–63.

Staring, Richard, G. Engbersen, H. Moerland, and N. de Lange. 2004. *De sociale organisatie van mensensmokkel*. Kerkebosch: Amsterdam.

Stop the Traffik. n.d. "The Chocolate Campaign." http://www.stopthetraffik.org/chocolate campaign/.

Surtees, Rebecca. 2008. "Traffickers and Trafficking in Southern and Eastern Europe: Considering the Other Side of Human Trafficking." *European Journal of Criminology* 5 (1): 39–68.

Surtees, Rebecca. 2007a. "Trafficking Victims in SEE—What We Know, What We Need to Know." Mensenhandel: achtergrond en aanpak, Conference, Vrije Universiteit Amsterdam, October 31.

Surtees, Rebecca. 2007b. "Trafficking of Men—A Trend Less Considered." *Global Eye on Human Trafficking* 1 (December): 1–2. International Organization for Migration.

Surtees, Rebecca. 2006. "Child Trafficking in Southeastern Europe: Different Forms of Trafficking and Alternative Interventions." *Tulane Journal of International and Comparative Law* 14 (1): 1–46.

Surtees, Rebecca. 2005. "Child Trafficking in Sierra Leone." UNICEF, Geneva. http://www.lastradainternational.org/lsidocs/244%20Child%20Trafficking%20in%20Sierra%20Leone%20(UNICEF).pdf.

Svensson, Naomi. 2006. "Extraterritorial Accountability: An Assessment of the Effectiveness of Child Sex Tourism Laws." *Loyola of Los Angeles International and Comparative Law Review* 28: 641–664. http://ilr.lls.edu/documents/Article6Svensson_000.pdf.

Tiefenbrun, Susan. 2007. "Child Soldiers, Slavery and the Trafficking of Children." Paper presented at the Symposium on Challenges for Children's Rights, Thomas

Jefferson School of Law, San Diego, California, March 2. http://works.bepress. com/cgi/viewcontent.cgi?article=1000&context=susan_tiefenbrun.

Tomesen, Remco. 2008. "Donor tenzij je nee zegt." *De Pers*, June 18, 3.

Tomiuc, Eugen. 2008. "World: UN, Campaigners Highlight Grim Reality of 'Happy Trafficking'." *Radio Free Europe Radio Liberty*, February 20. http://www.rferl.org/ features/features_Article.aspx?m=02&y=2008&id=4EC9DA3E-F08B-4412-9F1E-15B9AEA81347.

Tomiuc, Eugen. 2003a. "The Problem of Organ Trafficking." *Radio Free Europe Radio Liberty*, July 16. http://www.rferl.org/content/article/1142959.html.

Tomiuc, Eugen. 2003b. "Interpol Official Discusses Human Trafficking, Internet Pornography." Global Security. http://www.globalsecurity.org/security/library/news/ 2003/05/sec-030514-rfel-142137.htm.

Toneto, Bernardete. 2004. "The Price of a Slave in Brazil." Brazzill. http://www. brazzillog.com/2004/html/articles/feb04/p107feb04.htm.

The Transplantation of Human Organs Act. 1994. MedIndia. http://www.medindia.net/ indian_health_act/the-transplantation-of-human-organs-act-1994-authority-for-removal-of-human-organs.htm.

Tully, Andrew. 2008. "Experts Say Human Trafficking A Major Problem In U.S." *Radio Free/Europe Radio Liberty*, July 11. http://www.rferl.org/articleprintview/ 1183179.html.

UAE-UNICEF (United Arab Emirates-United Nations Children's Fund) Program. 2008. "The UAE-UNICEF Program Repatriating Camel Jockeys." http:// www.helpingcameljockeys.org/solution/uae-unicef_program.asp.

UNAIDS (The Joint United Nations Programme on HIV/AIDS). 2006. "2006 Report on the Global AIDS Epidemic." http://www.unaids.org/en/HIV_data/2006Global Report/default.asp.

UNDP (United Nations Development Program). n.d. "Trafficking and HIV/AIDS: The Link." Youandaids. http://www.youandaids.org/Themes/Trafficking.asp.

UNDP (United Nations Development Program). n.d. "Trafficking." Youandaids. http:// www.youandaids.org/Themes/Trafficking.asp#TraffickingSAsia.

UNDP (United Nations Development Program). n.d. "Anti-trafficking Manual Gives Romanian and Turkish Police Ammunition to Catch and Prosecute Offenders." http://europeandcis.undp.org/archive/?menu=p_cms/show&content_id=0F0C8366-F203-1EE9-BFD79D06036C6A65.

UNDPKO (United Nations Department of Peace Keeping Operations). n.d. "DPKO's Comprehensive Strategy on Sexual Exploitation and Abuse." http://www.un.org/ Depts/dpko/CDT/strategy.html.

UNDPKO (United Nations Department of Peace Keeping Operations). n.d. "Statistics." http://www.un.org/Depts/dpko/CDT/statistics.html.

UNESCO (United nations Educational, Scientific and Cultural Organization). 2003. "Clearing House on Trafficking Statistics." Press release, July 31. Trafficking Statistics Project. http://www.unescobkk.org/index.php?id=1022.

UN.GIFT (United Nations Global Initiative to Fight Human Trafficking). 2008a. "011 Workshop: Human Trafficking for the Removal of Organs and Body Parts." United Nations, Vienna. http://www.ungift.org/docs/ungift/pdf/vf/backgroundpapers/ BP011HumanTraffickingfortheRemovalofOrgans.pdf.

UN.GIFT (United Nations Global Initiative to Fight Human Trafficking). 2008b. *An Introduction to Human Trafficking: Vulnerability, Impact and Action.* Vienna: United Nations.

UN.GIFT (United Nations Global Initiative to Fight Human Trafficking). 2008c. "006 Workshop: Criminal Justice Responses to Human Trafficking." United Nations, Vienna. http://www.ungift.org/docs/ungift/pdf/vf/backgroundpapers/BP006CriminalJustice Responses.pdf.

UN.GIFT (United Nations Global Initiative to Fight Human Trafficking). 2008d. "'Naked Facts' Fight Human Trafficking in Serbia." July 18. http://www.ungift.org/ungift/en/stories/naked-facts-fight-human-trafficking-in-serbia-.html.

UN.GIFT (United Nations Global Initiative to Fight Human Trafficking). 2008e. Workshop: "Technology and Human Trafficking." February 13–15. United Nations, Vienna. http://www.ungift.org/docs/ungift/pdf/vf/aidmemoirs/technology%20and%20human%20trafficking.pdf.

UN.GIFT (United Nations Global Initiative to Fight Human Trafficking). n.d. "About UN.GIFT." http://www.ungift.org/ungift/en/about/index.html.

UN.GIFT (United Nations Global Initiative to Fight Human Trafficking). n.d. "The Vienna Forum." http://www.ungift.org/ungift/en/vf/index.html.

UNIAP (United Nations Inter-Agency Project on Human Trafficking in the Greater Mekong Sub-region). n.d. "Human Trafficking in the GMS." http://www.no-trafficking.org/content/About_Human_Trafficking/about_human.htm.

UNICEF (United Nations Children's Fund). 2006a. "UNICEF Welcomes Child Demobilisation in Southern Sudan." News note, April 24. http://www.unicef.org/media/media_33579.html.

UNICEF (United Nations Children's Fund). 2006b. "UN Launches Integrated Disarmament, Demobilization and Reintegration Standards." News note, December 18. http://www.unicef.org/media/media_37796.html.

UNICEF (United Nations Children's Fund). 2005. "Trafficking in Human Beings, Especially Women and Children, in Africa." http://www.unicef-irc.org/publications/pdf/trafficking-gb2ed-2005.pdf.

UNICEF (United Nations Children's Fund). 2003. *End Child Exploitation; Stop the Traffic!* UNICEF, United Kingdom.

UNICEF (United Nations Children's Fund). 2001. *Child Trafficking in West and Central Africa.* UNICEF, West and Central Africa Regional Office.

UNICEF (United Nations Children's Fund). n.d. "Trafficking Violates the Entire Spectrum of Children's Rights." *The State of the World's Children.* http://www.unicef.org/sowc06/profiles/trafficking.php.

UNICEF (United Nations Children's Fund). n.d. "Child Trafficking: Sexual Exploitation." http://www.unicef.org/protection/index_exploitation.html.

UNICEF (United Nations Children's Fund). n.d. "Factsheet: Child Trafficking." http://www.unicef.org/protection/files/ipuglobaltrafficking.pdf.

UNICEF (United Nations Children's Fund). n.d. "Factsheet: Child Soldiers." http://www.unicef.org/emerg/files/childsoldiers.pdf.

UNICRI (United Nations Interregional Crime and Justice Research Institute). 2006. *Trafficking In Human Beings and Peace-Support Operations,* Turin, Italy: UNICRI.

UNICRI (United Nations Interregional Crime and Justice Research Institute). n.d. "Counter-Trafficking: Peace Support Areas." http://www.unicri.it/wwd/trafficking/peacekeeping/index.php.

UNIS (United Nations Information Service). 2001. "Philippines Government Launches A National Action Plan Against Trafficking In Human Beings." October 30. http://www.unis.unvienna.org/unis/pressrels/2001/cp398.html.

United Kingdom Human Trafficking Centre. 2007. "Human Trafficking in the U.K." http://www.ukhtc.org/uk.htm.

United Nations. 2006. Report of the Secretary-General, "Preventing, Combating and Punishing Trafficking in Human Organs," Vienna, February 21. http://daccessdds. un.org/doc/UNDOC/GEN/V06/513/17/PDF/V0651317.pdf?OpenElement.

United Nations. 2005. General Assembly Security Council, "Children and Armed Conflict," A/59/695–S/2005/72, Vienna, February 9. http://daccessdds.un.org/doc/UNDOC/GEN/N05/215/07/PDF/N0521507.pdf?OpenElement.

United Nations. 2000a. *Protocol to Prevent, Suppress and Punish Trafficking in Persons, Especially Women and Children, Supplementing the United Nations Convention Against Transnational Organized Crime.* http://www.uncjin.org/Documents/Conventions/dcatoc/final_documents_2/convention_%20traff_eng.pdf.

United Nations. 2000b. *Protocol against the Smuggling of Migrants by Land, Sea and Air, Supplementing the United Nations Convention Against Transnational Organized Crime.* http://www.uncjin.org/Documents/Conventions/dcatoc/final_documents_2/convention_smug_eng.pdf.

United Nations. n.d. "Child Soldier's Stories." http://www.un.org/works/goingon/soldiers/stories.doc.

UNODC (United Nations Office on Drugs and Crime). 2008a. "Preventing Human Trafficking." http://www.unodc.org/unodc/en/human-trafficking/prevention.html.

UNODC (United Nations Office on Drugs and Crime). 2008b. *Responding to Trafficking for Sexual Exploitation in South Asia: India.* Vienna: UNODC.

UNODC (United Nations Office on Drugs and Crime). 2008c. *Challenges to the Implementation of the National Plan of Action Against Trafficking in Persons, Brazil.* Vienna: UNODC.

UNODC (United Nations Office on Drugs and Crime). 2008d. *First Regional Anti-Trafficking Conference in Eastern Africa: Vulnerabilities of Conflict and Post-Conflict Countries, Uganda.* Vienna: UNODC.

UNODC (United Nations Office on Drugs and Crime). 2008e. *High-Level Expert Meeting on Children and Armed Conflicts, Côte d'Ivoire.* Vienna: UNODC.

UNODC (United Nations Office on Drugs and Crime). 2007. "Compendium on Best Practices on Anti Human Trafficking by Law Enforcement Agencies." http://www.ungift.org/docs/ungift/pdf/knowledge/compendium_practices.pdf.

UNODC (United Nations Office on Drugs and Crime). 2006a. "Trafficking in Persons, Global Patterns." http://www.unodc.org/pdf/traffickinginpersons_report_2006-04.pdf.

UNODC (United Nations Office on Drugs and Crime). 2006b. "Trafficking in Persons, Global Patterns, Appendices." http://www.unodc.org/documents/human-trafficking/HT-globalpatterns-en-appendices.pdf.

UNODC (United Nations Office on Drugs and Crime). 2006c. "Toolkit to Combat Trafficking in Persons." http://www.unodc.org/pdf/Trafficking_toolkit_Oct06.pdf.

USAID (United States Agency for International Development). 2008. "Clergy Joins Fight against Human Trafficking." May 2. http://www.usaid.gov/locations/europe_eurasia/press/success/2006-10-07.html.

USCIS (United States Citizenship and Immigration Services). 2006. "International Marriage Broker Regulation Act Implementation Guidance." July 21. http://www.uscis.gov/files/pressrelease/IMBRA072106.pdf.

U.S. Department of Defense. n.d. "T.I.P. Awareness Training." http://www.dodig.osd.mil/TipTraining/index.htm.

U.S. Department of Health and Human Services. 2004. "HHS Announces Anti-Trafficking Hotline, Awareness Effort." March 11. http://www.hhs.gov/news/press/2004pres/20040311a.html.

U.S. Department of Justice. 2008a. "Attorney General's Annual Report to Congress on the U.S. Government Activities to Combat Trafficking in Persons Fiscal Year 2007." May. http://www.usdoj.gov/ag/annualreports/tr2007/agreporthumantrafficing2007.pdf.

U.S. Department of Justice. 2008b. "Federal Jury Convicts Anchorage Man in the First Sex Trafficking Trial in the District of Alaska." February 6. http://anchorage.fbi.gov/doj/pressrel/2008/aksextrafficking020608.htm.

U.S. Department of Justice. 2007a. "Assessment of U.S. Government Efforts to Combat Trafficking in Persons in Fiscal Year 2006." September. http://www.usdoj.gov/ag/annualreports/tr2007/assessment-of-efforts-to-combat-tip0907.pdf.

U.S. Department of Justice. 2007b. "Attorney General's Annual Report to Congress on the U.S. Government Activities to Combat Trafficking in Persons Fiscal Year 2006." May. http://www.usdoj.gov/ag/annualreports/tr2006/agreporthumantrafficing2006.pdf.

U.S. Department of Justice. 2007c. "Nine Charged in Sex Trafficking Ring Involving Minors." August 9. http://www.usdoj.gov/opa/pr/2007/August/07_crt_597.html.

U.S. Department of Justice. 2007d. "Transcript of Attorney General Alberto R. Gonzales, Assistant Attorney General Wan Kim, and Senior Department Officials at Pen and Pad Roundtable on Human Trafficking." Press release, January 31. http://www.usdoj.gov/crt/speeches/crt_speech_070131.html.

U.S. Department of Justice. 2007e. Case Updates: "United States v. Calimlim (Wisconsin)." *Anti-Trafficking News Bulletin* 3 (3). http://www.usdoj.gov/crt/crim/trafficking_newsletter/antitraffnews_aug07.pdf.

U.S. Department of Justice. 2006a. "Assessment of U.S. Government Efforts to Combat Trafficking in Persons in Fiscal Year 2005." September. http://www.usdoj.gov/ag/annualreports/tr2006/assessment-of-efforts-to-combat-tip.pdf.

U.S. Department of Justice, Bureau of Justice Statistics. 2006b. "Federal Prosecution of Human Trafficking, 2001–2005." October. http://www.ojp.gov/bjs/pub/pdf/fpht05.pdf.

U.S. Department of Justice. 2006c. "United States v. Telichenko." *Anti-Trafficking News Bulletin* 3 (3). http://www.usdoj.gov/crt/crim/trafficking_newsletter/antitraffnews_dec06.pdf.

U.S. Department of Justice. 2002. "Florida Man Part of Mexican Trafficking Ring Pleads Guilty to Involuntary Servitude Charges." September 13. http://www.usdoj.gov/opa/pr/2002/September/02_crt_525.htm.

U.S. Department of Justice. n.d. "Child Exploitation and Obscenity Section." *Child Sex Tourism.* http://www.usdoj.gov/criminal/ceos/sextour.html.

U.S. Department of State. 2008a. *Trafficking in Persons Report 2008*. Washington, D.C. http://www.state.gov/documents/organization/105501.pdf.

U.S. Department of State. 2008b. "Côte D'Ivoire." July. http://www.state.gov/r/pa/ei/bgn/2846.htm.

U.S. Department of State, Bureau of Democracy, Human Rights, and Labor. 2008c. "2007 Country Reports on Human Rights Practices: Japan." March 11. http://www.state.gov/g/drl/rls/hrrpt/2007/100522.htm.

U. S. Department of State, Bureau of Democracy, Human Rights, and Labor. 2008d. "2007 Country Reports on Human Rights Practices: China." March 11. http://www.state.gov/g/drl/rls/hrrpt/2007/100518.htm.

U.S. Department of State. 2008. "Immigrant Visas Issued to Orphans Coming to U.S." http://travel.state.gov/family/adoption/statis/stats_451.html.

U.S. Department of State. 2007. *Trafficking in Persons Report 2007*. Washington, D.C. http://www.state.gov/g/tip/rls/tiprpt/2007/.

U.S. Department of State. 2006a. *Trafficking in Persons Report 2006*. Washington, D.C. http://www.state.gov/documents/organization/66086.pdf.

U.S. Department of State. 2006b. "Fact Sheet: Distinction between Human Smuggling and Trafficking." April, Human Smuggling and Trafficking Center. http://www.state.gov/g/tip/rls/fs/2006/69386.htm and http://www.state.gov/documents/organization/69496.pdf.

U.S. Department of State. 2006c. "Introduction." Embassy of the United States Moscow, Russia. http://moscow.usembassy.gov/bilateral/bilateral.php?record_id=report_trafficking_2006_intro.

U.S. Department of State. 2004. *Trafficking in Persons Report 2005*. Washington, D.C. http://www.state.gov/g/tip/rls/tiprpt/2005/46606.htm.

U.S. Department of State. 2005. *Trafficking in Persons Report 2004*. Washington, D.C. http://www.state.gov/g/tip/rls/tiprpt/2004.

U.S. Department of State. 2003. *Trafficking in Persons Report 2003*. Washington, D.C.

U.S. Department of State. 2002. Congressional Research Service. "Trafficking in Women and Children: The U.S. and International Response." March 18. http://fpc.state.gov/documents/organization/9107.pdf.

U.S. House Committee on International Relations. 2002. "The U.N. and the Sex Slave Trade in Bosnia: Isolated Case or Larger Problem in the U.N. System." Hearings before the Subcommittee on International Operations and Human Rights, 107th Congress, 2nd session. http://commdocs.house.gov/committees/intlrel/hfa78948.000/hfa78948_0f.htm.

USICE (Immigration and Customs Enforcement). 2007a. "Fiscal Year 2007 Annual Report." http://www.ice.gov/doclib/about/ice07ar_final.pdf.

USICE (Immigration and Customs Enforcement). 2007b. "Human Trafficking Indicators."November.

U.S. Mission to the European Union. 2005. "Fact Sheet: Sex Trafficking, The United States, and Europe." January 6. 2005,http://useu.usmission.gov/Article.asp?ID=9B7A69F1-A6B3-48C8-9736-E9A52392B477&L=En.

U.S. Senate. 2004. "Human Trafficking: Mail Order Bride Abuses." July 13. http://bulk.resource.org/gpo.gov/hearings/108s/96804.pdf

Valentine, Sandrine. 2003. "Trafficking of Child Soldiers: Expanding the United Nations Convention on the Rights of the Child and its Optional Protocol on the

Involvement of Children in Armed Conflict." *New England Journal of International and Comparative Law* 9 (1): 109–178.

Van Dongen, Menno. 2007a. "Een geraffineerd spel." *De Volkskrant*, May 12, 26.

Van Dongen, Menno 2007b. "Pooierbroeders konden jaren hun gang gaan." *De Volkskrant*, February 13, 3.

Van Dongen, Menno 2007c. "140 meisjes uit Nigeria in prostitutie verdwenen." *De Volkskrant*, October 25, 3.

Vocks, J., and J. Nijboer. 2000. "The Promised Land: A Study of Trafficking in Women from Central and Eastern Europe to the Netherlands." *European Journal on Criminal Policy and Research*, no. 8: 379–388.

Vocks, J., and J. Nijboer. 1999. *Land van belofte: een onderzoek naar slachtoffers van vrouwenhandel uit Central- en Oost-Europa.* Groningen: University of Groningen, Department of Criminology.

Waging Peace. 2008. "Trafficking and Forced Recruitment of Child Soldiers on the Chad/Sudan Border." June 6. http://www.wagingpeace.info/files/20080606_WagingPeaceReport_ChildrenSoldiers.pdf.

Walt, V. 2007. "Comfort in a Cold Place." *Time*, February 19, 30–33.

War Child. 2007. "Child Soldiers: The Shadow of Their Existence," March. http://www.warchild.org/news/projects/ChildSoldierReport_/childsoldierreport_.html.

Watchlist on Children and Armed Conflict. 2008. No Safety No Escape: Children and the Armed Conflict in Sri Lanka," April. http://www.watchlist.org/reports/pdf/sri_lanka/ENGLISH%20REPORT%20LR%20p.pdf.

Watchlist on Children and Armed Conflict. 2006. "Struggling to Survive: Children in Armed Conflict in the Democratic Republic of the Congo," April. http://www.watchlist.org/reports/pdf/dr_congo.report.20060426.pdf.

Watchlist on Children and Armed Conflict. n.d. http://www.watchlist.org/.

Webber, A., and D. Shirk. 2005. "Hidden Victims: Evaluating Protections for Undocumented Victims of Human Trafficking." *Immigration Policy in Focus* 4 (8). http://safestate.org/documents/HT_Hidden_Victims.pdf.

Weissbrodt, D., and Anti-Slavery International. 2002. "Abolishing Slavery and Its Contemporary Forms." RR/PUB/02/4, para 19. www.antislavery.org/homepage/resources/Weissbrodt%20report%20final%20edition%202003.pdf.

Wessells, Michael. 2007. *Child Soldiers: From Violence to Protection.* Boston: Harvard University Press.

Wetmore, J. 2002. "The New T Visa: Is the Higher Extreme Hardship Standard Too High for Bona Fide Trafficking Victims?" *New England Journal of International and Comparative Law* 9 (1): 159–178. http://www.nesl.edu/intljournal/vol9/wetmore.pdf.

Wijers, M., and L. Lap-Chew. 1999. *Trafficking in Women, Forced Labour and Slavery-Like Practices in Marriage, Domestic Labour and Prostitution.* Utrecht: STV.

Wolak, Janis, David Finkelhor, and Kimberly Mitchell. 2005. *Child-Pornography Possessors Arrested in Internet-Related Crimes: Findings From the National Juvenile Online Victimization Study.* Alexandria, VA: National Center for Missing & Exploited Children. http://www.missingkids.com/en_US/publications/NC144.pdf.

World Vision. n.d. "U.S. Federal Law Regarding Child Sex Tourism." 18 U.S.C. 2423 (modified April 30, 2003 with the passage of the PROTECT Act). http://www.worldvision.org/get_involved.nsf/467ea108653d7ec987256fb4006c09b1/

df2eab2634bed631882571d80062ed70/$FILE/U.S.%20Law%20Regarding%20
Child%20Sex%20Tourism.pdf?Open&lid=CST_Law&lpos=rightnav.

Wynter, A. 2006. "Deadly Passage." International Red Cross. http://www.redcross.int/
EN/mag/magazine2006_2/index.html.

Yousafzai, Sami, Ron Moreau, and Marie Bourreau. 2008. "The Opium Brides of
Afghanistan." *Newsweek*, April 7, 38–40.

Zakaryan, Varduhi. 2007. "Gyumri's Human Trafficking Victims." *Hetq* online, January
15. http://www.hetq.am/eng/society/0701-worker.html.

Zimmerman, Cathy. 2003. *The Health Risks and Consequences of Trafficking in
Women and Adolescents.* London: London School of Hygiene and Tropical
Medicine. http://www.lshtm.ac.uk/hpu/docs/traffickingfinal.pdf.

Index

About the Author

ALEXIS A. ARONOWITZ received her PhD in Criminal Justice from the University at Albany in New York. She is an Assistant Professor and Academic Advisor at University College, Utrecht University, the Netherlands and works as an independent consultant on human trafficking. She has served as a staff member and consultant on projects in the field of trafficking in human beings for the United Nations Interregional Crime and Justice Research Institute, the United Nations Office on Drugs and Crime, the United Nations Division for the Advancement of Women, the International Organization for Migration and other international organizations. She is also the author/coauthor of three U. N. reports and numerous book chapters and journals articles on the subject.